PENGUIN BOOKS

CAMPING WITH THE PRINCE

Thomas A. Bass, author of *The Eudaemonic Pie*, first
traveled to Africa when he was seventeen. Seventeen
years later he returned for two years to write *Camping
with the Prince*. He lives in upstate New York with his wife
and daughter.

Thomas A. Bass

Camping with the Prince

AND OTHER TALES OF

Science in Africa

PENGUIN BOOKS

For Bonnie and Maude

PENGUIN BOOKS
Published by the Penguin Group
Viking Penguin, a division of Penguin Books USA Inc.,
375 Hudson Street, New York, New York 10014, U.S.A.
Penguin Books Ltd, 27 Wrights Lane, London W8 5TZ, England
Penguin Books Australia Ltd, Ringwood, Victoria, Australia
Penguin Books Canada Ltd, 2801 John Street,
Markham, Ontario, Canada L3R 1B4
Penguin Books (N.Z.) Ltd, 182–190 Wairau Road,
Auckland 10, New Zealand

Penguin Books Ltd, Registered Offices:
Harmondsworth, Middlesex, England

First published in the United States of America by
Houghton Mifflin Company, 1990
Reprinted by special arrangement with the Houghton Mifflin Company
Published in Penguin Books 1991

1 3 5 7 9 10 8 6 4 2

Copyright © Thomas A. Bass, 1990
All rights reserved

The lines on page 187 are from "Revolution" by John Lennon
and Paul McCartney. Copyright © 1968 Northern Songs Ltd. All
rights for the U.S., Canada, and Mexico controlled and admin-
istered by SBK Blackwood Music Inc. under license from ATV
Music (MACLEN). All rights reserved. International copyright
secured. Used by permission.

LIBRARY OF CONGRESS CATALOGING IN PUBLICATION DATA
Bass, Thomas A.
Camping with the Prince and other tales of science in Africa/
Thomas A. Bass.
p. cm.
Originally published: New York: Houghton Mifflin, 1990.
Includes bibliographical references and index.
ISBN 0 14 01.4870 1
1. Africa—Description and travel—1977— 2. Bass, Thomas A.—
Journeys—Africa. 3. Scientific expeditions—Africa. 4. Science
and civilization. I. Title.
DT12.25.B37 1991
916.04'328—dc20   90–20765

Printed in the United States of America

Except in the United States of America, this book is sold subject
to the condition that it shall not, by way of trade or otherwise, be
lent, re-sold, hired out, or otherwise circulated without the pub-
lisher's prior consent in any form of binding or cover other than
that in which it is published and without a similar condition
including this condition being imposed on the subsequent
purchaser.

Contents

Ex Africa semper aliquid novi.
There is always something new out of Africa.

PLINY THE ELDER

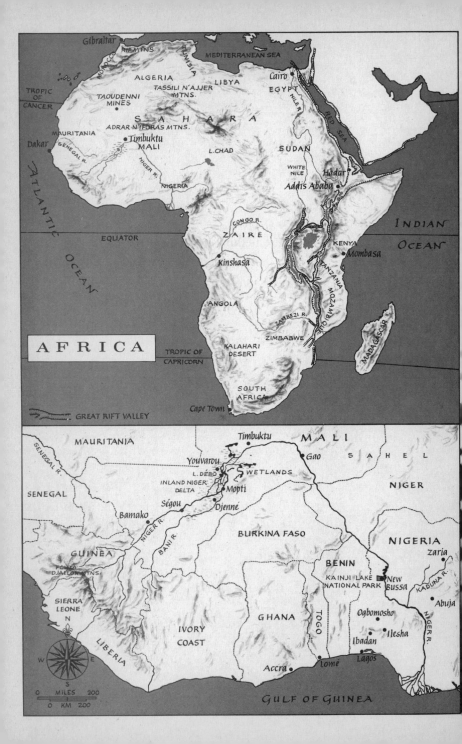

AFRICA

Gibraltar
RIF MTNS
MOROCCO
TUNISIA
MEDITERRANEAN SEA
TROPIC
OF
CANCER
ALGERIA
LIBYA
Cairo
TASSILI N'AJJER
MTNS.
EGYPT
TAOUDENNI
MINES
S A H A R A
NILE
ADRAR N'IFORAS MTNS.
MAURITANIA
Timbuktu
MALI
SUDAN
RED SEA
Dakar
SENEGAL R.
L. CHAD
WHITE
NILE
Hadar
NIGER R.
Addis Ababa
NIGERIA
ATLANTIC OCEAN
EQUATOR
CONGO R.
ZAIRE
INDIAN
OCEAN
KENYA
Mombasa
Kinshasa
TANZANIA
MOZAMBIQUE
ANGOLA
ZAMBEZI R.
MADAGASCAR
ZIMBABWE
TROPIC OF
CAPRICORN
KALAHARI
DESERT
SOUTH
AFRICA
Cape Town
GREAT RIFT VALLEY

MAURITANIA
Timbuktu
M A L I
SENEGAL R.
Youvarou
Gao
S A H E L
L. DÉBO
WETLANDS
NIGER
SENEGAL
INLAND NIGER
DELTA
Mopti
Ségou
Djenne
Bamako
NIGER R.
BANI R.
BURKINA FASO
NIGERIA
GUINEA
zaria
FOUTA
DJALLON MTNS.
BENIN
KAINJI LAKE
NATIONAL PARK
New
Bussa
KADUNA R.
SIERRA
LEONE
Abuja
N
GHANA
Ogbomosho
IVORY
COAST
TOGO
Ilesha
LIBERIA
W   E
Ibadan
NIGER R.
S
Lagos
Accra
Lomé
GULF OF GUINEA
0   MILES   200
0   KM   200

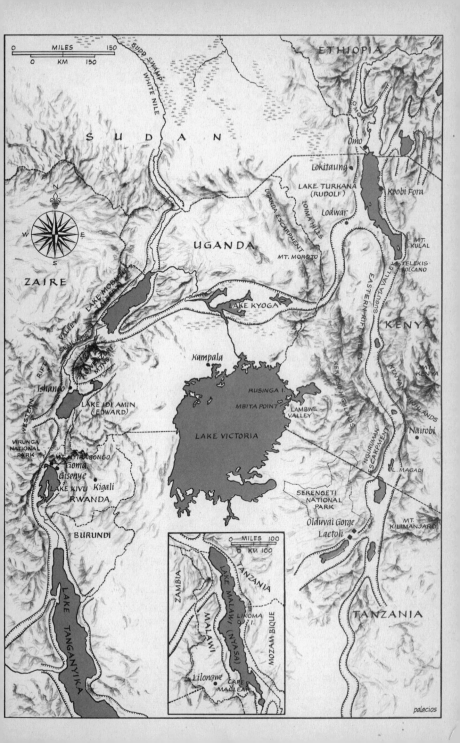

Preface

Over a period of two years, from 1985 to 1987, I accompanied
seven scientific expeditions into Africa. These ranged the length
of the continent from Timbuktu to the Zambezi River, and the
subjects under investigation also varied widely. To learn about life
in desert wetlands, I camped with Bozo fishermen on the edge of
the Sahara. I dove into Lake Malawi to observe fish sex and trapped
tsetse flies with Masai warriors in the Rift Valley. I studied slash-
and-burn agriculture in the tropical rain forests of West Africa
and queried Turkana herders about their knowledge of famine.
I hunted wild viruses on the Niger and excavated archaic bones
and stone tools on the shores of Lake Idi Amin Dada.

I had traveled to some of these places before. As a teenager I
burned up a lot of miles driving along the east coast of Africa,
floating down the Congo, and hitchhiking up the western hump.
Skipping my last year of high school, I convinced my parents to
let me substitute a grand tour of Africa for the tamer European
variety. I arrived in Swaziland on September 6, 1968, to find the
entire country gathered in the national soccer stadium. British
officials, wearing top hats and tails, were handing over the scrolls
of independence to King Sobhuza II, who was dressed in leopard-
skin robes.

Surrounded on three sides by its bellicose neighbor, Swaziland
is a handkerchief in South Africa's breast pocket. There was war
to the east in Mozambique, and some of the students in the mul-
tiracial boarding school where I taught English could attend classes
only by hiking surreptitiously across the border. From my first
moments in Africa, I felt the uneasy fit between contemporary
politics and traditional life.

My early travels on the continent shocked me into a kind of sensory overload. I returned home mute from having experienced too much and understood too little. For fifteen years I nursed the idea of getting back to Africa for a second look. One of the things I had learned in the meantime is that I like to travel with scientists. Scientists pay attention. They know the names of things, like birds and flowers, that I am always forgetting. They ask intelligent questions, and they make good explorers. The best of them are both critical and self-critical. When I conceived the idea of writing about science in Africa, I thought I would borrow my companions' spectacles to take a closer look at some African realities that I had previously glimpsed only in passing.

As I began tracking down researchers, whose whereabouts were often obscure, I discovered that two years' traveling could have turned into twenty. A letter from Nancy Thompson-Handler, who studies pygmy chimpanzees in the heart of the Zairean rain forest, included the following directions to her front door: "The only feasible way to reach Ndele is to walk thirty-five kilometers, much of the way through swamp forest. And this is only the end of the journey. If you are lucky enough to get a flight to Boende, the nearest city one hundred and twenty kilometers away, you must still drive over unimaginable roads and heart-stopping bridges and rely on a ferry that is often out of service. If you are not lucky, you have to do this journey from Mbandaka, so you must face five hundred and fifty kilometers of misery."

Another letter gave me the name of Oyewale Tomori and described him as "a skilled administrator, with strong ethical, philosophical, and humanitarian views, who is now fighting to rejuvenate virus research in Nigeria against political and financial odds." I wrote to Tomori and asked if I could join him in the field. He sent back a note with the dates when he expected to be searching for new viruses at Kainji Lake on the Niger River. There was no way to telephone him. No time for another exchange of letters. So that was all I had to go on when I caught a flight to Lagos.

Africa is a scientific treasure house. Endowed with fabulous examples of physical and cultural diversity, it pushes the boundaries of the known world. For the scientists described here Africa is a conundrum, a series of questions that in many instances can be answered, if they can be answered at all, only on *this* continent. When did humans first start using tools and fire? How do species evolve? Where do AIDS and other new viruses come from? Is our planet getting hotter and drier and, if so, what can be done about it?

Africa is a limit case. It offers scientists the most extreme examples of theoretical problems posed in various disciplines, ranging from human evolution and the evolution of species in general to the theory of famine, the spread of deserts, the rise of new viruses, and the special problems of tropical entomology and tropical agriculture. Africa is also a test case for the study of science and technology in the third world. What happens when this Western enterprise is translated into non-Western cultures?

The seven scientific subjects that make up the seven chapters of this book extend from paleoanthropology and evolutionary biology to economics and ecology, from medicine and insect physiology to tropical agriculture. I could have written seven more chapters, and perhaps I should warn the reader about the selective nature of my choices.

It would have been easy to compose a narrative filled with gloomy predictions like those I encountered at the Hôtel Muhabura, which lies at the base of Rwanda's Virunga Mountains. Here I met two Dutchmen, high officials in the World Bank, who were visiting mountain gorillas in the Parc National des Volcans. The World Bank is partly responsible for the fact that these remarkable primates are nearly extinct. The bank financed the building of pyrethrum plantations that chopped down all but the most inaccessible parts of the gorillas' forest habitat. The plantation scheme was quickly doomed by the development of synthetic pyrethrum, but the gorillas have not been allowed to reclaim their original land.

Since the Dutchmen and I were traveling in the same direction, they offered to chauffeur me to Gisenye, a town on the northern shore of Lake Kivu. I would walk from there across the Zairean border into Goma. We reached Gisenye in time for lunch at the Hôtel Méridien, where we sat beside the pool under a trellis of bougainvillea. We stared across the white tablecloth toward an azure lake dotted with fishermen in dugout canoes. Three salads and a bottle of mineral water cost forty dollars.

When I finally screwed up my courage to ask the World Bankers what they thought they were doing with their lives, they erupted into a torrent of confessional apologies. "I would quit if I had the nerve," said the senior agriculturist, who developed the pyrethrum industry in neighboring Kenya. "We're part of a mafia of high-level bureaucrats that's involved in recycling ideas from the 1950s and calling them new."

"The disastrous consequences of foreign aid are obvious to all of us," the other Dutchman, an economist, told me. "Look at the European milk powder and sugar sitting in front of you. These 'gifts' to Rwanda have destroyed the local dairy and sugar industries. And why is this? Because Europe has mountains of milk that it has to dump somewhere, and the sugar beet producers are an important lobby."

"We lie to our own people," said the agriculturist. "Not one of us is willing to stand up and tell the Europeans and Americans what's really happening in Africa. The current is rushing downstream at ten kilometers per hour. On a good day I think I may be pushing against it at the rate of two kilometers per hour. On a bad day I think I'm rushing headlong downstream like everyone else."

Comments like these can be heard around swimming pools all across Africa, and I repeat them not for what they say about the continent, but for what they tell about European perceptions of it. Our prejudices are daily confirmed by the news out of Africa. The subtext of these reports is one of hopelessness and passivity. Flip sides of the same reality, the ineffectual European and the submissive African are both scrambling to survive a sinking ship.

On a continent littered with white elephants — the bleaching bones of animals and aid projects alike — I could easily have reported on the failure of Africa, an image that flatters our feelings of superiority and generosity. But I chose to travel farther, often to very obscure places, for a glimpse of something else taking place on the continent, something risky and complex and thus hard to gauge in its success.

I believe there is an African counterforce working against entropic doom, and I have tried to write about this other reality, one informed by traditional knowledge and resourcefulness, one im-

bued with the intelligence of conscious acts, which may be undertaken for selfish reasons but which nonetheless work to the common
good. Because I believe that revelation lies in the telling detail, I
have avoided generalities about a continent not my own. Instead
I offer test cases — ideas in action — that are meant to convey the
incredible richness Africa offers the inquiring mind.

Camping with the Prince

I looked around and found that the sight before me did not answer my expectations. I had formed a totally different idea of the wealth and grandeur of Timbuktu.

René Caillié

RIGHT FROM THE START I know that nothing about this trip is going to go as planned. Last week the flight from Paris to Bamako was knocked out by Saharan sandstorms. Today the problem is European fog. Camped around me at Charles de Gaulle airport are students in ill-fitting suits, girls coifed in spiky topknots, and Malian businessmen laughing over a copy of *Le Canard Enchaîné*. An airline hostess tells us to report for dinner at the local Holiday Inn. The bus gets lost in the fog. We drift for an hour before ending up exactly where we started, and then the journey begins all over again.

After lifting off in the middle of the night, our plane sneaks into Bamako at dawn, when the wind is down. We are the first people to land there in a week. The cabin door opens to let in the particular smell of Africa. At its base is what the French call *le goût de terroir*, the acrid odor of earth. Overlaid on top of this is the ripeness of greening plants and decaying vegetable matter and the chalky taste of sweat and dust.

The African sun has already started baking the day into a tropical casserole. At the immigration desk I am told that my papers are not in order. Only after a long discussion does their order become apparent. I clear customs at the heels of a tout and allow myself to be plucked into a taxi for the ride across the Niger into Bamako. The river is brown and weedy, the town an overgrown bazaar of mud streets and cinderblock façades.

I check into the Grand Hôtel, shower, and walk to a nearby bank. After four false starts, I find an institution capable of changing dollars into CFA, which used to stand for "Colonies Françaises d'Afrique," but now signifies "Communauté Financière d'Afrique."

Three hundred dollars goes in a window and comes back out as 144,036 CFA. This huge wad of bills, thicker than *Bleak House*, is almost illegible with grime. I spend the rest of the morning hunting down other scraps of paper—visas, photo permits, fiscal stamps. Then I hear an interesting bit of news. Cobb is in town.

"He usually stays at Les Hirondelles," says the British consul. This small hotel on the outskirts of Bamako is frequented by East German construction crews and EEC functionaries traveling on per diem. "I haven't seen him for a couple of days," the consul says. "So he might have left by now."

I run out of the office and grab a taxi. *"Plus vite! Plus vite!"* I shout at the driver, as we career through town in a cloud of dust.

Dust and drought compose much of the news out of West Africa these days. The Sahara is moving south, we hear. The desert sands are pushing in front of them a wave of refugees. One of these waves has washed into the inner delta of the Niger River—the great wetlands south of Timbuktu, which for a thousand years has nurtured dwellers on the desert's edge. But now the sand has started blowing over the delta itself. The grass and fish are disappearing, and this once-rich land has begun to generate its own forms of dislocation.

To learn why things have gone wrong in the Niger delta, I have to talk to Stephen Cobb. Cobb runs a project designed to figure out if the desert is moving south and, if so, what can be done about it. But he doesn't want to see me. He lives four hundred miles from the nearest telephone. So I have no proof that he doesn't want to see me. But my letters have gone unanswered. My cables have disappeared into thin air.

Confirmation of my suspicions finally came in a message relayed through his employers in Switzerland. "We're sorry," they said, "but for the moment he's quite adamant." Headquarters explained he was suffering from stress. Cobb and his wife, Alison, along with Jamie Skinner, the project ornithologist, Richard Moorehead, its sociologist, and their Malian counterparts, had barely settled in Youvarou, a fishing village one hundred and thirty miles south of Timbuktu, when the Cobbs were told that Prince Philip, Duke of Edinburgh, was coming to visit.

Lodging a prince in a mud house on the banks of the Niger is no easy matter. For plumbing, there is a pit toilet in the yard, and not far from it is the well that you and your night watchman used to drink from until he died recently of cholera. The unfinished house next door has no roof. Your house has no beds. A three-hour jolt over a dirt track takes you to the nearest airport, which is closed because of the weather.

I am in Paris when I get a phone call telling me that if I want to see Cobb I have to go camping with the prince. Someone has come up with the bright idea of getting me into the delta by attaching me to the royal retinue. I am a bit nervous about the arrangement. It may be an American bias, a vestige of revolutionary fervor, but I have trouble making small talk with royalty. What if the prince and I have to share a mud hut? On the advice of a friend, I go out and buy a bush jacket. The epaulets give it an air of gravity, and I am told that in a pinch I can sleep in the thing and wake up the following morning looking relatively presentable.

I inform Switzerland I'll accept their plan on one condition, that I be allowed to fly on my own from Paris to Mali, where I will try to find Cobb before the prince arrives. This is my only hope of talking to him before we get swallowed up in royal protocol. As for what I can expect to find in Africa, my Swiss contact gives me two pieces of news. First, the Air Mali flight from Bamako to Timbuktu no longer exists; the airplane has just crashed and killed everybody on board. Second, it is already so hot, even in March, that everyone in Youvarou is sleeping on the roof.

On arriving at Les Hirondelles, I rush into the hotel dining room to find a solitary couple eating a late lunch of *steak frites*. The first thing I notice about Stephen Cobb is his rower's chest, convex and muscled under a shirt opened three buttons at the neck. He wears blue jeans and rubber sandals cut from auto tires. His gray eyes stare out at me from a narrow face, square-jawed and burnished with the ocherous tones of a malaria victim who has taken too much sun. Lanky and leathery like her husband, Alison Cobb shakes my hand and asks, "Shall we sit down?"

This greeting, formal, reserved, delivered with the clipped locution of the educated English, marks the tone of their conversation, even between themselves. Stephen tells me he is late. A week late. Otherwise I never would have found him in the capital lunching at three o'clock in the afternoon. They are leaving momentarily for Mopti, a nine-hour drive to the north, and then traveling another three hours to Youvarou. Yes, I can ride with them to Youvarou, if I am willing to straddle the gearshift. But I should expect no more favors until after the prince's visit. I agree to the terms, and within hours of arriving in Africa, fresh off the night flight from Paris, I find myself swaying around potholes in a Land Rover roaring toward the desert.

North of Bamako we drive through a forest of tenacious, small-leafed trees, including kapoks and baobabs that look as if they have been stuck in the earth root side up. This forest has plenty of strolling room between the trees, although underground, where taproots and tendrils are competing for every available drop of water, space is doubtless tighter. Along the roadside march women carrying on their heads calabashes full of milk, bundles of forage, stacks of reeds, and baskets loaded with millet, sorghum, mangoes, raw cotton, animal hides, and chickens. A second line of transport rolls along on bicycles freighted with cassava, mounds of dried fish, sheep, and goats. Donkey carts full of dung and bricks merge onto the highway, while the final link in the procession consists of lorries top-heavy with cattle and sacks of donated Canadian grain.

Every few miles we slow for roadblocks at police checkpoints. This will become a familiar sight in Mali: civil servants collecting their wages directly from the people. "They usually wave us through because of our international plates," says Stephen. "But if you stop to pay all the bribes between Bamako and Mopti, a nine-hour trip takes twenty-four."

We stop for dinner in a town where the only illumination comes from kerosene lamps. Walking down an alleyway, we enter an open courtyard furnished with a well, a cooking fire, and some three-legged stools. A woman serves us bowls of rice sauced with peanuts and peppers. Holding empty bowls of their own, a dozen boys watch us eat. "*Les garibous,*" says Alison, pointing to the boys. "Koranic students whom Allah commends to our charity." When we give them half our dinner, the boys praise the mercy of God.

"You see," a Malian friend later explains to me, holding his palm in front of my face, "some fingers are longer than others, just as some people in life possess more than others. But if we share among ourselves, then it serves to make us more equal. It's the opposite in your country, isn't it?"

The forests to the north get drier and dustier until they thin out into sandy wastes and plains of baked laterite covered with leafless bushes. The wind fills with migrating soil, and the road diverges into multiple detours, with one track looking exactly like another. Our headlights surprise a Twareg, a blue-robed nomad from the desert. His belongings are bundled behind him on a splay-footed camel. The camel is headed south. "This is two hundred kilometers below the normal range for camels," says Stephen. "You can tell something very strange is going on."

We stop for the night at Ségou, the major town on the southern boundary of the delta. The medieval capital of the Songhai empire, Ségou was where the Scottish explorer Mungo Park in 1796 "saw with infinite pleasure the great object of my mission — the long sought for majestic Niger, glittering in the morning sun, as broad as the Thames at Westminster, and flowing slowly *to the eastward*."

Ségou later served as administrative capital for the greatest colonial project in French Africa. Using forced labor recruited from Upper Volta, the French in 1932 built a dam and canals sufficient to irrigate a million hectares of land in an ancient watercourse known as the Dead Niger. The French were hoping to emulate the Manchester cotton merchants who had dammed the Blue Nile to build the Gezira scheme, the world's largest farm. But the Office du Niger, as the French project was called, never succeeded in turning the Niger delta into a cotton plantation. Embarrassed when their scheme was compared to the Nazi concentration camps, the French had to find another source of labor after the Second World War. But by then the project was already suffering from the waterlogging and salinization that would doom it. Production has now dropped to twenty-eight thousand hectares of rice — cotton is no longer grown — and most of the area has reverted to a soupy bog into which tractors and cows have been known to sink without a trace.

That night I sleep fitfully in a concrete guest room appended to a textile factory. The factory processes cotton trucked in from Senegal, and Alison Cobb tells me it makes very bad fabric. The warp is off square, and when you cut the material it goes out of true. I keep thinking of the fog I left behind in Europe and the red ball of dust I found in Africa, until the two images merge into something truly obscure.

We leave at sunrise and drive north into a thickening haze. By noon we are running along the dike that leads to the island city and three mosques of Mopti. Sitting at the confluence of the Bani and Niger rivers, this Venice of Africa used to be approachable in the rainy season only by boat. But this year the canals are bone dry, and some of the flood plain surrounding the city has been scraped into vegetable gardens. Other sections are covered with the mat houses of Twareg and Bella refugees from the desert. Crowded with bush taxis, motorbikes, and pedestrians walking shoulder to shoulder in its dusty streets, Mopti itself is swelled with a dry-season influx that has tripled its normal population of twenty thousand.

Koranic students with begging bowls ply the mud-walled city yelling, "*Allah garibous!*" A boy leads a blind *griot* down the street as the *griot* sings a praise song mixing local news with the great deeds of his benefactors. The Mercedes of a rice merchant driving to the mosque for midday prayers cuts a wake through the populace. On the far side of the city, dozens of merchants squatting on the riverbank shout up their goods. "Sardines! Sony Walkmen! Tomatoes! Mopeds!" The cacophony of items for sale includes everything from tape cassettes to tablets of salt carried by camel from the Taoudenni mines above Timbuktu.

It will take us another three to four hours to drive from Mopti to Youvarou. After being ferried across the Niger on a steel barge, our Land Rover rolls into a thorn scrub terrain filled with green monkeys, black bush chats, yellow wagtails, and mourning doves perched in the deep green crowns of *Diospyros* trees. Termite mounds point skyward like red fingers at salute. We set off on a one-track *piste* that disappears at times into dry lake bottoms and river beds. The only traffic we encounter is a truck delivering food aid and a Peugeot bush taxi swaying under an impossible load.

A plume of red earth trails behind us as we race over the bed of Lake Débo. Clumps of tussock grass and *Ziziphus*, an inedible bush, give the illusion of greenery to land that has actually been grazed to dust. Fulani herders, who in Neolithic times husbanded animals in what is now the middle of the Sahara, stand guard over their hump-backed cattle. The Fulani, or Peul, as they are known in French West Africa, with their elongated bodies wrapped in togas, and straw platter hats on their heads, look like visitors from outer space. Of course, to them the *toubabs* in their Land Rover must look equally strange.

We crest a sandy ridge, and there below us, unfurling like a golden sash laid over the brown land, lies the Niger. A mile wide, the river fills the horizon. "To see the Niger flowing through the desert is one of nature's wonders, as incongruous as the umbrella on the operating table made famous by the surrealists," said Sanche de Gramont. Birds flock over the sluggish current. Pirogues pull inverted Vs in their wake. It will ultimately get banked against the Sahara and spun from north to south, but here in the delta the Niger runs like a great highway straight to Timbuktu.

Given the anomaly of rivers that rise in tropical highlands and flow north to the Sahara, three of Africa's greatest wetlands lie in the Sahel. This band of arid savanna, which edges the desert and takes its name from the Arabic word for "shore," receives no rain for nine months of the year and then a scant foot or two that falls in bursts between June and September. An immense tract stretching across Africa from the Atlantic Ocean to the Sudan, the Sahel would be largely unpopulated were it not for the watered oases provided by the Senegal River valley, Lake Chad, and the inland delta of the Niger.

The Niger River possesses not one but two deltas: a mangrove swamp on the Atlantic coast rich in fish and hydrocarbons, and an inland delta blessed in its own fashion. Rising in the Guinean highlands of the Fouta Djallon mountains, almost within sight of the ocean it later rejoins, the Niger passes through a dusty stretch of Sahelian forest before coming to the clay plain of the inland delta. Here the river, swollen with summer rains from the mountains, transforms itself into a moving lake sixty miles wide and two hundred miles long. By August, Djenné and other towns in the southern delta have become islands, and by January the flood has peaked at Timbuktu.

Because of the Niger flood, what would otherwise be a semiarid steppe surviving on ten inches of rain a year is converted annually into a mosaic of lakes and streams. Green islands rise out of the water, their shores fringed with the mat houses of Bozo fishermen, who ply the river in canoes made of dom palms stitched together with hibiscus twine. Rimaïbé farmers plant rice at the river's edge. A long-stemmed floating grass known as *bourgou* sprouts in the flooded meadows, and then as the waters recede in the southern delta, Fulani and Twareg nomads lead their herds northward through the newly revitalized pasture. For a thousand years these wetlands supported the black empires of West Africa and anchored the southern edge of the Saharan trade routes. They nurtured the medieval fortunes of Timbuktu, and today they assure the livelihood of a million fishermen, farmers, pastoralists, and nomads.

Arranged into carefully synchronized patterns of land use that have survived for millennia, these desert wetlands produce eight times as much plant matter per acre as the average wheat field. A half-dozen Malian tribes have worked out elaborate protocols for sharing this common ground as it cycles from flood plain to pasture for a million cattle and three million sheep and goats — the highest density of herds in all of Africa. Now that the Nile, Senegal, Volta, and Zambezi rivers have been dammed and channeled, the Niger delta preserves the last of the continent's great flood plains.

A safe harbor for nomads throughout the Sahel, the delta is also a refuge for millions of birds. Three hundred and fifty species either breed or winter here. As snow settles over the northern hemisphere, most of the herons, egrets, ibises, and terns empty out of Europe and Asia north of the Himalayas. To reach their wintering grounds in Africa, birds coming from the Arctic Circle will fly up to ten thousand miles in a month-long journey across Siberia, the Caucasian steppes, the Black Sea, and a desert as large as the United States.

Like most other visitors to the Niger delta, I have come in the spring, after the flood and before the rains. This is the one season when passable roads exist. I have also come a couple of years after the worst Sahelian drought in recorded history. Following a string of bad years beginning in the late 1960s, the flood failed completely in 1984. The delta that year received less than a third of its usual

volume of water. By the summer of 1985, three fourths of the
stock in the area had died for lack of pasture. How many people
died is unknown.

In the common view of the matter, as presented in newspaper
articles and TV specials, Africa is suffering from desertification.
Borrowed from the French, the word denotes the ecological degradation of land evolving from a more to a less productive state.
But the concept also entails a host of presuppositions about land
use and people. In the case of Africa, it is assumed that the continent is overgrazed, overpopulated, and now permanently
wracked by drought. Aided by man and beast nibbling away at its
desiccated margins, the Sahara, according to popular report, is
creeping southward at the rate of ten, twenty, thirty miles a year.
    "Anyone possessing some knowledge of the desert-country types
can come and study the stages, quite sufficiently clear cut once the
eye is attuned to discerning them, by which the desert has through
the centuries, assisted by man, advanced over rich and fertile regions." This was written in 1937 by Edward Stebbing, a forester
whose remarks characterize what was then, and is again today,
accepted opinion about Africa. Stebbing and his latter-day colleagues specialize in drawing maps showing the "present advance
of sand."
    The problem with Stebbing's view is that little evidence supports
it, and some contravenes it. It is true that a drought in the 1930s
simultaneously desiccated Africa and the American Dust Bowl. But
conditions later returned to normal, and both parts of the world
witnessed exceptionally plentiful rainfall in the 1940s. As West
African farmers pushed their fields northward into areas that had
once been reserved for grazing, the amount of land under cultivation greatly increased. African nations fought for their independence in the midst of these bountiful times, and no one
suspected that the rain-fed harvests would disappear as quickly as
they had come.
    In fact, these cycles of wet and dry years have characterized the
climate of Africa for the past two thousand years, and one has to
look even further back in history to find the long-term changes
that Stebbing was so quick to identify. Once Africa actually did

have sand dunes blowing over what are now tropical rain forests. At the end of the last glaciation, fifteen thousand years ago, the Kalahari Desert stretched into the Congo basin, and massive dune fields can still be found lying far to the south of what today marks the edge of the Sahara. Reaching three hundred miles into tropical Africa, these Saharan dunes have been colonized by grasses and trees, but when photographed from outer space, they reveal the serried waves of what was once a great sand sea.

If the African climate has been drier at various times in the past, it has also been wetter. One of these humid periods, beginning in the sixth millennium B.C., coincides with the Neolithic revolution —the stage in human history when plants and animals were domesticated and city living was invented. Signs of these wetter times still exist in the form of olive trees clinging to mountaintops in the middle of the desert.

Other evidence of major shifts in the weather comes from the thousands of cave paintings scattered throughout the Sahara. They record the remarkable trajectory of land passing from savanna to desert, in images that themselves appear to get dried out, wrung free of swamp and marsh, cleansed of zebra and giraffe, and finally toasted to a sandy brown. The oldest paintings, dating from 5500 B.C., show hippos and fish swimming in Saharan lakes and hunters chasing elephants over well-watered plains. These are followed by drawings of pastoralists whose herds are so prolific that the multicolored animals tumble out of the picture. Then come chariots and warriors on horses and camels, which had disappeared from North Africa until the Romans reintroduced them in the second century A.D.

If the Saharan climate has remained relatively stable for the past two thousand years, there are two possible exceptions when it may have been wetter than it is today. The Greco-Roman-Byzantine era, Africa's Golden Age, witnessed plentiful rainfall feeding rivers and oases in what is now the Libyan Desert. This water allowed the North African territories to supply both the bread and elephants for Roman circuses. A second wet period may have occurred during the Middle Ages, which are also known as the Dark Ages—in part because it rained a lot. From the ninth to the fourteenth centuries a succession of great empires rose on the southern edge of the Sahara. Ghana was the first of these, but its capital at Koumbi Saleh—with a square mile of stone buildings and two square miles of outlying cemeteries—now lies buried under sand in the middle of the Mauritanian desert.

In 1324 the emperor of Mali, Mansa Musa, crossed the Sahara on a pilgrimage to Mecca accompanied by five hundred slaves carrying golden staffs and another hundred camels laden with gold. His arrival depreciated the metals market in Egypt by twelve percent. It also sparked fabulous tales of Timbuktu and the Niger delta on which the city's wealth was based. The area flourished as part of the Songhai empire until the sixteenth century, when a new form of technology, Portuguese ships, and a new source of gold, the Americas, weakened it beyond repair. Fought over by competing groups, the delta recorded great famines every ten years, and then every five years. In 1738 half the population of Timbuktu died of famine. Ninety years later, when Timbuktu was "discovered" by the Frenchman René Caillié, this once-prosperous city, with eighty thousand inhabitants and two universities, had been reduced to a miserable village of twelve thousand souls.

"I looked around and found that the sight before me did not answer my expectations," said Caillié. "I had formed a totally different idea of the wealth and grandeur of Timbuktu." The fabulous city "presented, at first view, nothing but a mass of ill-looking houses, built of earth. Nothing was to be seen in all directions but immense plains of quicksand of a yellowish-white color. The sky was a pale red as far as the horizon; all nature wore a dreary aspect, and the most profound silence prevailed; not even the warbling of a bird was to be heard."

Stephen Cobb has been given a tough nut to crack, a scientific puzzle with too many pieces and no obvious solutions. Employed by the Swiss-based International Union for the Conservation of Nature and Natural Resources (IUCN) as director of a $730,000 project financed by the German government and the World Wildlife Fund, he is charged with studying the Niger delta and thinking of ways to solve its drought-exacerbated problems. He will design a mix of small-scale development schemes, wildlife reserves, and buffer zones regulated for multiple use by all the competing forces in the region. After drawing up a management plan for the delta in its entirety, he is supposed to mount an experiment that will demonstrate the effectiveness of his plan.

The stakes in this venture are high for everybody involved. Cobb's project is IUCN's largest, and it marks a revolutionary departure for the organization. Since its founding in 1948, this consortium of five hundred government and environmental groups has employed a variety of traditional measures for protecting plants and animals. But there is growing concern in the organization, as its Red Data Books record the demise of one species after another, that these standard procedures—such as the establishment of parks and international controls on the traffic in wildlife—are no longer working. When it was founded, IUCN thought about conservation in terms of individual species. Then, after launching a campaign to save tropical rain forests and plants, it began to think in terms of environments. But a crucial element was still missing from the equation. Only belatedly and with great trepidation has IUCN begun to think about people.

Plants, animals, and environments have to be put back in a social matrix—which they never left in the first place—to see what people do with nature and how they benefit from conserving it. IUCN has to generate hard-nosed economic arguments for conservation. It has to be more aggressive in countering development agencies like the World Bank, which has been financing the destruction of tropical rain forests at the rate of a hundred acres a minute. They have been archenemies since the beginning of the environmental movement, but conservation can no longer exist apart from development. Ducks in the Niger delta will not be saved while nomads die, and the two causes are really part of the same struggle anyway. Desert wetlands preserved as working resources are good for *both* ducks and people. The new theme at IUCN headquarters is "development based on a healthy environment," and Project 9016, with Stephen Cobb at the helm, was launched in 1984 as the flagship for reaching this goal.

The stakes are also high for the Malian government, which has been watching the country's major assets die on the hoof and wither under a killing sun. International experts bearing multimillion-dollar contracts have been advising the government to dam the

Niger and channel it into agricultural projects. Do the conserva-
tionists really have something better to offer? They think so, which
is why Prince Philip is coming to town. Wearing his twin hats as
vice president of IUCN and president of the World Wildlife
Fund — which will later change its name, along with its perspective,
to the World Wide Fund for Nature — the prince is going to talk
with the president of Mali about Cobb's project and ask him to
support it at the highest level. For a wildlife ecologist who spent
the happiest years of his life living alone studying elephants in
Tsavo National Park, Stephen is about to get a strong dose of
politics mixed into his science.

In the spring of 1984 Stephen and Alison Cobb drove overland
from England to Mali. After crossing the Strait of Gibraltar into
Morocco and traversing the Rif Mountains, they dropped into the
waterless ergs of the Algerian desert and then traveled south across
the Niger to Bamako. Bamako is the capital of what was once
known as French Sudan, a former colony twice the size of France
itself and now the largest country in West Africa. It is also among
the poorest. Two thirds of Mali is either desert or Sahelian scrub,
and the country's seven million inhabitants are reported to have
a yearly per capita income of one hundred and sixty dollars. After
becoming independent in 1960, Mali flirted with state socialism
and transferred its young intellectuals from the Sorbonne to Patrice Lumumba University in Moscow. The Soviet Union provided
the helicopters that defeated a Twareg insurrection in 1963. Part
of the tragedy of Mali and other Sahelian countries is that their
political independence coincided with the *sécheresse*; impoverished
nations veering from right to left and back again have proved no
match for a killing drought.

Stephen was planning a quick visit to the capital, a round of
hand shaking at various government offices before getting to work
in the delta. But his quick visit became a nightmare. Everything
he touched turned into paperwork. As gracious and charming as
they may be in private life, government officials in Mali stand in
relation to the country's citizens like suckerfish to whales. "They
tied me up in knots," he says. "Wherever I went they asked me,
'Who is your special man?' I was supposed to be paying someone

full-time to run around and do the paperwork. I was driving a new Land Rover they hadn't seen before, so the police kept stopping me. I spent three hours a day for a month refusing to pay bribes. It was all extremely depressing, but I learned patience."

At the end of their month in the capital, the Cobbs renegotiated the dozen police checkpoints on the road between Bamako and Mopti and found themselves back on the banks of the Niger. They ferried across the river and drove to Youvarou, the small fishing village on whose outskirts they would build a house. Construction, expected to take two months, took six. Stephen succumbed to a bout of malaria that left him unconscious for hours on end. Their night watchman died of cholera. "One night he was smiling, saying, 'My family is at peace. I am at peace,' and the next morning he was dead." Supplies shipped from Europe got lost in Dakar, as did the mail from IUCN headquarters, including the payroll. Stephen reached into his pocket one morning to find himself flat broke.

Ten months after their arrival in Mali, the Cobbs were visited by two officials from Switzerland. There are no telephones in Youvarou, and the mail, even when Stephen delivers the last hundred miles of the route himself, takes a couple of months to arrive. The officials brought news that Prince Philip planned to visit Youvarou and survey the project firsthand. "At least we knew they hadn't forgotten us," says Stephen. "With the prince coming, they must have thought we were doing *something* right."

When I met him near the end of his first year in Mali, Stephen had accomplished less than he wanted, and some of what he *had* accomplished gave him new grounds for worry. He had hired a staff of four people and imported an airplane to fly transects over the delta. These aerial surveys, conducted by a pilot and three observers flying at a hundred fifty kilometers per hour, two hundred feet off the ground, were meant to canvass the human, animal, and bird populations down below. The technique had worked nicely in East Africa, where Stephen had had no trouble distinguishing elephants from zebras. But telling sheep from goats is another matter, and people's tribal affiliations are impossible to spot from the air. One unsettling discovery Stephen made was the existence of over a thousand square kilometers of dead forest.

Seeing all these withered trees gave him a scare. It brought home the magnitude of the disaster afflicting Sahelian Africa and made him wonder about the merits of *any* development project in the region. It was all well and good to talk about the economic benefits of a healthy environment. But what if the desert was blowing a hundred and fifty miles south of its usual border? How could any environment survive this onslaught?

A job description of Stephen's work in the Niger delta would range from scientist and medic to ombudsman and ecological practitioner. His contract called for him to do basic research on the flora and fauna of the region, survey its human and animal populations, establish a system of reserves for protecting wildlife, particularly the large numbers of birds, draft a management plan for the area based on the idea of overlapping "zones of multiple use," doctor local Malians, provide them with clean water, voice the concerns of the people to the government, and design a pilot project to demonstrate the economic benefits of a healthy environment. He was most worried about the last item on the list. "In three years it's hard to *demonstrate* anything in Africa. Particularly in a part of the world as complex as this."

As for managing natural resources in the delta through reserves and zones of multiple use, Stephen explained the concept as follows. "To understand the idea of zones in the delta, all you have to do is stand on my roof. As you look out over the Niger, you see cattle grazing its shores and birds lining the riverbank. Farther out you see fishermen casting their nets and pirogues filled with *bourgou* being poled upstream. An engineer surveying the river from my rooftop might imagine a world full of dams and polders and rice paddies producing surplus crops for the people of Mali. I look out and see something entirely different: a wonderfully productive ecosystem that for a thousand years has supported an intricate mix of wildlife, pastoralists, fishermen, and farmers, each of them moving in discrete cycles through space and time, according to the rise and fall of the river."

A thirty-nine-year-old ecologist who wrote his dissertation on Kenyan elephants, Stephen took a roundabout route to gain his expertise in wetlands ecology and the politics of science in Africa. It was only after flunking his A-levels in modern literature that this son of a neurophysiologist and graduate of the Shrewsbury

School "decided to get on with it and become a biologist." He took a job as a scaffolder's mate digging the Victoria line of the London Underground and enrolled in a college of further education. The second time around he tested well enough to get admitted to Oxford.

Shrewsbury is in the Shropshire hill country, and Stephen had always been "keen on birds at school." Birds took him to Africa for the first time at the age of nineteen, when he spent a summer banding waders in Tunisia. Then in 1968 he shipped out on a cargo boat for Dar es Salaam and worked for six months as odd-job man at the Serengeti Research Institute. Among other assignments, he counted impala from the air and studied lions with the zoologist George Schaller. "The lions were mostly asleep. It was nothing much, but I learned that I liked Africa and wanted to get back as soon as I could."

Stephen returned the following year to look at genets, small spotted cats, on the shores of Lake Turkana, and then he put together enough money for a longer stay in Kenya's Tsavo National Park. At the time Tsavo was losing its trees. It was also losing its browsing animals, like elephants, who were being replaced by grazers. Elephants die in private, and all Stephen could find of their remains was a handful of jawbones. Only after he got an airplane and started flying transects over the park was he able to map the distribution of animals in relation to its shifting climate. "It was a useful bit of baseline work," he says of his doctoral dissertation. "Part of it involved a computer program for analyzing aerial surveys, which I later sold to a number of users. That was back in the old days, when all you wanted to know was a number."

Stephen's next African assignment was much trickier, and it threw him into a dilemma he was likely to face again in Mali. What happens when a scientist, hired to advise the government, is banished for reporting bad news? Is the research itself a failure because of its inability to affect public policy? In 1981 Stephen was tapped by an Anglo-Italian consulting firm to direct the range ecology and aerial surveys in a study of the Jonglei Canal, which was then under construction south of Khartoum. At two hundred and twenty-five miles—longer than the Panama and Suez canals put together—the Jonglei Canal will divert the White Nile from the Sudd swamp, where half the river currently evaporates every year.

As Alan Moorehead wrote in his book *The White Nile*, "There is no more formidable swamp in the world than the Sudd. The Nile loses itself in a vast sea of papyrus ferns and rotting vegetation, and in that foetid heat there is a spawning tropical life that can hardly have altered very much since the beginning of the world."

Stephen and Alison spent eighteen months in the Sudd living in a Dinka hut whose door was four feet off the ground. With no navigable river channels, it was impossible to travel during the six-month rainy season, except by hiking through the mud. Alison, trained as a biotechnician, did laboratory analyses and local doctoring in the morning, and then retreated into her hut in the afternoon, when the temperature would climb to a hundred and twenty degrees Fahrenheit. Working with four permanent staff members and fifteen visiting scientists, Stephen surveyed the swamp. He balanced the canal's benefits (improved transportation and farming) against its drawbacks (deterioration of grazing lands and spread of waterborne diseases) to conclude that the Sudd and its inhabitants would be better off without the Jonglei Canal. When he handed his ten-volume report to the Sudanese authorities in 1983, they threw it in the wastebasket and tried to finish what they had already started. "Faced with translating scientific results into political action," Stephen says, "the project ended a complete failure."

In Youvarou the Cobbs are busy preparing for the royal visit, so they send me next door to stay with their sociologist, Richard Moorehead, and their ornithologist, Jamie Skinner. Jamie, at twenty-seven, is younger than Richard and less experienced in the field, but he is politically savvy about things that Richard prefers not to think about, like the protocol of royal visits. They make a good team. While Stephen is preoccupied with the logistics of running the project, Jamie and Richard carry on its scientific work.

When they first came to Mali in the fall of 1984, Richard and Jamie found they liked each other and decided to build a house together. They hired a mason who worked in mud bricks, and just about the time I arrived in Youvarou they were putting the finishing touches on a delightful Moorish palace of whitewashed rooms laid out around a central courtyard of sand. Decorated with Fulani wedding blankets and pottery funerary urns, this inner cloister was open to what, in better days, would have been a crystalline blue sky.

Walking up the staircase to the newly finished roof, I discover a breathtaking view of the Niger, which flows in front of the house like a silver thread inlaid between ocher bands of sand. Away from the river lies a dusty plain dotted with the occasional thorn tree or bush. As windswept and unwelcoming as it looks, there are always people in sight. A Twareg leads his camel to water. A woman carries a bowl of fish on her head. A boy chases his goats to pasture. Later we will take our sleeping mats up to the roof and lie there listening to the whirring *trrr, trrr* sound of long-tailed nightjars courting over the desert.

The house sits several hundred feet back from the river, but it looks as if a small rise in water would flood the site. Jamie confirms my suspicions. "We built our house on sand," he says. "If the rains ever come back, we're going to disappear under a lake of water. It was supposed to be a short-term project anyway."

A Scottish zoologist trained at the University of London, Jamie had come to Mali from another African assignment at Lake Ichkeul in Tunisia. The most important of the remaining freshwater lakes that once lined the southern shore of the Mediterranean, Ichkeul is a national park and haven for millions of ducks and water birds. But when the six dams being built on its inflow rivers are finished, Ichkeul will be turned into a wheat field and a salt pan. "That's the problem with wetlands in arid countries," Jamie says. "They all get dammed or farmed or used for power production. The problem with wetlands in humid countries is that they all get polluted."

Jamie and I are driving through the delta one evening looking at roosting birds. Crowned cranes strut through meadows hopping with larks and black-tailed godwits. Swallows eating flies dart overhead, and the air is filled with flocks of ruffs from the Arctic Circle. After crossing the desert at the end of their journey, these birds are sometimes so tired that they literally fall out of the air. Having burned up all their body fat, they desperately need water, tree cover, and food. But if these are missing from the desert's edge, one can walk out in the morning to find the cold corpses of warblers and nightingales huddled behind the tussocks of grass from which they sought shelter in the night.

Evening settles over the delta, and the harmattan blows a wall of dust off the Sahara. Our *piste* disappears into a dry lake bed. Out of the red cloud surrounding us loom Fulani herders in their flying-saucer hats. I look over at Jamie's face, flushed by the wind, and notice something unusual. His gold, wire-rim spectacles are polished like no one else's in Mali. I swear there is not a speck of dust on them.

"Birds get massacred in the slide to monoculture," is Jamie's succinct way of characterizing one problem with developing the Niger flood plain. As precious as they are, these waters are bound to be developed. But developed for whom? A nomad looking over the delta sees a landscape in motion, an array of shifting opportunities overlaid by an ancient network of social relations. A Western engineer, on the other hand, sees a resource waiting to be exploited, a good place to build dams and other projects cast in concrete.

The engineers have already largely succeeded in channeling West Africa's wetlands into polders, rice paddies, and other irrigation schemes. Reworking the same idea that motivated the Office du Niger, they are launching a spate of new projects supposedly designed to counter desertification in the Sahel. Overlooked or ignored in these schemes is the fact that every technological fix attempted in the Sahelian wetlands over the past fifty years has failed. Either the technology was wrong for the culture, or the technology itself was faulty. Permanent waterworks require social hierarchies to run them: managers on top, workers below. But the network of relationships in the Sahel tends to stretch horizontally among peers rather than vertically between figures of authority. Twareg women, for example, exercise a degree of independence encountered nowhere else in the Moslem world. The Frenchmen running the Office du Niger discovered these facts about Sahelian life when they were forced to import slave labor from outside the region, but the lesson seems to have been forgotten.

The land itself has also resisted the imposition of Western technology. The soils have proved too fragile to support the irrigation projects already built in the Sahel. Most of these have been plagued by waterlogging and salinization before finally being abandoned. A telling example comes from the agricultural schemes on the Senegal River, which, along with Lake Chad and the Niger, used to be the third great wetlands in the Sahel. Two new dams at the headwaters and mouth of the river will put an end to its existence as a seasonal flood plain. But they will do nothing to alter the fact that other irrigation projects already built along the Senegal have greatly impoverished the lives of its riverine citizens: every newly created acre of paddy field has resulted in four acres of flood plain reverting to desert.

The figures are no more encouraging for the Niger delta. Over the past fifteen years more than one hundred million dollars have been invested here in cattle-ranching and rice-growing schemes. During the drought of 1984, this Sahelian herd totaled a million well-watered cattle, but two thirds of them died for lack of pasture. Their plight was worsened by the conversion of twenty percent of the delta from grazing land to rice polders that produced no rice that year. Undaunted by its previous failures, the World Bank is investing another fifty million dollars in the delta for irrigated agriculture. A further threat to the area comes from twenty dams planned for the river all the way back to its headwaters in the Fouta Djallon in Guinea.

In the face of this onslaught, Jamie's original assignment was little more than a holding action. He was supposed to survey the delta and find a watery ark to be set aside as a national reserve for the ducks and water birds that winter here. Many of Africa's parks have been established under similar conditions. They represent an amelioration of doubtful policies, an itch in the conscience of northerners as they work their will on the south. Cynics might say that establishing a bird reserve in Mali is of particular interest to European duck hunters worried about their supply of fowl. Whatever the motive behind it, Jamie abandoned the project when he realized there was no way the delta could be turned into a park.

"You can't tell someone not to eat a pelican when they're hungry," he says. "And pelican eating itself is less of a threat to the bird populations than other factors."

In a locale that shifts from dusty plain to watery world in a matter of days, where mud, marsh, and flood make transportation impossible for six months of the year, it is impossible to establish and police a European-style park. "Most of what you do in conservation is untenable here. When the flood arrives you're surrounded by a sea of water. So forget about driving your car. Then when the flood recedes you're surrounded by mud. So you can't travel by boat either."

Late in 1984 Jamie sent a report to Switzerland explaining why he wanted to drop the idea of bird reserves in the delta. The birds are threatened locally by four trends: the extension and intensification of agriculture, the use of contact poisons on cropland, the destruction of *bourgou* pasture through overgrazing, and the hunting of ducks and other waterfowl by the Bozo. But in Jamie's opinion, none of these trends is alarming, and all are relatively benign compared to other threats lying upstream.

"In fact the desired reserve system exists already — it is the thousands of square kilometers of seasonally flooded pastures managed traditionally for fishing and grazing activities, neither of which excludes healthy bird populations," his report concluded. "While current land use practices continue, the role of the conservationist will be to fine-tune improvements at the local level of resource use, which will probably have few dramatic effects. The single most long-reaching contribution to be made is in ensuring the water supply, and let the vast surface area and tradition do the rest."

Jamie was the first project member to demonstrate the benefits of marrying conservation to development. By fine-tuning some local improvements — undramatic as they may be — he created one of the few success stories to be found in the crisis-ridden Sahel. Jamie had become alarmed about the thirteen species of heron that breed in the delta. While touring the region by airplane, boat, and car on his bird surveys, he counted close to two hundred thousand herons in five large colonies. But the thorn forests holding these colonies were under seige, and they looked about ready to join the twenty *Acacia kirkii* woodlands that have been chopped down within recent memory. Jamie chose a forest near the fishing village of Bouna to see if he could design a strategy for saving the remaining woodlands.

Lying in a heavily trafficked part of the delta, the Bouna forest revolves seasonally through a bird-fish-crop-herding system of great complexity. To explain how it works, one has to mention Cheikou Ahmadou, the Moslem *marabout* who organized a theocratic state in the delta in the nineteenth century. Ahmadou established the Dina system, which divided the plain into thirty-seven *leydi*, or districts, controlled by village elders. They maintained fishing and woodland reserves, organized access to resources, and managed their own indigenous, highly effective forms of conservation. Cattle crossings, fishing rights, and other rules were codified in Arabic texts known as *Tariki*. Remnants of this early attempt at environmental planning still exist in the delta, and Jamie thought they would make an excellent framework for his experiment.

As decreed under the Dina, a Master of the Water controls a forest when it is wet, and a Dioro—the nominal head of an old fighting family—controls it when it is dry. This authority over grazing rights has made the Dioros rich. But the migrant goat herders who pay the Dioros to use their forests also have to buy cutting permits from the Service des Eaux et Forêts. A permit costs twenty-five hundred CFA and allows the goat herders to construct thorn enclosures for guarding their animals at night. Anyone who builds an enclosure without a permit or who cuts live trees to feed his goats risks paying a stiff fine, fifteen percent of which, by law, goes to the agent levying the fine.

Jamie discovered that this system, with its peculiar mix of motives and power, actually encouraged people to chop down the forests. The goat herders expected to be fined no matter what they did. Slight damage to one forest would result in a collective fine of forty thousand CFA, while heavy damage cost fifty thousand. Regarding these fines as a supplementary tax, the herders thought it prudent to pay them and fatten their goats at the same time. The Dioro, as an absentee landlord, was content with his rent check, while the agent from Eaux et Forêts was happy to collect his salary on the job.

Jamie's basic idea was to give the people using the Bouna forest a greater say in running their own affairs. Goat herders know better than anybody that tree cutting and overgrazing damage their livelihood, but they lack the internal organization necessary to police the woodlands and mete out punishment to wrongdoers.

The matter is further complicated by class differences. The goat herders, a mix of Peul, Bella, and Serifi tribesmen, occupy the bottom rung of the social ladder.

Jamie drew up a plan for getting the Bouna forest declared a *forêt villageoise*. Newly created under Malian law, this status allows forests to be run by a committee of users. From the perspective of Eaux et Forêts, this is like giving the fox the key to the chicken coop. But for the goat herders and Dioros, it represents a rare chance for grassroots democracy. Eight people would sit on the management committee: three fishermen, two Dioros, two elected goat herders, and the local agent from Eaux et Forêts. Redundancy on the committee is owing to the difficulty of convoking a quorum of nomads.

The first problem encountered in setting up the *forêt villageoise* lay in deciding who "owned" it. The law states that a forest must belong to a village and that a village can stretch no farther than six kilometers from its center. This works quite nicely in southern Mali, which is densely settled, but not in the Sahel. If anyone "owned" the forest, it was the Fulani Dioros, but they lived twenty-five kilometers away. The only local candidate for ownership was the Bozo fishing village at Bouna. So the question was settled, at least in theory, by giving official ownership of grazing land to fishermen, who most of the year had no use for it. This apparently nonsensical solution actually managed to sidestep a number of potentially volatile arguments among the Dioros.

Next, the ground rules for using the forest were laid down. The Dioros would retain their traditional rights to the area. No acacias would be cut either for enclosing or feeding goats. Herders would have to make their fences out of mimosa and other weedy shrubs. The number of animals would be limited. This would give herders better pasture and a potentially useful sanction, because someone violating the rules could be expelled. Arguments would be settled by elected camp leaders and the larger management committee. Anyone going against communal decisions would be delivered up to Eaux et Forêts, which would enter the area only on request.

Everyone stood to gain from the arrangement. The Dioros would conserve a rent-paying resource. The herders would pay fewer fines for better pasture. Eaux et Forêts would maintain its position of ultimate authority in the area. And the herons would have someplace to sleep at night.

Prince Philip is traveling to Mali in his private capacity as head of the World Wildlife Fund, or so Stephen Cobb has been told. He wants a quiet tour of the delta with time out for bird watching. Not believing that princes have such a thing as a private capacity, dozens of Malian officials are besieging Stephen for an invitation to join the royal entourage. The president of Mali himself would have insisted on coming, were it not for the unlikely event that George Bush, then vice president of the United States, was going to be visiting Mali at the same time as His Royal Highness. Stephen is also alarmed by the list of journalists covering the event. It includes reporters from the *Guardian* and *Observer* in England, Agence France Presse in France, and a Swiss TV crew. Stephen turns away most of the prospective gate crashers and sets to work finding beds for the others — people too high up in the Malian government to risk offending.

The prince will be traveling light, with a couple of WWF advisers, a bodyguard, and the royal physician. The Europeans will spend the night with the Cobbs. The Malians will stay next door with Richard and Jamie, and the journalists will be lodged somewhere else. The logistics of preparing for this onslaught has become the Cobbs' major obsession. Stephen has driven to Bamako for plates and cutlery. Alison has bought material and sewn sheets and napkins for His Royal Highness, or "HRH," as she calls him. They have stocked the liquor cabinet and arranged the linens, while fearing up to the last minute that a sandstorm will cancel his visit.

The day the prince is supposed to arrive, I wake to a white sun filtered through clouds. This is an improvement over a red sun filtered through dust, but the harmattan is still blowing strongly off the desert. Green bee eaters flit through the acacias. In front of me the river bustles with stilts and terns and bands of crocodile birds scooting along the shore. Next door the chortling sounds of guinea hens rise from Stephen and Alison's courtyard.

Stephen has driven to Mopti to meet the prince's plane, while Alison bustles around the house preparing for his late-afternoon arrival. She supervises the building of a fireplace in the back yard for roasting lambs. She sends runners scurrying off for charcoal. She lines up the household help and instructs them in protocol. "You address him once as 'Your Highness,' and then after that you call him 'Sir.' "

The prince is already several hours late as day fades into evening. I am standing on Richard and Jamie's roof, scanning the river with a pair of binoculars, when the cry goes up around me. "*Ils arrivent! They're coming!*" Across the plain I make out a caravan of six Land Rovers eating each other's dust. The red one in the lead is driven by Stephen, and next to him sits the prince. The cars roar up to the house. Out tumble HRH in khaki safari clothes and a top slice of the Malian government, including the ministers of state planning and natural resources, the head of the national political party, and the governor of the Fifth Region. The Malians are wearing resplendent, three-piece *boubous* in powder blue and egg-shell white. According to the protocol outlined by Alison earlier in the day, this is a crucial moment. The Moslem Malians, who refrain from alcohol, have to be segregated from the prince as soon as possible.

The Malians are steered in my direction. HRH is ushered into the Cobbs', and the two houses are surrounded by armed guards. Suddenly the prince emerges on the neighboring roof within a stone's throw of me. His schedule calls for a shower and tea, but he seems to have moved straight to the cocktail hour. Looking rather glum, with his jaw set in a hard-mouthed frown, he walks to the edge of the roof and trains his binoculars on the river. The day is fast sinking into crepuscular gloom. The Niger is the color of rusted iron except where a kingfisher, diving for his dinner, has poked a gray hole in the water. HRH drops his binoculars onto his chest and settles into a deck chair across from mine. Alison plants a Union Jack in a pot of sand, thereby alerting the staff to his royal presence.

My own roof is suddenly filled with flapping *boubous*; the Malians have come up for an evening promenade. Joining them on their rooftop circuit, I find myself chatting with Dybary Diallo, minister of state planning and possibly the second most important person in the Malian government. An imposing man who studied engineering in France, Diallo knows the Latin Quarter as well as the

Niger delta. He quizzes me on his former Left Bank haunts, and we are pleased to discover that we share a fondness for the old La Coupole.

Moslems and Christians reunite for the lamb roast and then separate again to sit in their respective courtyards. Representing the mix of royalty and money that drives the WWF engine, the prince is accompanied by two businessmen. One of them used to run an airline and the other owns a chemical company. The airline man forgoes his after-dinner *digestif* to join the Moslems in their courtyard. He mixes praise for the intelligence of his hosts and the beauty of their country with pointed remarks about the need to conserve it. He also mentions the generosity of the Western donors. If Diallo finds the discussion condescending, he is too polite to say so. Instead he tells a story about food aid. Now that the United States is encouraging the sale of donated food on the open market, American rice has bankrupted many local producers, some of whom have been driven to suicide.

Later in the evening I walk a half mile inland from the river to find the journalists lodged in a concrete shed. They had not been invited to dinner. Scraps from the lamb roast were delivered to their door, but they have run out of water. The man from the *Guardian* says he has never been treated so badly in all his years as a journalist. The scrappy Yorkshireman from the *Observer* frets about there being no story here. The Swiss TV crew is embroiled in the palpable animosity of a lover's quarrel between the producer and her cameraman. Everyone is thirsty.

I learn from the journalists that the prince's trip is already littered with social mishaps. HRH found python skins for sale in the lobby of the Hotel Kanaga in Mopti. At the official reception in the hotel dining room he chided his host, the governor, for his laxity in protecting an endangered species. The governor, in turn, spoke about the need to sedentarize nomads. Stephen followed with a disquisition on the theory and practice of aerial surveys. The journalists voted thumbs down on all three presentations.

I have already heard of another faux pas marring the prince's tour. The caravan of Land Rovers was late in reaching Youvarou because Stephen, more familiar with flying than driving across the delta, got lost on the way. Richard had warned him that the route was tricky, especially on the dry bed of Lake Walado, where tracks veer off in every direction. Only belatedly, with an entourage of Malian officials turning in his wake, did Stephen discover that his compass had jammed and he was driving in circles. This ticked the prince into a rage. What kind of project are they running with a director who gets lost going home? The prince's physician was also in a dither, as the snake bite serum in his medical kit was supposed to be kept refrigerated.

If very little goes right the first day of the prince's visit, nothing goes right the second. He rises early. Accompanied by his body-guard, he is driven to the river for a sail on the Niger. Kassoum the boatman, for reasons that remain obscure, fails to arrive with the newly outfitted pirogue. The prince peers through the dust at several species visible from shore and then returns to breakfast.

His official day begins with a speech delivered in the *forêt morte*, a stand of dead trees near Youvarou. To get there, we drive in a caravan of Malian functionaries, soldiers, and journalists down a sandy track into what was formerly a forest of *Acacia scorpioides*. This once-green world used to stretch for ten miles in every di-rection. During the flood, men in pirogues would float in here to cut wood. But not since the drought of 1973 has the water level been high enough to reach the forest, and without their yearly inundation, the trees have died. All the large mammals that used to live here — gazelles, panthers, oryx, and antelopes — have dis-appeared.

As we pull up in a sandy cloud, I look out to see the prince stationed before a backdrop of leafless trees bleached stone gray in the desert sun. We pile out of our cars and face him at a re-spectful distance. As we have seen no other human beings for many miles, we are his only audience. A hawk-faced man with a beaked nose and blue eyes, the prince is dressed in beltless slacks fastened with Velcro, a salmon-colored shirt, and a straw hat. "He doesn't *look* like a prince," I hear a *boubou*ed Malian say to his companion.

The TV camera rolls. HRH begins speaking about the Sahelian drought, how there is really very little that can be done about it, save for building a kind of Noah's Ark, a reserve for protecting the indigenous flora and fauna from the people who would otherwise use them up. If the rains ever return, people can draw on this ark to revitalize their world. If the rains do not return, they will have to practice birth control and expect less out of life.

"Do you know how much the population of India increases every year?" asks the prince.

"Oh, no," mutters the man from the *Guardian*. "He gives the same bloody speech wherever he goes."

". . . It increases by twenty million people. That's more than the population of London, and the country simply doesn't have the infrastructure to handle that big an increase."

After the speech in the *forêt morte*, we drive back to the river to see trees that are still alive. These stand in a *forêt classée*, one of the woodland reserves that used to supply the colonial steamers that plied the Niger. It is not mentioned, and I doubt that anyone attending the event remembers that the once heavily forested banks of the river were largely cleared to fuel these boats.

The prince asks a forestry official how he plans to keep the trees alive. "When these die," says the man, "we will have to replace them with new drought-resistant species." Finding the answer insufficient, the regional head of the political party steps forward to say that a canal should be dug from the Office du Niger north to Youvarou. "This will allow us to irrigate all the region in between."

"That's not a viable solution," says the prince, turning on his heel and grimacing.

Alison and her staff have worked all morning making cucumber sandwiches and other goodies for a royal picnic. Stephen thinks he has found a nice place to stop under a tamarind tree halfway between Youvarou and Mopti, but once again his timing is off. The prince and his entourage fail to reach the tree until midafternoon. HRH is not pleased with the site. He leans against the fender and wolfs down a cucumber sandwich before commanding Stephen to drive on. The governor has no time to protest that he, too, has laid on a royal picnic farther down the road, complete with sheep roasts and tribal dancing. When HRH's group zooms by without stopping, the governor is furious at the insult of having his party spurned.

"God, it's depressing," says the prince in his last words to Stephen.

As for the enormous quantities of cucumber sandwiches left over from the royal picnic, they eventually make their way into the outstretched bowls of the Mopti *garibous*, who praise God for showering them with such munificence.

After building their house, Jamie and Richard hired two young Bozo fishermen to keep it in order. Jet black like their fellow tribesmen and strong enough to carry two hundred pounds on their heads, Siné Konta and Ngolo Tiao were amiable teenagers with no experience whatsoever in keeping a house in order. Giving them a task, like cooking eggs and potatoes, required a preliminary discussion about how the eggs should go on the stove after, long after, the potatoes. It was usually easier to send one of them into town to buy a chicken or fish already cooked. Dinner would arrive in a large bowl. Beers would be produced from a kerosene refrigerator, and we would sit together at a table in the courtyard eating rice balls dipped in sauce, while conversing in French, Bozo, Fulfulde, or one of the dozen other languages spoken in the delta.

By the time the prince arrived in Youvarou, the household was facing its first domestic crisis. To help with the crush of last-minute arrangements, Jamie and Richard hired Aminata. Aminata has the blue tattooed lips that the Fulani find so beautiful, but she is actually a Rimaïbé, from the tribe of former slaves who used to grow crops for their pastoral overlords. She and the boys chased each other around the house and laughed a lot about the *toubabs* and their funny way of doing things. But when they found themselves in Aminata's company, Ngolo and Siné were incapable of lifting a finger. If you asked Ngolo to get water from the well, Aminata drew it. In spite of the increase in staff, Richard and Jamie had effectively cut their labor force in half and added an extra layer of bureaucracy to the chain of command.

With the equanimity of an old Africa hand, Richard's standard response to domestic crises is to get in his boat and shove off downstream, where he beaches at a fishing village, and spends his days studying a world whose traditional customs he greatly admires. "The Bozo are tough and resourceful and immensely knowledgeable about fishing and survival. I'm still learning new things every time I visit them. If this weren't the case, I'd quit the project in a minute."

Richard invites me to accompany him on one of his river trips to the village of Aoré, where we will watch the great gathering of Bozo fishermen that marks the opening of the waters. Life in Mali demands a certain patience. So it is not until midday, following long stretches of apparent inactivity, that Kassoum the boatman announces our departure. After piling four cots, a roll of grass mats, and a trunk full of lanterns and cooking utensils onto his head, Ngolo leads us out the front door and down the loamy banks to the river. Already loaded with a dozen passengers, our pirogue sports a freshly woven grass canopy and a billowing sail in the form of Kassoum dressed in his new *boubou*. Both improvements are owing to Prince Philip's recent visit, although, unfortunately, HRH never managed to see them.

With polers bow and stern leaning smartly to their task, our needle-nosed craft glides midstream for a peaceful descent down the Niger. To clarify what might be a confusing bit of geography, "down the Niger" for the first thousand miles of its existence means north toward Timbuktu, where the river hits a band of ancient dunes at the Tossaye Sill and bends like a giant question mark around the edge of the desert. West Africa's longest river then retreats sixteen hundred miles southward to empty into the Atlantic Ocean at the Gulf of Guinea.

Except for a hint of grass along the bank, and the forest reserve we had visited with Prince Philip, the shore on either side is bare of vegetation until we come to a garden plot fenced with thorns. "That's the beginning of private property," Richard says. "It happens when resources are scarce. This year for the first time people have been allowed to fence off land along the river. This plot is owned by a civil servant who hires Fulani to tend it."

Looking like overgrown gondolas taken out of service on the River Styx, pirogues loaded with dried fish pole their way upstream. Moving in the opposite direction, we lead the procession of boats heading to Aoré. Around a bend in the river we sight the ostrich eggs that adorn the roof of the mosque. Dom palms and tamarinds wave over mud houses glowing red in the afternoon light. We come abreast of two buildings decorated with arabesques and geometric designs. Traditionally occupied by Aoré's young men, the houses are empty.

On beaching our pirogue we are met by a delegation of elders dressed in scarves and dusty *boubous*. They lead us into a courtyard behind the mosque, where we sit on mats facing each other in a circle. Our eyes turned to the ground, we begin the formalities. How are your family, your relatives, your animals? All are well, *Alhamdoulahi*. A crowd of women and children push their way into the courtyard to stare at us. A girl in a pumpkin-colored dress breaks out laughing whenever I look in her direction. Speaking in French that is translated by Arsiké, his research assistant, into Bozo, Richard explains our mission.

"We have come to study the life of people living in the Cercle de Youvarou," he says, referring to the local district and the town from which it takes its name. "We have heard there are problems because of the *sécheresse*, the drought, but also because the old systems, founded in the time of Cheikou Ahmadou, are breaking down. I want to know how in the past you divided the river and managed the fishing. Do you have customs that should be reestablished? We are beginning by talking to the people who live here, because you know best how to manage your lives."

Nervous about speaking in front of his elders, Arsiké talks softly and stares at his sandals, but the speech is well received. The men say they will be glad to tell us about fishing in the old days, before the *sécheresse*. But first the river has to be surveyed and boundaries set for the collective fishing that opens the following day. We walk back to the Niger, where Arsiké produces a metal tape measure from Richard's briefcase, which he carries on his head as part of his duties as *enquêteur*.

Another young man from the village, wearing blue jeans and cowboy boots, grabs the tape from Arsiké and stretches it down the riverbank. Each Bozo seine net swings an arc of eighty meters. In the old days, the most venerable of Aoré's fishermen used to measure the distance in cubits, one of which equals the length of the forearm from the tip of the middle finger to the elbow. The job goes faster with a tape measure, but still there are arguments. One group of fishermen wants an extra section of riverbank. Other people, who have come from as far away as Timbuktu and Gao, hold out for choicer allotments. Twenty of us, in a gesticulating, windblown flock of *boubous*, dispute our way down a mile of riverbank on the eastern shore, then pole across to divide another half mile on the western shore.

For three months this stretch of river is held in reserve for collective fishing by Mali's sixty thousand Bozo, who migrate through the delta according to the seasons announced overhead by the passage of the Pleiades. The Bozo are the original inhabitants of this world. They call themselves the Sorogo and Kélinga. "Bozo" is the Bambara word for "fish eater," but they seem not to mind the name. After all, what harm lies in being called a fish eater? The Niger used to be such a bountiful river that the Bozo worked it with harpoons. They leaned from their pirogues to spear Nile perch, known locally as *capitaine*, that weighed a hundred pounds or more. They attracted horse fish at night with the aid of torches and gathered tilapia into hand nets worn like water wings. But the good years have given way to lean years, and the annual catch of a hundred thousand tons has shrunk by half. Instead of two hundred nets on the river, Aoré will be lucky this year to see thirty.

Aoré was once a sizable town, home to four hundred people. But now it is largely abandoned, and we have no difficulty finding an empty house to borrow for the night. The village is muffled in heat and silent except for the rattling of dom palms and the chirping of *mange milles* pecking seeds out of the jujube trees. The only human voices are those of boys climbing the tamarinds for a harvest of leaves. Boiled into a bitter broth, the leaves will replace the milk missing from the evening meal.

As darkness settles around the chocolate-colored buildings, we sit drinking tea. Besides Ngolo, Kassoum, Arsiké, Richard, and me, the room is filled with girls from the village who have come to visit us in giggling groups of three and four. It is actually Arsiké they have come to visit. Like most of the other young men born in Aoré, who in better times would be fishing the river, he has gone away to find work, and now that he is back, everyone wants to know if life is better elsewhere.

Later, when we hear drums, we walk to the river to find fifty or sixty pirogues pulled up on shore. In front of them glow the embers of fires built on the beach. Over the water come the piping of flutes and chanting of dancers being poled from the far side.

The music echoes across the river. It piles into rhythmic layers of sound until suddenly, without warning, everything is swallowed up in the monotonous drone of the harmattan. This northeasterly wind off the Sahara, companion to a plague of seven lean years and seven again, kicks sand in our faces. It chokes us with dust and obscures the way home. It rattles our shutters and begrudges us a fitful sleep while we wait, like everyone else, for the stillness that sometimes returns at dawn.

It is no less windy in the morning, only hotter. So we take our mats outside and stretch them under the leeward wall of our house, where we breakfast on Nescafé and rice cakes. Greetings unfurl around us like arabesques in an illuminated Koran. *Jamwali?* Have you slept in peace? *Kori jamwali*. Nothing troubled our sleep. *Sagomèni*. As we would have wished. And how are your wife, children, animals, in-laws? Everyone and everything is doing splendidly. Spoken with eyes averted, these lies are topped off with a hearty chorus of *Alhamdoulahi*, invoking the name of the prophet.

Barefoot and unshaven, sitting cross-legged on the mat next to mine, Richard knows how to wait patiently while formalities shade into facts. In his mid-thirties, of medium height and build, he wears drawstring pants and a white shirt that looks positively stylish in the middle of a sandstorm. His pleasant, nut-brown face is highlighted by an ironic curve to the eyebrows and a mass of shaggy black hair. The ease with which he takes to African village life bespeaks his dual provenance. An Australian father supplied the self-sufficiency. An English mother, who spent much of her life in Italy, inspired the white shirt.

Three village elders come to visit us after breakfast, old men with creased faces, wispy gray beards, and skullcaps on their heads. One of them tells us he is seventy-four, which means he has outlived the average Malian by thirty years. We repair to the back room of our house, unroll our mats over the dirt floor, and sit in a circle drinking tea and talking about life in the old days.

"There used to be big fish in the river, enough so that everyone, villagers and strangers, ate well." As they speak, I watch the long, ebony faces of the men, which are high-cheeked and shiny under their cotton caps. They slurp their tea as a sign of appreciation. When excited, they move their fingers like fish in the current or lean backward into a corner and spit.

"Aoré used to control the deep holes all the way from Youvarou north to the next big village. Every third cast of the nets was owed to us as rent. Now we have rights only to the river directly in front of us." They explain how the stars regulated the fishing season, which opened after the departure of the Pleiades in May. Now fishing begins much earlier, in March.

"The village has always had a *djitigui*, a Master of the Water descended from the founding family. Because he was related to the river spirit, the *djitigui* could swim underwater and either aid or hinder you in catching fish." He opened the season and divided the river. But now that the founding family has moved away, the head of the village youths directs the fishing.

Richard draws a map of the Niger and its islands on a piece of paper. He places the map on the floor and asks the old men to point out the traditional fishing reserves. They tell him that before 1960, when Mali became independent and control of the river passed from Aoré to the state, there were ten reserves instead of two, and each was protected for an extra three months of the year.

Richard thanks the men and gives them money for kola nuts. "Two hours is the limit for interviews," he says. "After that, everyone gets tired."

We stretch our legs with a walk to the river. The fishing should have begun. It is already late in the day and the wind is up, but the pirogues are beached. The fishermen sitting next to them are mending nets and talking among themselves. It seems there is a problem with the strangers from downstream. Refusing to pay the traditional fee for using Aoré's waters, they are threatening to skip the collective fishing altogether and work the river later on their own. "The river belongs to the state," they say. "It belongs to all of us." But they are also afraid, if the argument goes on too long and word of it gets back to Youvarou, that armed agents from Eaux et Forêts will come and demand a state licensing fee of thirty dollars per net.

The wind and the argument last all day. Richard and I return to our house to drink endless cups of tea. We chat with village elders in the back room and town youths in the front. The old men chew kola nuts and spit in the corners; the young men discourse on their inalienable rights. Referring to the money to be gained from renting the river to strangers, one of the elders summarizes the crux of the argument. "Since there are so few fish in the river, we have no choice but to fish the fishermen."

I find myself getting irritable from too much tea and talk. I turn to Richard, reclining on his mat, and ask him how he feels. "Either way it goes," he says, "whether they fish or not, we're getting important information."

I suddenly realize this is what being a social scientist in the field is all about. You put yourself in the midst of conflict, let it wash over you, keep your notebook at hand, and then take all these scraps of reality home and try to make sense of them. Sitting out a sandstorm south of Timbuktu, we are learning about the area's economy and lines of authority. It feels as if nothing is happening, but we are actually watching Bozo society unravel at the seams.

The harmattan is still blowing the following day when the strangers capitulate and pay twenty-five hundred CFA per net, about five dollars, to the village. Moving quickly now, they stake one end of their nets to the riverbank. The other is stretched midstream by pirogue and then pulled ashore in a furious burst of paddling. Standing in water up to their waists, men and women seize the lines and heave mightily to land the catch. Other people, wading into the current with raffia hand nets strapped to their arms, scoop up any big fish trying to escape.

Hundreds of men and women are chanting and singing while gathering their nets hand over hand. It is a colorful scene, for the Bozo are a handsome people who dress with style. But I notice that few of the men wearing hand nets are bringing up fish. Of the one hundred and fifty species reported to live in the Niger, the catch produces nothing more exceptional than dogfish, catfish, carp, and the occasional eel among a poor showing of Niger sardines. A single *capitaine* is pulled from a river that used to teem with them. On the far shore, where the strangers are fishing, many of them harvest little more than the spiny oyster shells that tear their nets.

At the end of the day, families sort their catch into piles and rest on the riverbank. They tie grass mats to their boat paddles and mount them in the sand as windbreaks against the harmattan. The wind thickens with dust as it blows over men and women lying wrapped in blankets on the ground. Instead of satisfaction at the end of a good day's work, there is a worrying wind and the anxiety of too little food for too many mouths. Night falls and people lie down to sleep among the oyster shells. In the morning, they will pole downstream to Timbuktu and another day of fishing, or give it up and head for the shantytowns of the Ivory Coast.

Like his father, Alan Moorehead, who wrote about the continent in his books on explorers and natural history, Richard is an Africanist. He had already spent a year and a half in the delta, studying family economies in a Bozo village, and had gone back to England to write up his work for a master's degree at the University of Sussex, when Stephen Cobb tapped him for a return engagement. People talk about culture shock, by which they usually mean the absence of comforts from home, but in Richard's case the process worked in reverse. After nine months among the Bozo, living on fish and rice, he feared more than anything else the prospect of going home.

"I had what you might call a nervous breakdown. I was in Mopti, ready to leave. All I needed to do was cash a check. But I developed a block against signing my name. I would go to the bank, stand in line, and then have to go home when I couldn't sign the check. This went on for a week. I tried getting drunk and everything else I could think of to trick myself into doing it. Finally I lay in a dark room all day until the moment came when I could jump up and sign my name. I ran to the bank, cashed the check, and *bang* I was on my way to Bamako, where I got on an airplane and kept my eyes shut tight all the way to London."

Glad for the chance to return to Mali, Richard bought a Land Rover and spent three weeks driving from England to Africa in the fall of 1984. His assignment was to figure out how the old systems of land use in the delta could be integrated into a plan for conserving it. "Tradition is a powerful force here," he says. "I try to work inside these societies, to take all their productive lines and see them as a whole. These are sophisticated, practical people who have known about conservation and multiple-use reserves for a long time."

One evening, with the moon rising over us as we sit in the courtyard of his house talking, I ask Richard about the future of the delta. "If you want to conserve resources and raise the standard of living," he says, "you have to be hard-nosed about who's in this game for what. The idea of walling off the delta into a park is ostrich behavior. The Malian government is broke. They have to get revenue out of here.

"From their perspective, they have two choices. They could build a dam across the top of the Niger near Timbuktu and turn the delta into a rice plantation. Rice growing, when it works, is more productive than nomadic economies. You have sedentary rather than mobile forms of production, and the government likes these schemes. But damming the river is politically a very hairy issue. It would probably result in war with Nigeria. Even without a dam at Timbuktu, the government plans to build a million hectares of irrigated rice fields. The environmental consequences could be disastrous, and it will make the area more vulnerable to drought. Instead of three lines of production, from fishing, farming, and pastoralism, you'll have only one.

"An entirely different approach to development would encourage rational use of the delta by the people who live here. They've been practicing a risk economy for years. The Dina was a system of multiple land use that imposed a balance on resources and their exploitation. The population has tripled since then, but the Dina gives you a blueprint to go on. You plan for drought. You assume minimum natural resources and use this as your base. And then you tackle the thorny question of controlling the number of strangers let into the area."

I ask Richard if he has learned anything new about the delta since his return, and he gives me a grim report. The social arrangements that once governed the area are collapsing. Farmers are cutting *bourgou* and selling it to herders who traditionally grazed it for free. Civil servants are staking off garden plots along the river on what used to be common ground. The fishing communities are breaking up under the pressure of too many people and too few fish.

Everyone knows things are bad in the delta. But Richard very quietly and methodically is demonstrating exactly how bad they really are, and some of his findings have come as a big surprise, even to him. After returning to Mali, he embarked on a series of household studies. He monitored the income and expenses of one hundred and fifty representative families in twelve delta villages and two nomadic groups. A family in this case was defined by the French term *marmite*, which literally means a "cooking pot." A *marmite* includes all the people in a household or nomadic group who produce and consume their food together. Harvests, fish yields, demographic trends, household budgets, and debts all became raw data for Richard and his *enquêteurs*, who were trying to figure out the strategies people employ for surviving drought.

This kind of work can be a delicate business. "People won't tell you how many animals they have, or what they paid for their new boat. Their replies are geared either to what they expect you'll give them, or what they expect you'll take away. Expectation A leads to exaggerated accounts of expenditures and needs. Expectation B leads to minimized accounts of income. 'Last month I spent a fortune on cooking oil, millet, milk, and rice. My income? Nothing at all.' But a workable method for dealing with responses like these is to assume that income is comparable to expenditures, and then fill in the blanks on the balance sheet."

What Richard discovered in his household studies is that people are teetering on the thin edge of survival, and to keep from falling over, they are doing two things. They are diversifying their activities: fishermen are dabbling in farming and farmers are beginning to fish and everyone is trying to graze a few animals. Second, they are pushing the land and water harder: reducing the size of the mesh in their nets, cultivating more rice and millet, cutting trees for forage. They are also relying on wild grains, berries, and other famine foods. *Bourgou* seeds and lotus fruits from water lilies kept many people alive in 1984.

Along with his village surveys, Richard embarked on another study of the delta. He had a hunch that something was wrong with its terms of trade. Economists use this concept to describe the balance sheet for a nation. How much money does it make from exports versus the amount paid out for imports and interest on the national debt? Mali and the rest of Africa currently have negative terms of trade, which means they pay out more than they earn or receive in aid. Richard wanted to see if these national imbalances were reproduced at the local level. Was it true, as it appeared, that the delta was financing a state bureaucracy that gave it very little in return?

Taxes in Mali are levied on the means of production—boats, plows, nets, and carts—regardless of their earnings. If you own a pirogue and owe taxes on this piece of capital equipment, your nets will be impounded until the money is paid. Your only recourse at this point is to become indebted to the fish merchant, who advances you the money and thereby turns you into his laborer. The consequences of this tax policy were generally known, but the amounts of money involved were a complete mystery.

"What I thought would be a simple six-month project to find out how much money had been taken out of the delta versus how much had been reinvested since 1973, when a lot of aid money started pouring into the area, turned into one of the most frustrating eighteen months of my life. It was a lesson in the fact that information equals power. Reports were out of print or had been eaten by termites. People had left their jobs carrying with them unique copies of all the crucial documents, which they then hid under their beds. One person admitted that in the absence of any information he had made up his statistics from scratch. I met another official in a completely bare office. 'Monsieur,' he said, 'what you see here is everything I know about my mission.' The World Bank has a computer in Bamako with a massive memory and nothing in it. The building is nicely air-conditioned, though, which makes it a very good place to go in the hot season."

Through sheer doggedness, Richard verified his hunch about declining terms of trade in the delta. In 1984, during the worst drought in its recorded history, the taxes and fines taken out of the area by the Service des Eaux et Forêts were double those levied in 1973. In 1985, a total of 135,230,705 CFA was removed from the delta in taxes, while only 35,000,000 CFA was returned in the local budget. No wonder the trees are being chopped down and the land overgrazed and overfished. People already weakened by drought are carrying on their backs the government officials who fine them every time they fall in the dust.

The drought of 1973 put the Sahel on the map—the map, that is, of Western consciousness. An unknown part of the globe suddenly flickered onto our TV screens, where "Sahel" became synonymous with drought, famine, and irredeemable misery. There are no precise figures on the number of people who died in 1973. Estimates range from one hundred thousand to two hundred and fifty thousand, out of a total nomad population in the affected area of two and a half million. Nightly on the news we watched hungry pastoralists tumble out of the desert into relief camps, where measles and other diseases took their own swift toll. We were surprised at how slowly emergency food arrived in this remote part of the world. And then our concern passed into the professional hands of aid agencies in Washington and Paris, who busied themselves with the Jobian task of rehabilitation. They drew up plans for saving the Sahel with multimillion-dollar investments in shelterbelts, boreholes, roads, dams, irrigation schemes, and other capital projects known collectively as development.

"Development, the eighth plague of Egypt," says one critic of these plans. He and others see development as part of the problem, not the solution. The spread of agriculture into marginal lands, the clustering of animals around boreholes, the emphasis on cash crops over food crops—development of this sort has made West Africa vulnerable to drought in the first place. These facts have become common knowledge by now. But in the absence of new ideas, aid money keeps flowing in the same channels. "Everything that has been undertaken in the region up to the present," says the French geographer Jean Gallais of development projects in the Niger delta, "has served only to establish an urban power which is largely parasitical and profoundly resented by the rural people."

After gathering information on taxes and household economies, Richard started fine-tuning his data with seasonal adjustments. If a one-and-a-half-ton pirogue costs fifty thousand CFA, this equals one month's revenue for a family when the fishing is good, but four months' revenue during the hungry season. Heaven help you if you have to buy a boat in the bad part of a bad year. When Richard stopped to think what people really needed to keep their culture intact, the answer was money. He conceived the idea of setting up *caisses communautaires*, village-based banks capable of loaning families money when they most needed it. He also thought up an elegant experiment for testing what people would do with the money once they got it. He would give all the families in his study the princely sum of seventy-five thousand CFA, about a hundred and fifty dollars.

"Seventy-five thousand CFA buys you fishing nets, grain, clothing, eight goats, or a wife. If somebody buys fishing nets, they're making a capital investment. If they buy a wife, they're investing in labor. This is important when you realize that half the children born in the delta die in the first year of life. There's no way I could lose from the scheme. Anything a family did with the money would be data.

"An experiment like this would put meat on the argument that people in the countryside really know what they're doing, that they're smarter than anyone else in marshaling their assets through seasonal lines of production. There's a lot of talk by development experts about the 'coping strategies' of poor people moving among resources. But the basic fact is that you have to improve their standard of living so they don't use up their resources in the first place. If a strategy works for someone in the delta, it's accepted like wildfire. You don't need big money to succeed here. You need big ideas. We're not short of money, but we are short of ideas."

As soon as the Malian government got wind of Richard's scheme, they put a stop to it. "Giving money to individual families would have allowed us for the first time to poll local opinion and track people's real needs and interests. But it goes against the conventional, moral approach to development, which imposes ideas on people in the countryside—new stoves, irrigation projects, tree planting—without asking them what they want." The final blow to the project came when IUCN refused to support it. "I was naive," says Richard. "I was led by the nose. I thought finding out the truth about the delta's economy would result in good being done.

I was thinking in terms of a showdown between IUCN and the World Bank. But it doesn't work that way. Even if you know what needs to be done, the powers that be won't necessarily allow you to do it."

At our last meeting I find Stephen Cobb sitting in his office. The wind is rattling the shutters and blowing papers across his desk. A sandstorm has cut visibility to a hundred feet. The sun glows with the eerie orange light of a holocaust fireball. "God, this is nasty," he says, stooping to pick up some Malian bank notes that have blown onto the floor. "I'm not particularly good at keeping track of these things anyway, and this doesn't help."

I look out the window to see a turbaned figure plowing into the wind. "There's no way you can really describe to people what it's like to have sand up your nose and in your teeth," says Stephen, following my gaze.

Since he spotted the thousand hectares of dead trees from his airplane, Stephen has been thinking a lot about the weather. He is perplexed that the weather on the western side of the African continent seems to be the inverse of that on the east. There had been no shortage of rain when he was living in the Sudd. In fact the Nile was exceptionally high in the 1960s and 1970s. This led him to entertain the idea of compensatory rainfall. Was West Africa suffering from East Africa's gain?

"I don't think desertification comes from the malign hand of man and hoof, even if the malign hand of man accelerates things," he says. "I think we're dealing with a profound shift in the climate. This is part of a long-term global phenomenon that includes changes in winds and composition of the atmosphere and vegetative cover. If this is true, then there is astonishingly little we can do about it, other than asking less of the land, with fewer animals and people, less intensive exploitation, a lowering of expectations — which are all politically and socially hard to accept.

"On the other hand, maybe we're only facing a kind of belt tightening until the return to better years. If this is the case, then there is plenty of scope for action. Desertification is a hard thing to judge," he says. "Certain species of trees may look dead, although they are not. They have seeds in the ground waiting to regenerate, which can happen extremely rapidly, and there's an enormous wealth of seeds in the Sahel."

If he is witnessing a long-term change in climate, Stephen wonders if the best thing he can do is give people in the delta a ticket south. "You don't solve global problems at the local level. I just hope we're not raising any false expectations."

As he sits on the banks of the Niger watching the world around him dissolve into a cloud of dust, Stephen thinks he is seeing "the inescapable evidence of climatic change." He could be wrong, but that's what it feels like. There is little solace to be found in reviewing weather data for the past two thousand years, but the historical record does contain one item of interest: Roman Africa, the Sahelian empires of the Middle Ages, and the Dina of Cheikou Ahmadou all managed to nurse agricultural plenty out of resources nearly as meager as those available today. Doing so required an ecological feel for what the land could offer and a wise investment in husbanding its resources. The key seemed to lie in political organization, control of grazing and fishing rights, small-scale irrigation projects, and seasonal use of land that was replenished through reserves and various cycles of cropping and grazing. Stephen is no emperor or sheik capable of imposing his will on people, but these old techniques look to him like the only hope for preserving what remains of West Africa's greatest wetlands.

Two years after our trip to Aoré I meet Richard again in London, where he is taking a break from life in the field. We spend the afternoon visiting his former wife, picking up his young daughter for a weekend visit, and talking about Mali, where there have been some changes.

"I've been back to Aoré three or four times to see how the families are doing," he says. "The collective fishing in 1985 was such a nightmare that it wasn't worth turning up to get fined by Eaux et Forêts, and the rice harvest was a disaster." A food-for-work project had dammed a riverside marsh and leveled it into a rice paddy. They planted ten tons of seed from the Office du Niger and another fifty tons from the World Bank, but it was Asian paddy rice, the wrong kind for growing in flood conditions, and they lost the entire crop. The next year a French volunteer built a sluice gate meant to control the water level in the marsh. But she went on holiday just before the flood reached Aoré. The gate broke, and again the entire crop was lost.

On the other side of the balance sheet, Richard reports that the millet harvest has been good and that the fishing in 1986 was five times better than the previous year. This patchy state of affairs—the rains arrive but the flood fails, the millet flourishes while the fish are nowhere to be found—is the complex story of life in the delta over the past fifteen years. It counters the simple idea of desertification, which assumes an inexorable advance of desert southward.

"I don't believe in this desert-moving-south business," Richard says. "There have been rains in arid parts of the desert, and conditions recently have been so good that camels were able to make three rather than two trips to the salt mines at Taoudenni. It's true there have been a string of lean years following the 1973 drought, and that the losses are beginning to compound themselves. I'm sure resources have become scarcer in the delta, but I'm not sure it's going to keep happening. For all we know, the dead forest where Prince Philip gave his speech could come back to life."

Richard tells me that IUCN Project 9016, which is nearing the end of its first three-year contract, is itself about to be reborn. Several Scandinavian governments are putting up a million and a half dollars for Phase II, which will be even more emphatic in linking community development with conservation. Stephen Cobb has resigned as director, and Richard will be the new head of the project. "IUCN is moving into rural development," he says. "That's the name of the game from now on."

They are hoping to accomplish this through a number of experimental, village-based initiatives. Richard expects these to resemble what Jamie has already started in the Bouna forest. "Organizing people on the move is a tricky business that we may finally know enough to accomplish. The project will also work on changing property rules and stopping Eaux et Forêts from fining people. They in turn will have to get together and agree among themselves on how to use the land."

Stephen and Alison Cobb are moving back to their house in Oxford. Mali was never really his cup of tea, and the details of running the project seem to have overwhelmed him from the start. His airplane broke down after a couple of aerial surveys, and he never found the time to figure out how fast the grass grew and the fish reproduced.

During our last conversation, Stephen had talked about the difficulty of translating his East African experience to the other side of the continent. He regretted the absence of large mammals, which had been given "the hammer blow" in Mali during the 1973 drought. He found the country "overgoverned" and the people "dispirited" by an administration that was either arbitrary or incapable of enforcing its rules. It was a nation that believed unswervingly in God and the sword, but for Stephen, the God of Islam was depressingly fatalistic, while the country's administrative sword—doubly sharp for having been ground on the twin stones of French colonial discipline and Marxist ideology—was "imposing a new kind of pain on the citizens of Mali, that of being governed by their own people."

In recent news from Youvarou, Richard tells me that Ngolo is an *enquêteur*-in-training and Siné has become a professional birder who can spot a fish eagle at five hundred yards. "He's perfect for the job. Instead of mediocre functionaries protecting birds in the delta, what you want is fishermen like Siné." But the most intriguing news is the fact that Jamie Skinner is famous all over northern Mali. Under the Fulani clan name of Jimmy Diallo, he is the hero of two hit songs blasting from tape decks throughout the delta.

Richard thought up the idea of having a *griot*, one of the local bards, compose a song about Jamie's forest project. If you want to educate someone in an oral culture, where only one child in ten ever attends school, you have to sing the news. Intrigued by Richard's idea, Jamie approached Bara Sambarou, the best-known *griot* in Mali. His fee for singing at weddings is thirty cows, all the same color, and a round-trip ticket to Mecca. Jamie got him for a steal at fifty dollars. The song Sambarou recorded about Jimmy Diallo's work in Youvarou was such a success that he made a second tape specifically about heron colonies in the *forêts villageoises*. This was an even bigger success. It skyrocketed to the top ten on the *griot* charts, selling thousands of copies all the way from Burkina Faso to the Ivory Coast.

As Sambarou warms up his three-string Fulani guitar, the tape begins with a reverberating back beat, a skipping melody of seven notes played over and over again. He hums to himself for a few seconds, waiting for the muse to arrive, then launches into song. He weaves a half dozen imaginary voices, including his own authoritative baritone, into an exhorting, flattering dialogue addressed to "the Fulani people of the world." Excited voices flying across the higher registers are reassured by the knowing explanations of Jimmy Diallo, "our *toubab*, a friend to men, animals, and plants."

Sambarou lays out the facts of the heron project. He explains how the birds eat grasshoppers and mentions other benefits from keeping woodlands in place. He lists by name all the people involved, flattering their intelligence and exhorting his audience to follow their example. "If we refuse their propositions, then we can expect to harvest in the future nothing but broken pots." The performance sounds something like an Indian raga mixed with the evening news as sung by John Lennon and Yoko Ono.

Following an interlude of variations on the melodic line, side one concludes with an imaginary dialogue between Jimmy Diallo and a goat herder caught cutting down a tree. The man receives a lecture on the benefits of woodland. Then Jimmy Diallo declares he is "only a messenger bringing the news," and that everything else depends on the people involved.

On the flip side Sambarou sings about reforestation. He praises everyone involved in a tree-planting project at Akkagoun and tells his audience to follow their lead. Two years after reseeding the area, "Akkagoun today reminds us of the years of happiness. The trees are growing nicely. *Bourgou* flourishes across the woodland. *Vetuvaria* grass, long absent from the area, has returned in force. I sing of this to let you know that man, instead of sleeping through the day or counting solely on the will of God, can accomplish something in life."

"We must rise out of our torpor," Sambarou sings in his own

voice. "As a heritage to our children, it will not suffice to leave only money, animals, and gold. By wasting our world, we will find ourselves one day faced with nothing. Future generations will say to us accusingly, 'I have never seen an antelope or a hippopotamus.' To really know the value of something, it must first be lost. The abuse of man has put an end to the existence of many things. But now it is time to put an end to our abuse."

The Dudu World

It makes no sense to me to separate science from technology, technology from ethics, or ethics from religion.

Freeman Dyson

WHEN I ARRIVE in Nairobi everyone is talking about the dead Luo. He has already been embalmed twice, but if he remains unburied much longer he will have to be embalmed again. Hundreds of fellow tribesmen loiter around the city morgue waiting for a chance to grab the body. Down the street at the Court of Appeal another crowd watches the dead man's wife, who is not a Luo, argue that *she* has the right to his remains. Two graves have been dug, one outside the man's house in Nairobi, and another at his birthplace in Luoland, three hundred miles west on the shores of Lake Victoria. It will take five months before Kenya's highest court decides into which grave to put the body.

Other than the initials S. M., I never learn his Christian name. But everyone knows what you mean when you say "Otieno" or "the dead Luo," and everyone has an opinion on where his body should go. "A man's house is not his home," I am told. "You can choose to live wherever you want, but your final allegiance will be to your people."

Others argue that a man should be buried wherever he wants. "The Luo are a backward people possessed by spirits. We have to get beyond this kind of tribalism if Kenya is to become a modern nation." Some say the case is really about money, that the estate will follow the body. Others, including the man's widow, say it is about sex. A patriarchal tribe is trying to erase the social gains of women in Africa. Otieno was a progressive man—a Kenyan, not a Luo, he said proudly—who tried to free himself from the spirit world of the ancestors and adopt the single spirit of modernity. But is such a project possible in late-twentieth-century Africa?

Otieno was a wealthy lawyer who suffered from hypertension

and died of a heart attack at the age of fifty-five. He left no will, but his wife and nine children testify that he had renounced all tribal customs and wished to be buried on his Nairobi estate over-looking the Ngong Hills. In 1963, the year of Kenya's independence from Britain, Otieno had crossed tribal boundaries to marry Virginia Wambui, a Kikuyu woman. The Kikuyu are the largest and most progressive of Kenya's dozen major tribes, and Nairobi is the showplace for their commercial talents. The Luo are the second largest tribe and among the least progressive. A Nilotic people related to the tall pastoralists of the Sudan, they scratch out a living on the shores of Lake Victoria. In spite of their sup-posed backwardness, the Luo consider themselves the aristocrats of East Africa. They may be plagued by the spirit world of the ancestors, but they also produce the foremost scientists and intel-lectuals in Kenya. So much for generalizations about tribalism in Africa.

Kenyans joke among themselves about the tribe known as the waBenzi, the newly rich Africans who drive Mercedes-Benzes. Otieno was one of them. A silver-haired, imposing man good at defending bank robbers in criminal cases, he enjoyed reciting Shakespeare and watching Perry Mason reruns on his VCR. Otieno refused to teach his children the Luo language. They were cir-cumcised according to Kikuyu custom and sent abroad to school. One of Otieno's sons, who has interrupted his studies at William Paterson College in New Jersey to fly home for the trial, denounces his Luo relatives as "lazy" and "uncivilized."

Virginia Wambui, who goes by her maiden name, is a resolutely modern woman. Coming from a wealthy family of judges and public officials, she fought in the Mau Mau uprising and was in-terned in a colonial prison for three years. Of the four children she bore out of wedlock before marrying Otieno, one was the result of being raped by a white soldier in prison. After her marriage, she ran unsuccessfully for parliament, emerged as Kenya's leading feminist, and served as treasurer for the United Nations confer-ence on women held in Nairobi in 1985. According to Luo custom, when a man dies, his male relatives raid his house and carry off whatever property they wish. But as Otieno's relatives complain in court, by the time they got to his house Wambui had "even locked the toilets."

The main witness for the Luo plaintiffs in the trial is Otieno's younger brother, Joash Ochieng Ougo, who looks very much the country bumpkin next to his city kin. Ochieng testifies that his brother's angry spirit will sabotage his life if the body is not buried on the ancestral farm. A violation of tribal law will produce a restless ghost capable of revenging itself through car accidents, house fires, and birth defects. For putting himself and others at risk, Ochieng will be spat upon by his fellow clansmen. "Can you not explain to these ghosts and spirits that it is not your fault?" asks Wambui's lawyer in cross-examination. "No," Ochieng replies. "This is because you cannot catch these spirits or talk to them."

One hundred and fifty-four days after his death, surrounded by three cabinet ministers and a crowd of ululating women, S. M. Otieno is buried by court decree in the spring-green hills of Luoland. His wife and children do not attend the ceremony.

I was ignorant of the Otieno case before arriving in Nairobi in the spring of 1987, but not of the fact that the man I have come to meet, Thomas Risley Odhiambo, is a Luo. A former colleague has described him as the smartest man in East Africa. Many people say he is a visionary leader. Someone else characterizes him as remarkably gifted at making donors reach for their checkbooks.

My first meeting with Odhiambo, a sturdy, round-faced man in his mid-fifties, who is wearing a crisp shirt and tie, lasts six hours. I am weary by the end, but as far as I can tell, he could talk for another six. Odhiambo gives precise, at times eloquent, answers to my questions, recalling events down to the day and hour when they happened. In his office at the International Centre of Insect Physiology and Ecology, Odhiambo sits behind a desk covered with ordered piles of documents. Beside him are four black telephones, one of which is connected, he tells me, "directly to the government." Talking through lunch, which is served to us at a conference table in his office, Odhiambo rules no subjects out of bounds, although at times he raises his eyebrows in alarm at the impetuous observations I tend to make when excited.

Odhiambo is not without a sense of humor, which he displays when recounting his upbringing in colonial Kenya and his early work as an entomologist for the Tea Research Institute of East Africa. "The head of my department told me he could not conceive of an African being an entomologist. Africans didn't even grow tea. It must be remembered, of course, that they were forbidden to do so by law."

His employers were no more encouraging at his second job, at the Ugandan Ministry of Agriculture, where Odhiambo disobeyed his superiors to become the first black man in East Africa to publish a scientific paper in an international journal. "When they discovered I was doing research, they told me not to waste the department's time and to get back to curating the insect collection. So I did my research after office hours and on weekends. The hurdles made me climb them because they were there. I'm not one to get ulcers or bear resentment; it's too expensive."

Odhiambo was born in Mombasa in 1931, the first of eleven children fathered by a telegraph clerk in the colonial postal service. Mombasa is an Indian Ocean port on the opposite side of Kenya from Lake Victoria, but Odhiambo informs me that his "ancestral home" is Ng'iya, a village on the eastern shore of the lake that happens to be quite close to S. M. Otieno's ancestral home. "We don't call them tribes," Odhiambo says, correcting me. "I belong to the Luo ethnic group. We are a Nilotic people, part of a larger group of nationalities whose birthplace is the Sudan, but that today covers much of East, West, and Central Africa, from Mali down to Zambia. The Nilotes are quite different from the Bantu, both in language and traditions."

"Was yours a Christian family?" I ask.

"Christian with antecedents," Odhiambo replies.

Schooled by missionaries and the *Encyclopaedia Britannica*, Odhiambo entered Makerere University in Uganda to earn a college degree in the natural sciences. He then spent six years curating collections of tea and cotton insect pests — and doing research on his own — before starting his undergraduate education all over again at Queens College, Cambridge. Odhiambo lived for six years in England, a period of his life that he describes as intellectually exhilarating but physically painful.

"They very generously placed me in the oldest and most historic part of the college. It had no heat, and the bathrooms were down in the basement. My first year I was in pain, really in pain. But when they realized I had a problem, they were kind enough to allocate me extra blankets and as much coal as I needed, so that I could keep a fire burning in my sitting room twenty-four hours a day.

"I was the only African in the college and older than most of the students—I was twenty-eight at the time—but they accepted me on equal terms as an intellectual, and the problems I had had in Kenya and Uganda disappeared. I took zoology, botany, physics. I wanted to do the whole thing. I took history and philosophy of science. I wanted to understand the thinking behind science and the growth of science over the ages. And then all the societies and clubs you could join! It was like a supermarket; every day was a special day."

Odhiambo wrote his doctoral dissertation at Cambridge on the reproductive physiology of the desert locust. Feeling the tug of "nationalistic sentiments" and obligations to a wife and three children, he decided to return to Africa as a lecturer in zoology at the newly established University of Nairobi. Among his other talents, Odhiambo is an organizational genius. Everything he touches turns to structure. Along with scores of more specialized societies, he has either founded or directed the Kenyan, African, and third world academies of science. But his greatest organizational feat, and the one that would become his life work, sprang from an article he wrote in 1967 for *Science* magazine. Discussing "Science for Development," Odhiambo argued that Africa has to embrace the scientific method—not just its technological results, but the world view inherent in doing science—if it wants to get beyond the "colonial interlude." He called for developing "centers of excellence" in Africa that would act as "powerhouses for the initiated and for those wishing to be initiated in research."

Along with its practical suggestions, Odhiambo's article raised larger questions about the philosophical implications of science in Africa. How receptive are Africans to this Western idea? How can something that was an engine of the colonial enterprise now drive the continent forward on its own? Why are there so few African scientists? Poor teaching and no jobs form part of an answer, "but is it not possible," Odhiambo speculated, "that there may be something in the cultural attitude and social philosophy that may discourage a tradition in science?"

Answering his question, Odhiambo wrote, "It is my view that the African's monistic (one world) view of nature has proved an impediment to his becoming a natural scientist." Odhiambo elaborated on this statement by explaining the Nilotic concept of *jok*, which refers to both the body and the spirit that moves it. "One cannot dismiss this concept as merely superstition or a form of animism. *Jok* permeates the Nilotic idea of the universe, of existence, and of destiny" so deeply that nothing distinguishes the living and the dead for these Africans other than the life force, the *jok* that animates them. "Plants, animals, inanimate objects, God, spirits, and men" all share to a lesser or greater extent in this diffusion of energy.

"In this African philosophy there is no sharp distinction between the subjective and objective worlds." In Europe such a distinction led to the development of science. Where the European world view is static and dualistic, that in Africa is dynamic and unitary. "As for the African, his monism has deprived him of the choice between either science or mysticism; instead, he has concentrated his intellectual powers in devising a vastly intricate social and communalistic system." Odhiambo concluded by saying that "science, in the modern sense, has no firm foundations in African society."

If Odhiambo's analysis is correct—not only for the Luo but also for Africa's eight hundred other ethnic groups—then how will they seize the key to scientific power? Realizing the need for a radical solution, Odhiambo called for the creation of a New African. He wanted to "reach the basic root of the problem, his monistic world view, and modify it in a manner in which he can begin to regard Nature apart from himself and other beings."

Odhiambo proposed to begin at the beginning and make no compromises while training Africans into the international cadre of scientists. "There is only one measure in science," he tells me during our first conversation. "The yardstick of excellence.

"Africa in the last two centuries has gone through probably the worst period in its history. That we have survived without going mad is due in part to our sense of immortality, the belief that the dead can oversee the affairs of the living. It is a comforting thought to know that the living and the dead are one and the same. The only thing that distinguishes them is what in English is vaguely

known as *energy*. The less you have of it the more you become
nonliving. The more you have of it the more you are living, or
you may even become a god.

"This African way of thinking is synthetic, rather than analytical.
Its truths are arrived at by an additive process that makes them
ever more complex and multifaceted. The analytical approach, on
the other hand, is reductive. It ends up with a partial truth that
is easier to explain for its being an approximation. Unless the
African can learn to use analytical tools better, even against his
own instincts—indeed, in this case, become schizophrenic about
it—then I have a feeling we're not going to get very far. I myself
am schizophrenic. I believe that analytical tools are very powerful
and that we should use them. When I'm thinking science, I think
analytically. But I don't bring these methods into my general life.
There I leave them out."

"Schizophrenia can be a risky condition," I comment.

"The Japanese have practiced it very successfully," Odhiambo
replies. "They have their culture. They have their technology. It
can be done, but one has to think about it deliberately and say,
'These are my compartments. I will not be muddled about it. I
will have my scientific life and my cultural life, and I will not live
one inside the other.'

"My own feeling is that if Africa can rationalize its strengths and
incorporate science into its culture, we will have a very powerful
instrument. Instinctively I am relying more on science than most
African thinkers, who are counting on change in the geopolitical
situation. I may be totally wrong, but that's my instinct."

Confronted with multiple crises of drought, famine, debt, disease,
and political instability, Africa suffers calmly at the hands of experts whose prior solutions have contributed to today's disasters.
The patient has been sick so long that one grows suspicious of
both the doctors and the diagnosis. The continent is littered with
failed attempts to transfer technology from the northern to the
southern hemisphere. Fish packing plants that have never seen a
fish. Vaccination programs that when discontinued result in epidemics. Irrigation schemes whose major output is a plague of waterborne diseases. According to Odhiambo these projects have

failed, and will continue to fail, because they jumped a necessary step in third world development.

"We don't need any more fire brigades," he says emphatically. "In an atmosphere of crisis it's natural to want to take shortcuts. Africa has been sold the idea that it can transfer technology from other parts of the world to solve its problems. But it won't work, and we've lost a quarter of a century because of this simplistic view. I believe instead that basic scientific research is what is going to bring Africa to a position where it can control its destiny."

Odhiambo's article in *Science* immediately struck a resonant chord. Carl Djerassi, one of the inventors of the birth control pill, had recently sketched a similar model. Using his own case as an example, Djerassi described how he first synthesized the chemical agents used in oral contraceptives while working at a small laboratory in Mexico. In the wake of his efforts, a country that had previously performed no basic research in chemistry developed, in the short space of ten years, into a world center of steroid chemistry. Djerassi outlined how similar endeavors could be launched. Start with an international cadre of postdoctoral research fellows, choose the best scientists in the world to lead them as visiting directors of research, and then set everyone to work on problems with "ultimate economic pay-off and a maximum multiplication factor" throughout the developing world.

Blending his own and Djerassi's ideas, and aided extensively by the American Academy of Arts and Sciences, the National Academy of Sciences, and other friends in the United States and Europe, Odhiambo and a secretary declared the International Centre of Insect Physiology and Ecology—ICIPE—open for business in 1970. The first postdoc arrived to work in a garage that flooded in the rainy season, and the budget was improvised from week to week while Odhiambo traveled the world convincing academies of science from Sweden to Japan and agencies from the World Bank to OPEC to support his efforts. "The route to pest control will be through basic research on some of the most difficult problems in Africa," he told them. In conference rooms on six continents he enumerated "lists of what are the pests and what are the approaches." The lists have changed over the years, as research developed or donors demanded, but always central to Odhiambo's message has been the importance of insects to life in the tropics.

If human beings live on this planet as the guests of green plants, then plants and animals can be said to survive—or fail to survive—as the guests of insects. Since the first cockroach appeared on earth three hundred million years ago, insects have evolved into as many as thirty million different species, of which one million have been discovered. Insects account for eighty-five percent of all animal life, and someone has calculated that the combined weight of the earth's insects is twelve times greater than that of its human population. In Africa the termites and ants alone outweigh all the mammals put together.

The mosquito and the tsetse fly have dictated the lifestyle and distribution of human populations across the continent. The Arabs penetrated only as far into Africa as the tsetse fly allowed before sleeping sickness killed them and their horses. Armed with malaria and yellow fever, the mosquito defended West Africa from colonial settlement by turning it into the "white man's grave." Of course, the people who suffer most under this burden of insects are the Africans themselves.

Given the importance of insects to life in the tropics, one might be surprised to learn that ICIPE is the only research institute in the world devoted exclusively to the study of insects. "It was never easy for people to understand what we wanted to do," Odhiambo says. "And it's only now in Africa, when so many development projects have failed, that people are beginning to realize how important insects are.

"Entomology is a key issue here because of the devastating impact of insects on tropical health and agriculture, but also because of their decided importance, if we want to make use of them, for food and other products. We have to move beyond our reliance on highly poisonous chemicals, which are counterproductive in the long run, to the management of insect populations that could just as well be our friends as our enemies."

Odhiambo has intriguing ideas about the potential usefulness of insects. "Did you know that termites make excellent chicken food?" he asks me. "It seems quite sensible to incorporate these and other insects into our livestock production systems. Insects also have an extremely acute and diverse chemical language whose content may be very close to that of our own spoken language. Just as we have telescopes for extending our vision, there is no reason why we couldn't borrow the language of insects to develop chemical telescopes for looking into the natural world."

Unlike many of his colleagues in the northern hemisphere, when Odhiambo looks at tropical Africa he sees a unique constellation of opportunities. Africa for him is full of potential discoveries and applications in entomology, medicine, natural products chemistry, and a host of other sciences. If someone gave him the money, he could establish a dozen institutes like ICIPE that would benefit from doing science in Africa.

"One of the richest biotas in the world is concentrated here. We have special resources even in those areas that people say are not particularly important in the tropics, like the physical sciences. The equator is one of them. Not everyone has an equator. Much of astronomy is based on polar or subpolar research, while the equator remains to be exploited. Mathematics has been invented more than once in Africa, by the Yoruba, the Shilluk, and others. I have a feeling that an African institute dealing with mathematics and astronomy would flourish fairly fast."

Odhiambo the visionary imagines a time when *jok* and science no longer oppose each other. Schizophrenic Africa will heal itself when the spirit world of the ancestors embraces the scientific methods of the West. "We will be surprised to see what comes out of this union of synthetic and analytical abilities," he says. "While adopting analytical tools, we should keep on pursuing how to manage this other tool of synthesis, because it will give us the whole picture, which, after all, is what we want. The analytical approach is very powerful, but it does not give you the whole picture. When methods exist for reaching scientific truth through synthetic means, then the African will be on his own."

Odhiambo gives me an example of what he means. "Psychiatry is far more advanced in Africa than anywhere else in the world. And why is this? The use of drugs through herbal medicine is only one element, and not the most important. The major element is the personality. Traditional healers look at someone's relationship with his people, his family and clan. His relationship with the dead, his ancestors. It's only after that that a drug might be given, and in fact the herbal cure is normally directed by the dead.

"Some of the plants are very ordinary. One can isolate the active ingredients, but when a medical doctor administers them, nothing happens. We are talking about a holistic approach, and I believe that African governments have lost a great deal by insisting, as the laboratory-oriented medical doctors told them to, on knowing the active ingredients. When the traditional healers come to the laboratory, they give you the herbs, but they don't give you the secrets. The pharmacopoeia is more than the chemical. Our training as doctors, even those of us who are African doctors, has not allowed us to penetrate the real secret of traditional psychiatry."

Thomas Adeoye Lambo, a friend of Odhiambo's and a former ICIPE adviser, conducted a famous experiment in the 1950s. Next to the psychiatric hospital he directed at Aro, in western Nigeria, Lambo built an African village of huts that doubled as consulting rooms. He hired a dozen witch doctors and moved his patients and their relatives into the village. With colleagues from Cornell University, he began a comparative study of mental illness in New York City, Nova Scotia, and the Yoruba area of western Nigeria. The study revealed that mental illness is equally prevalent in all three places. "We exploded for the first time the myth of the 'happy savage,' " said Lambo.

Impressed by the success of traditional healers in treating schizophrenia and other psychological disorders, Lambo analyzed their incantations to find "that they had been using free association long before Freud put this on paper," not to mention other techniques such as group therapy and behavior modification. "I was then determined that I would depart from the established order in psychiatry to start something new, to have an approach which had some affinity towards the local culture. And therefore I started the village community mental health services."

Lambo continued to place his patients in Aro and neighboring villages. He mixed traditional techniques with family and group encounters, drugs, and other Western methods to arrive at a therapy that cost one eighth as much and was much more effective than that practiced next door in the Aro hospital. Thirty-five years after his first experiments, Lambo's village method for treating mental illness has been adopted in dozens of countries across Africa and Asia.

*

Quickly outgrowing its Nairobi garage, the International Centre of Insect Physiology and Ecology has by now expanded into an eight-million-dollar-a-year institution employing forty senior scientists and nearly as many graduate and postdoctoral students. Its charismatic director and unusual research — on everything from inducing abortions in tsetse flies to making plants smell unattractive to crop pests — have put ICIPE on the map as a world center of insect science.

"The idea was actually very simple," Odhiambo tells me about founding ICIPE, which he pronounces "eeceepay." "Get the very best people, and then if you have more money, put buildings and equipment around them." Until recently money was in short supply, so ICIPE's headquarters consists of a number of rented houses and wood-frame barracks perched on the banks of the Masonga Wai River, which flows through the hillside campus of the University of Nairobi. Working conditions are much better for the crop pest scientists who occupy a new field station on the shores of Lake Victoria, and life should improve for everyone else at ICIPE when the laboratories open in a new thirteen-million-dollar complex being built outside of Nairobi at Duduville, whose Swahili name means Bug City.

Looking for ways to control insect pests in the tropics, ICIPE mixes pure and applied research, outreach and training programs. It cuts a wide swath across disciplines to work on human and animal health as well as agricultural pests. The four core programs concentrate on crop pests, livestock ticks, tsetse flies, and other insect vectors of human diseases. Crop pests such as mealybugs, mites, shootflies, and stem borers can make the difference between survival and famine for small farmers. Ticks carry diseases that can kill a cow in a matter of days. Tsetse flies spread sleeping sickness across an area of Africa larger than the United States. Mosquito-borne malaria is a leading cause of death among children in the tropics. Solving any one of these problems would be a major accomplishment. ICIPE tackles all of them at once. It even stretches the meaning of the word "insect" to include ticks and mites, which are technically only the cousins of insects.

At Odhiambo's invitation, I spend several weeks visiting ICIPE laboratories and traveling with scientists in the field. Because the center's research projects are scattered from one side of Kenya to the other, my visit turns into a scientific safari across East Africa. Rather than the usual postcard varieties, the game being tracked are creatures like spider mites, ticks, and tsetse flies.

From Nairobi's Wilson Airport, the Flying Doctors carry Mrs. M. U. Arara and me in a needle-nosed Beech Baron over the wall of the Rift Valley, across the manicured tea estates of the Kericho Highlands, and down to the steamy shores of Lake Victoria, where we land at Homa Bay in front of a tin hut and a lemon tree. There is no sign of the car that is supposed to drive us to Mbita Point, where ICIPE has built a new laboratory for studying crop pests. We wave goodbye to the pilot. After extracting two stools from the hut, Mrs. Arara and I pass the morning sitting under the lemon tree. Dressed in high heels and a brilliant floral robe with matching headband, this senior secretary in ICIPE's Outreach and Training Unit has been sent to accompany me into the bush. I am initially embarrassed by her presence, for it indicates that headquarters has mistaken me for an important person. But the logistics of African travel being what they are, I appreciate having a companion during my not unexpected delay.

Among other things, Mrs. Arara and I talk about insects, not as scientists talk about them, but as local farmers might. We exchange recipes on how to cook the many varieties of locusts, termites, and army worms that are eaten in Africa. We discuss a number of traditional ways to protect crops from insects. Store your grain in clay pots covered with a cap of cow manure and ash, or hang your maize over the fire, where the smoke and soot will keep it safe from weevils.

When I inquire about the large red fingers of earth thrust up beside the runway in front of us, Mrs. Arara arranges her skirt and gives me a lesson in how to demolish a termite mound. She pokes a stick into the honeycomb of sunless chambers. As the blind workers scurry to mend the breach in their walls, she explains that ordinarily the next step would be to pour urine on them. She warns me to avoid being bitten by the soldiers, whose heads contain a gland full of irritating liquid. We continue digging until we come to the central chamber where the queen, interrupted in the process of being fed by her retainers, reposes like a large white sausage.

She is the progenitor of the hundreds of thousands of termites now rushing to her defense.

"Run on absolutely totalitarian lines ... the termite mound is by far the oldest type of organized community found on Earth," writes S. H. Skaife in his book *African Insect Life*. The vast majority of its residents stop growing before their sexual organs have developed. These sterile workers and soldiers "can thus devote all their time and attention to unremitting labour for the State—without the distractions of sex."

It was not their social philosophy but another aspect of termite life that convinced the International Atomic Energy Agency in Vienna to finance an ICIPE study of termites. Because of their rare ability to extract energy from the cellulose in leaves and twigs—a process requiring enzymes that humans and most other animals lack—termites function like miniature biogas machines. Could scientists isolate these enzymes, build them into plant digesters, and thus use termite chemistry to generate alternate sources of fuel?

The cellulose in plants is tightly bound with lignin, the polymer support that gives plants the strength to stand up. Humans are incapable of digesting lignocellulose, but termites have just the right body chemistry required for breaking it apart and employing the sugar molecules released in the process. "We were going to steal their secrets and put them into our test tubes," said one of the scientists working on the project.

Within their colonies, termites operate their own plant digesters for turning lignocellulose into energy. These consist of large chambers lined with arching clay shelves full of digested cellulose. There workers tend fungus gardens that produce crops of white mushrooms. "The mushrooms are delicious," says Mrs. Arara, who, like many Africans, considers them a great delicacy.

The ICIPE termite project was recently declared a failure. Termite enzymes had been isolated and cultured, and some of these microbes did a good job of freeing cellulose from lignin. "But we found to our horror that the microbes breaking down lignin then used up the cellulose as fast as they released it," explained the project's former director. "After four years of hard work, we had succeeded in converting one form of inaccessible biomass into another. Termites proved too clever for us."

The project did manage to produce one practical result. ICIPE scientists are now able to grow termite mushrooms in the laboratory.

When the Land Rover finally arrives, Mrs. Arara and I embark on an hour's bone-wrenching ride down to the lake. We pass sisal plants with spiky green leaves and flowers perched on ten-foot stalks. Fences woven of euphorbia surround the ancestral homes of the Luo. The long rains are expected soon, but the land looks so dry and unpromising that it is hard to imagine anyone bothering to scratch it into a garden. Past the Ruri Hills we descend into swampy lowlands filled with papyrus and sedge. The sun pours down, and a great wall of humidity rises off the lake. Victoria is full of hippos, crocodiles, and bilharzia snails thriving in its weedy shallows. So the lake margin is generally off limits to humans, except the fishermen who sail their dhows out with the morning breeze and then back when the wind shifts in the afternoon.

We come to Mbita Point, a fifty-acre peninsula on which ICIPE built its field station for crop pest research in the late 1970s. The paved road, gate, and guardpost mark this as a world apart. Here twenty-five scientists, including graduate students and postdocs, develop resistant plant varieties and work on other techniques for helping Africa's "resource-poor" farmers — ICIPE's official clientele — prevail against insects. From a rocky landscape of mud huts and sisal, we suddenly enter a world of flower-lined avenues and staff houses in which everything, from hot water taps to telephones, miraculously works.

I am welcomed at the Mbita guest center "on behalf of the host country" and ushered into a lovely room with sliding glass doors and a balcony overlooking Rusinga Island. Arab dhows, some with blood-red sails and the rakish look of pirate ships, are running home for the evening. Behind them, floating like a brown smudge in the heat haze of a tropical afternoon, lies the island. Nothing more than a rocky outcropping populated with too many Luo farmers and their animals, Rusinga Island happens to be one of the most famous sites in Kenya. This is where Mary Leakey excavated Proconsul, the Miocene skull that launched the Leakey family on the first of its major anthropological discoveries.

Another famous skull lies interred on Rusinga, that of Tom Mboya, the Luo politician who was assassinated in 1969 when he appeared likely to succeed Jomo Kenyatta as Kenya's second president. Because it was Mboya's ancestral home, the island has become a kind of Luo shrine. A number of ICIPE scientists, studying subjects as diverse as crop pests and ticks, have been told to orient their field work around Rusinga. The island will serve as the test case for an integrated project uniting many of ICIPE's various lines of research. The idea may be a good one, but the locale seems suspect. Unlike Kenya's other farmland, which can be planted during both the long and short rains, the Lake Victoria region grows only one crop a year. The Luo by tradition are nomadic pastoralists, but the rinderpest epidemic at the turn of the century destroyed their animals and forced them into a sedentary mix of farming, fishing, and herding, none of which they pursue with great success.

Later that evening, as I sit alone with my dinner of roast goat and potatoes in a dining room built for a hundred people, I find myself giving way to morbid thoughts about the nature of overhead. I discover later, reading the numerous reports written on the subject, that some of ICIPE's donors have also reflected on the high cost of running an agricultural research station in such a remote and unpromising part of the country.

"Remote from what?" Odhiambo counters later when I repeat the criticisms about building a research station at Mbita Point. "All the crops and all our target pests, including tsetse flies and ticks, are there in abundance." He also reminds me that Luoland has no shortage of resource-poor farmers.

After dinner I walk over to Mbita's main laboratory, which is designed in the modular fashion of a Luo compound. Offices and workrooms surround a central courtyard, and each building is encircled by a shallow moat of water—a simple device for keeping ambulatory insects either in or out.

"What are you doing?" I ask the scientists whom I find working during the evening hours, and they are kind enough to answer my question.

Many people in Africa are involved in breeding insect-resistant plants. They start with a number of varieties, subject them to a barrage of insects, and then carry on with the survivors. But ICIPE is one of the few places on the continent doing basic research on why the survivors survive. One scientist shows me a photograph of a corn stalk magnified thousands of times by an electron microscope. What I once thought was relatively smooth suddenly appears as a mass of spikes and hairs. Can something as simple as hairiness make a plant resistant to egg-laying insects?

Among the researchers in the laboratory I meet Lu Qing Guang, a visitor from the Chinese Academy of Agricultural Sciences. The Chinese have an extensive program in the biological control of insects, and ICIPE is trying to emulate their success. "If insect life is so rich and abundant in the tropics, then there must also be many natural pathogens," Odhiambo told me before I went to Mbita Point. "In other words, insects might be controllable by their own diseases."

On the list of promising pathogens are several viruses and microbes and even a nematode, or microscopic worm, that carries a bacterium toxic to crop borers. ICIPE has also found a fungus that does a very good job of spinning a deadly cocoon around insect larvae. "Before the end of the year we'll start exploring production of nematodes and bacteria," said Odhiambo. "I think the tropics are going to be a surprise in many ways, and these are just some of the small surprises in store for us."

It is one thing to identify an agent of biological control, and another to get it out into farmers' fields. Gilbert Oloo, the lanky, soft-spoken Luo who heads ICIPE's program in biological control, recently traveled around the world on a shopping trip looking for insect delivery systems, the most successful of which he found in China. "The Americans are strong in production, but they don't care about success rates in the field. They just supply the package. The Chinese seem to have the best model for us to follow here in Africa. They operate at the level of the small farmer, where every commune is responsible for raising its own parasitoids."

A parasite that kills another parasite is known as a parasitoid, and the star performer in China—although it is actually indigenous to Africa—is the trichogramma wasp. One of the smallest insects in the world, this wasp provides tremendous service to farmers by destroying the eggs of fruit- and cereal-eating moths. "All across China farmers breed trichogramma wasps and collect them in these," says Lu Qing Guang, holding up a little plastic pagoda lined with sheets of waxed paper, where the wasps are raised on silkworm eggs before flying out to do their work. "Instead of silkworm eggs, we'll use an artificial medium for growing wasps here in Africa," he says. "We might also want to change the pagoda to some other shape."

To learn more about how their technology moves from lab to field, and vice versa, I ask Wellington Otieno to lead me back out through the ICIPE gate. A gap-toothed Luo who is the soul of courtesy, Otieno is an expert in biological control with a Ph.D. from the University of California at Berkeley. "With only fifty acres at Mbita Point," he says, "there's no way we can become a world of our own. We have to work on our neighbors' fields." He cites his own experiments as an example.

Otieno is using local roundworms, or nematodes, to attack the stem borers that kill maize and sorghum. The following morning, before we walk out through the gate, he takes me into his laboratory to show me a petri dish full of worms. Under the microscope I see a swirling ball of threadlike organisms searching for something to eat. "Nematodes move on a plant, while chemicals just sit there. The other nice thing is that insects aren't likely to develop resistance to worms." There are a hundred thousand nematodes in Otieno's petri dish. One or two is sufficient to kill a stem borer larva, and applying them requires nothing more than a backpack sprayer filled with a solution of water and worms. "Anyone in a week can grow enough nematodes to cover the average Luo farm."

"The good insect for a farmer is a dead one," says Otieno. "You want to spray and see them fall to the ground. Our problems are more basic than those facing commercial agriculture in the West. We're working to realize the potential of one acre; our people have to fill their stomachs before they can fill their pockets."

On leaving Mbita Point, Otieno and I walk along a dirt road lined with houses made of wattle and thatch. In front of us a stand of bananas and acacias serves as a barrier against grazing hippos. We have an appointment to meet Atieno Oguto, whom we find collecting chairs for us to sit on in the middle of her family compound. Surrounding us are the kitchen, a number of granaries, and various houses built for some of her nine living children. A compact woman with powerful hands, Oguto is not a resource-poor farmer. Her house has no electricity, but it has a telephone, and she and her husband own enough land to rent some of it to ICIPE for their experiments with nematodes and bacteria.

The local Luo word for what ICIPE sprays in her fields is *yadhkundi*, formed from *yadh*, meaning medicine, and *kundi*, meaning pest. "Now that they see it working, all my neighbors are curious to try ICIPE's *yadhkundi*," says Oguto. She herself has visited the laboratory and looked through a microscope at nematodes attacking corn borers. "The people at ICIPE are knowledgeable, and I'm glad to adopt their ideas," she says. "Science has made my life easier."

Like her neighbors, Oguto is an avid cultivator of ICZ, Kenya 511, and other improved varieties of maize. She plants most of her land with one of ICIPE's insect-resistant strains, which mature early and yield before the rains give out. The rest she plants with hybrid seed, which is more susceptible to drought and insects. "The ICIPE variety tastes very good, and we grow it as a kind of insurance policy. But you know it's the wrong color," she tells Otieno.

"I hadn't thought about it, but you're right," he says. "It's yellow, and we like our cornmeal white. Somebody should look into this."

Back at ICIPE headquarters in Nairobi I enter a wooden barracks identified as the Sensory Physiology Laboratory to find Sam Waladde, head of the unit, and Phil McDowell, an ICIPE research scientist, crammed into a corner office chock-a-block with electronic gear. There is too little room to sit facing each other, so we line up two chairs and a stool in front of an apparatus resembling the juggernaut machine in Kafka's "Penal Colony." A little dun-colored moth, condemned for doing tremendous damage as a stem borer, lies on a platform over which micropipettes are blowing air and pheromones. Hooked to the moth's antennae are electrodes wired into a succession of instruments, including a gas chromatograph, a four-channel magnetic tape recorder, an oscilloscope, a camera, and a computer. "The tape recorder alone," McDowell tells me, "costs as much as a duty-free Volvo." Known as the electroantennagram machine, this apparatus is designed to read involuntary confessions at the cellular level from a moth's antenna or a tick's nose.

"We're hoping to identify the full pheromone blend used by

females to attract males for mating," Waladde says. "What you want is a cocktail of molecules as complex as the language of the insect."

Pheromones are the molecular words used by insects to communicate among themselves. Insects and plants use other signals, known as semiochemicals, to communicate with each other. If scientists can learn to talk these languages, they should be able to direct insects among plants like boxcars in a switching yard. The idea is to get them on the wrong track. Insects have proved genetically plastic enough to mutate and develop resistance to insecticides. But there is no such thing as genetic resistance to language, which is why research on the sensory physiology of insects looks so promising.

Advances have been slow, though, even in the United States, where sex pheromones have been identified for over six hundred insect species. A recent article in a professional journal is entitled "Pheromones: As the Glamour and Glitter Fade — The Real Work Begins." McDowell warns me about other problems particular to Africa, where farmers often blame animals, birds, or drought for damage done by insects, especially those with complicated life histories. "It's all well and good to do high science, but then you have to take it into the field and get the local farmers to accept a technological package that looks to them like magic."

An aromatic cloud of pheromones that interferes with the signals males and females use to find each other is already employed commercially to control Egyptian cotton moths. ICIPE is experimenting with other pheromones that take advantage of insects' territoriality. After laying her eggs on a seedling, a sorghum shootfly will mark it with an odor that says "This space is taken." The next step for ICIPE scientists is to make entire fields signal that they are "taken."

In a neat twist to the standard approach, scientists are also trying to *attract* insects, but to the wrong plant. This research began with a simple question: why do sorghum shootflies deposit their eggs on sorghum and not on related plants, such as maize? When it was discovered that shootfly larvae thrive on sorghum but die on maize, which they can't digest, someone conceived the idea of baiting maize plants with the odor of sorghum. An insect that lays its eggs on the wrong plant is making a fatal mistake.

Chief blender of semiochemical cocktails at ICIPE is Ahmed Hassanali, an energetic man from the island of Zanzibar, who runs the chemistry research unit. One of Hassanali's assignments is to figure out the chemistry of plant resistance. Why are some plant varieties less susceptible to insect attack than others? "Insects would have wiped out plants long ago if they hadn't developed an exotic range of defense mechanisms," he says. At the chemical level, these defenses include everything from feeding deterrents to hormone mimics that keep insects from growing. "Every plant variety possesses a unique fingerprint of volatile compounds. Now we have to discover which ones are involved in insect-plant relations."

Hassanali also researches something called natural products chemistry, which involves isolating insecticidal agents in plants. "When I was growing up on Zanzibar we didn't have a refrigerator," he says. "Instead we used clove oil, cinnamon, and turmeric as antifungal and antibacterial agents for the preservation of food. We burned plants in the house at night to keep away mosquitoes. Something as simple as lining storage containers with neem leaves, which contain a very potent antihormonal insecticide, keeps them free of weevils. I was brought up on traditional medicine and have always been aware of the power of plants. Many people in Africa could grow their own organic, nonpersistent insecticides. It's ridiculous we're not capitalizing on this."

Chemical codes may be the most important form of insect communication, but a range of other signals—auditory, visual, thermal, and contact—also governs insect behavior. All of these are subject to ICIPE inquiry. Described to me as "the man with the tsetse love songs," Rajinder Saini is sweating in a closet-sized room full of flies when I first meet him. "They like it humid," he says, pointing to a chorus line of tsetses tethered in wax on a cardboard platform. He hands me a set of earphones and asks my pleasure. "Feeding songs? Larviposition songs? Love songs?" By the time we get to the end of the tape I imagine their high-pitched whine being used as an exquisite tool of torture. "Its peculiar buzz when once heard can never be forgotten," said David Livingstone of the tsetse. "Though this insect sang the feeblest note," Henry Stanley remarked, "it certainly did the most work and inflicted the most injury."

Other insect-borne threats to human health in the tropics are tackled by ICIPE's program in medical vectors, which includes all the biting flies and mosquitoes other than tsetses. The medical vectors program is headed by Mutuku Mutinga, a former student of Odhiambo's. Mutinga's specialty is sand flies — innocuous creatures except for their ability to transmit various parasitical diseases known collectively as leishmaniasis. Millions of people in the tropics suffer from either the cutaneous form of the disease, which resembles leprosy, or the visceral form, known as kala-azar, which inflates the liver and spleen until they burst.

Mutinga has discovered a wide variety of animal reservoirs for leishmaniasis, including the hyraxes that live in caves on top of Kenya's Mount Elgon. Hyraxes are hoofed animals the size of rabbits but related to elephants. Visitors to Africa's wild areas may be oblivious to the dangers, but medical researchers are acutely aware of those that exist at the boundary between wilderness and culture. Whenever they accidentally enter the natural cycle of disease transmission among animals, humans are at risk. Mutinga recently advised the Kenyan government *not* to clear leishmaniasis-infected rodents from an irrigation project north of Nairobi. He thereby spared the human population from becoming the new target of biting sand flies, which were happy to continue feeding on their original hosts.

When I ask Odhiambo to list the five major accomplishments of ICIPE, he names first the work of the tick program. Ticks cause tremendous damage to livestock in Africa. Several research centers are looking for vaccines against tick-borne protozoa such as East Coast fever, but ICIPE has taken the novel approach of trying to develop a vaccine against the tick itself. The idea was conceived by Rachel Galun, an Israeli endocrinologist who worked at ICIPE in the 1970s. While watching ticks jump on and off their hosts for the blood meal on which they survive, Galun wondered whether cattle could be vaccinated to produce antibodies that would make their blood lethal to ticks. Ticks feeding on vaccinated cows would be destroyed through the collapse of their own immune systems.

"We have established clearly that one can induce resistance in cattle to the tick itself," Odhiambo tells me. "This is a difficult concept. We are used to thinking of immunity against small organisms like viruses and bacteria. But here we are dealing with an antigen-antibody response between two multicellular organisms. This is an advance that was not expected. All along people poohpoohed the idea. They felt the only way to control tick-borne diseases was to vaccinate against the parasite. What we are saying is that eventually we will vaccinate against the tick. It's a new idea and a new strategy."

When Julio de Castro picks me up in his Land Rover for a Sunday drive onto the Athi Plains south of Nairobi, we head off looking for ticks. De Castro, a Uruguayan vet with a doctorate in animal parasitology, works on breeding tick resistance into Kenyan cattle. Apart from developing vaccines, stock selection of animals naturally resistant to ticks is a major avenue of ICIPE research.

After driving over savanna dotted with flat-topped acacias and grazing giraffes, we stop to look at a herd of Masai cattle. De Castro walks up to a bull and lifts his tail. "Now don't kick me," he says, picking off a tick. From the ears, neck, eyes, and rear end of the bull he gathers ticks. Ticks with inky carapaces and golden legs. Cream-colored ticks festooned with black arabesques. Ticks like little hot rods with metallic orange bodies.

"You see the problem?" says de Castro. "There are eighty species of ticks in Kenya. The most dangerous is the brown ear tick that carries the *Theileria* parasite responsible for East Coast fever. A well-fed tick can produce from four to five thousand eggs, which gives it infinite potential for expansion. But all it takes is a single tick infected with *Theileria* to kill a cow, especially the exotic strains people have tried to introduce into Africa.

"Whether you arrive at it through a tick vaccine or by identifying cattle with natural resistance, the goal is the same. We want to hammer the vector, not the disease. Don't worry for the moment about parasites or protozoa. Hit the carrier of the parasites. We're developing Trojan cows—immunized or resistant animals that will surprise ticks by giving them a bad meal."

On our way home de Castro detours to show me the Mathare Valley, which I have not seen on my half dozen previous trips to Nairobi. Down below us, in a narrow canyon denuded of vegetation, stretching as far as we can see in both directions through a haze of wood smoke and dust, lies the jumble of cardboard lean-tos, reed huts, plastic tents, and tin boxes that makes up the most notorious of Nairobi's slums. The only source of water for the thousands of people camped along its banks is the muddy river that flows along the bottom of the valley. Living here are Africa's new urban dwellers, its refugees, second sons, drought victims, and belated entrants into the cash economy. In 1982, on hearing the rumor that Kenya's president had been killed in a coup, the residents of Mathare Valley broke into an orgy of rioting and looting. Victims of bad reporting, hundreds of people lay dead in the streets after the army had come and gone.

When I next see Odhiambo, I tell him I have visited Mathare Valley and ask him an obvious question. "How can you justify spending money on advanced research when thousands of people in Kenya are suffering for want of clean water?"

"My own feeling is that we have to run on twin tracks," he says. "We have the longer-range problems that depend on science and technology. We must solve them. At the same time we must tackle these problems arising from urbanization and dislocation from the land. If we take only one track and not the other, we will be in worse trouble, because we will have no future in terms of strategies for the long term."

In 1981 ICIPE nearly collapsed under debt of a million and a half dollars, and the excitement of its founding gave way to a bureau-cratic retrenchment. In response to its fiscal crisis, ICIPE jettisoned its theoretical work on subjects such as termite communication. It had already abandoned the idea of visiting directors of research, who were replaced by permanent program leaders. Some people regret the passing of those heady days when ICIPE was an inter-national crossroads at which many of the world's great and soon-to-be-great entomologists met in the course of a year. Others argue that ICIPE remains the center of excellence Odhiambo wanted to establish in Africa and that certain tasks, such as the three-year graduate training program offered to students from a dozen Af-rican universities, it now performs better than ever.

Opinions also vary about the cause of ICIPE's crisis. Did the donors betray Odhiambo when they refused to finance pure research in Africa? Or were they merely tightening up the operation? "It was a time of accountability," someone tells me. "We had to come forward and justify our existence." Another scientist professes enthusiasm for the change. "I like the idea of catering to small-scale farmers. What would we do with another Max Planck Institute in Africa?"

Someone else tells me about the personal hardship of the crisis for Odhiambo. "He was shaken up by these charges that ICIPE wasn't helping the people it was supposed to help. He went ahead with the reorganization. He made our research more 'mission oriented.' But I still feel bad about it, because of my interest in good, fundamental science."

Odhiambo himself maintains that what he is doing now is not different from what he was doing in 1970, when ICIPE was founded. "Many people never understood our philosophy. From the very beginning we said, 'We must manage tropical insects.' We did not say, 'We must do basic research.' The goal has always been the same. In the beginning we lacked adequate information. We had generalized theories from the study of insects, but not particular knowledge of the species we were dealing with. But by 1980 we could see where we were going. The information had accumulated. We could begin to say, 'This goal can be reached by these means.'"

Speaking of himself in the third person, Odhiambo admits that dropping the idea of visiting directors of research cost him friends. "Many people felt that Odhiambo had become iconoclastic, which was not the case," he says. "Or that he had become racially minded, which he hadn't. But when all was said and done, everyone saw it was inevitable. There had to be a transition from Plato's Academy, where people come to sit at the feet of the Master, to a community of interactive scholars talking to other scholars on their own terms."

While ICIPE was weathering the change in scientific direction, it ran out of money. Donors told Odhiambo to cut a quarter of his budget. "I went to the staff and said, 'We have to tighten our belt. Is that what you want, or do you want us to close up shop?' We tried the first option, but people came back and said, 'This is not working. We can't cut off the water and electricity and everything else. We have to cut staff.' We discussed it among ourselves.

'Who can we forgo?' We found alternative jobs for everybody, but it was very painful."

This is when ICIPE dropped most of its work on termites and mosquitoes. "The termite work was fantastic," Odhiambo says. "It was cited all over the place. We were using termites to model chemical communication in insects. They have more vocabulary than we do. It's very diverse, highly selective. Because it's so complex, this chemical interaction can be a very effective way of controlling insects. We wanted to do it first with termites, and then move on to the others. We were using them as a meta-problem, but we couldn't get the donors behind us."

Mosquitoes provided another meta-problem for ICIPE, this time in insect genetics. Could insects be controlled by altering their genetic composition? "The idea," says Odhiambo, "was to introduce a deleterious mutation or a new gene into a mosquito that would make it ineffective as a carrier of the malaria parasite." But again the donors balked at ICIPE doing basic research. "The World Health Organization insisted at the time that the only effective method of controlling mosquitoes was by chemicals."

Donors occasionally drop into his office and suggest that Odhiambo get back to work on the problem of maize-eating termites or the scourge of malaria. "I tell them, 'Unless you can guarantee money over a long period of time, we're not touching it. We can give you advice, but to do research, we need a long-term commitment.' That's when the checkbooks start disappearing.

"We are a very strange institution, if one looks at it objectively. All the other major research centers in Africa are commodity oriented. Most donors do not believe that basic research should be involved. They are more interested in technology transfer than you would expect. ICIPE, on the other hand, is not commodity oriented. We are interested in a specific component that leads to crop production. It's only one element—although an important one in the tropics—and I can tell you it's not very easy for donors to understand."

On the last leg of my scientific safari, I drive south out of Nairobi over the Ngong Hills and down into the Rift Valley at Lake Magadi, which ranks as one of the strangest sights in Africa. This white bowl of sodium carbonate shines like a glacier under the midday sun. On the far side of the lake stretches the Sampu Plain, a dry savanna that gives way to acacia woodland as we approach the blue wall of the Nguruman Plateau. This side of the Rift Valley and all the fertile land below it belong to the tsetse fly. To be more precise, they belong to the deadly trypanosomes that cause the animal form of sleeping sickness known as nagana. Only the arid shores of Lake Magadi have been left to the Masai pastoralists whose thorn enclosures and dung houses hug the few small trees available for shade.

The Tswana people of the Kalahari Desert named the twenty-two species of *Glossina* flies and their unforgettable buzz *tsetse*. The bite of these big flies is nasty but tolerable, unless they happen to be infected with the blood parasite that causes trypanosomiasis. The human form of the disease is commonly known as sleeping sickness, because once the parasites have crossed the blood barrier into the brain, their victims sink into an incurable doze. By spreading the animal form of sleeping sickness throughout the tropics from the Kalahari to the Sahara, tsetse flies have effectively zoned much of Africa off limits to cattle raising.

Camped below the wall of the Rift Valley in prefabricated barracks are a dozen ICIPE scientists working on a project unique in Africa for its combination of high-tech research and low-tech solutions to the scourge of the tsetse fly. "I believe strongly in getting people together and letting them control their own lives," says Robert Dransfield, the thirty-seven-year-old British zoologist who runs the project. "If the fix comes from outside, it isn't going to work." For Dransfield to accomplish his goal among the Masai, who have a long history of resistance to external meddling, will verge on the miraculous.

The classic approach to tsetse control includes stripping the land of vegetation, killing all the animals on which the fly feeds, and bombarding the area from fixed-wing aircraft with DDT and other chlorinated hydrocarbons. Carried on for forty years over thousands of square miles, this method of tsetse control has temporarily pushed the fly back from the outer limits of its range. Some of this land is now being reinvaded, and elsewhere in Africa the fly is developing genetic resistance to chemicals. "The scorched-earth approach to tsetse control may really do more harm in the long run than leaving them there," Odhiambo had told me. "Our question is this, How can we have flies without their carrying the disease? Is there a way to make sure the parasite and the tsetse are not at the same place at the same time?"

To answer this question, Dransfield and his team moved to Nguruman in 1983 to begin a seven-year project. Aided by computer modeling, electric screens, and odor-baited traps, they started counting flies and monitoring how many contained parasites. Ecologists dotted live flies with oil paint and then recaptured them to estimate the size of the population. An epidemiologist wrestled Masai cattle to the ground and studied their blood for trypanosomes. A physiologist researched ways to induce abortions in tsetse flies. Rajinder Saini brought out his Uher 4400 tape deck to record their singing. And four Masai *morans*, young men trained as warriors, came to work as technicians sitting at the "disassembly line," a long table laden with microscopes where flies by the thousands are dissected and converted into data.

Once he knew enough about it, Dransfield in 1986 thought he could move from modeling the tsetse population to controlling it by means of traps. Originally designed to look like animals made of canvas and netting, tsetse traps have been used in Africa with limited success since the 1930s. But two recent improvements have made them increasingly effective: the addition of color — contrasting shades of blue and white being the most attractive — and odor, in the form of ox breath, acetone, or some other winning combination. There are probably as many trap designs being tested today in Africa as there are tsetse researchers, but Dransfield's team developed yet another model, possibly the most effective yet, which also has the distinct advantage of being inexpensive. A plastic bag, a handful of staples, a few feet of cloth, and some cow urine are all that's required to build a device capable of trapping twenty thousand flies a week.

Tsetse traps have a way of disappearing and getting recycled for other uses. This is a nuisance for the technicians deploying them and a danger to everyone else, because many of these traps are impregnated with insecticides. Dransfield discussed the problem with his Masai neighbors, who decided, while assembling their own traps, to mark them with the same brands they use on their cattle. The task of maintaining the traps got assigned to the young *morans*, who incorporated it, along with animal tracking and cattle rustling, into their training as warriors.

I walk out with the *morans* one morning to service some traps placed deep in the bush along a dry riverbed. The tangerine sky of an African dawn floats over the valley as we ascend into a forest of *ngoja kidogo*, the wait-a-bit bush, whose thorns make for slow going. Hadada ibis cackle at us from up in the trees. Baboons cough in the distance, and dik-diks and bat-eared foxes scamper away through the grass. With spears, pangas, and a lot of high-spirited yelling, the *morans* chase off the occasional buffalo that comes crashing toward us through the forest. My warrior companions, who double as technicians trained in identifying trypanosomes through Leitz microscopes, are good enough at spear throwing to split a vine at sixty feet.

Under a spreading crown of tropical figs we find our first tsetse trap. It looks like a miniature tent for extraterrestrials, with royal blue walls, a conical roof of nylon mesh, and a chimney made from a plastic bag. The trap works like a lobster pot: easy to get in, impossible to get out. Lured into the dark interior and then fooled into thinking they can escape through the plastic chimney, the flies die of dehydration. Servicing the trap consists of topping off the odor bait—a Kimbo shortening can full of cow urine—weeding the entrance, stapling up the genet bites, changing plastic bags, and walking off with a mass of dehydrated tsetses. Seventy traps scattered over a hundred square kilometers have already removed half of the million flies that once lived in the area.

If Dransfield's idea of giving local people the tools to control their own destiny sounds simple enough, it actually required great skill to implement. Dransfield is a bearded man with bright green eyes and a laugh of Swiftian vigor. His brown hair falls over his forehead in a wash-basin cut. His pants hang off his bottom. His fingernails are blackened with grease and dead tsetses. A hard-drinking, straight-talking Englishman who smokes and works around the clock, Dransfield is a polymath who rushes with gusto from computer programming to goat roasts. He knew he was on to something important at Nguruman, but when he tried to explain his ideas to the local Masai, they feared a land grab and "put up a wall of hostility against us."

The project was saved by love. On Dransfield's team was an epidemiologist named Rose Tarimo, an elegant, highly trained woman who likes to go out in the field and get her hands dirty. A Tanzanian who is part Masai, Tarimo knows how to gather people together into a *baraza* and explain things. At one of these meetings she asked if she could bleed and tag their cows, a delicate matter for the Masai, but crucial to understanding tsetse infection rates. After falling madly in love with her, giving her a necklace, and asking Dransfield for her hand in marriage, a local elder was the first to put his livestock in Tarimo's care. After that the project quickly developed the tissue of personal relationships without which the Masai would never have adopted it as their own.

Dransfield's idea of community participation is diametrically opposite the standard approach to tsetse control in Africa. A perfect example of that approach can be found west of Nguruman in Kenya's Lambwe Valley, which is not far from ICIPE's field station at Mbita Point. This once heavily settled valley is currently empty of people and designated as a national park. But it is surely the oddest national park in Africa. The forests have been cleared, the land carved into a grid of access roads, the animals killed. Since 1939 Lambwe Valley has been strafed from the air and saturated from the ground with DDT, dieldrin, malathion, endosulphan, and pyrethrum. It reeks of chemicals. In a landscape of deformed acacia trees fifteen feet high yet only two inches thick, a visitor is struck by the immense silence of a park denuded of birds, dragonflies, wasps, mammals—everything, that is, except tsetse flies. Happily doubling their population every month, the flies will soon be celebrating the golden anniversary of their resistance to chemicals.

Like many of Africa's parks, Lambwe Valley is a reservoir of disease—in this case, both the human and animal forms of sleeping sickness. That sleeping sickness exists here at all is a curious by-product of colonialism. In the European myth of the Dark Continent, Africa was ravaged by disease until the arrival of Western medical science. The truth is actually quite different. Financed by Belgium's King Leopold II, it was Henry Stanley and his steamboats in the late 1870s that transported the most dangerous species of tsetse fly upriver from its native home in the lower Congo, thereby introducing sleeping sickness liberally throughout Central Africa. The diseases that accompanied the early explorers nailed Africa into the coffin that the Arab and American slave trades had been building for four centuries. Joseph Conrad, who followed Stanley's path ten years later, would write in *Heart of Darkness* that the Congo by then had been turned into a forced labor camp full of men who were "nothing but black shadows of disease and starvation, lying confusedly in the greenish gloom."

As infected tsetse flies spread throughout Africa with colonial zeal, epidemics of sleeping sickness eventually claimed hundreds of thousands, if not millions, of lives. The problem was further exacerbated by the mistaken notion that survivors should be evacuated from infected regions. Sleeping sickness reached the western shores of Lake Victoria at the turn of the century. After two hundred thousand people had died, the governor of Uganda in 1907 ordered the area cleared, and its inhabitants and cattle were moved to the eastern side of the lake. He thereby laid the groundwork for the epidemics of sleeping sickness that have continued to afflict Kenya as recently as the 1960s.

At the end of a career in the colonial tsetse services, John Ford wrote a classic study of trypanosomiasis. Ford concluded that he and his colleagues "were feebly scratching at the surface of events that we hardly knew existed, and if we achieved anything at all, it was often to exacerbate the ills of the societies we imagined ourselves to be helping. . . . Unfortunately, with very few exceptions, it was psychologically impossible for men and women concerned in imperial expansion in Africa to believe that their own actions were more often than not responsible for the manifold disasters in which they found themselves caught up. The scientists they called in to help them were as ignorant as they of the problems they had to tackle."

Dransfield, who has taken Ford's warning to heart, believes that no effective measures against sleeping sickness will be developed in Africa without an understanding of the ecology and cultures in which they are expected to operate. I am curious what the Masai

themselves think about Dransfield's project. He suggests I visit
Ngoto Kinampet, who is known to everyone as Mama Jacob from
the Masai custom of naming women after their last-born son. The
Jacob in question is one of Dransfield's *morans*, and he and I drive
off into the bush one evening to find the *engang*, or cattle camp,
where his mother lives.

Descending from the forested edge of the Rift Valley into its
arid center, we bounce over savanna littered with red volcanic rocks
and the odd thorn tree. We follow a track etched by one or two
passes of a Land Rover through the grass until the path ends in
a maze of cattle trails. Jacob points to the horizon. It takes me a
while to discern the perfectly camouflaged thorn-bush enclosure
that his mother shares with three other families.

We find Mama Jacob up on the roof of her house massaging a
large mound of cow dung into a viscous paste. This is her mortar
for patching the roof and sealing it against the coming rains. Built
in the shape of an elongated igloo, the entire house, inside and
out, is constructed of cow dung plastered over an armature of
twigs and reeds. Mama Jacob is well known for her skills in house
building—in the valley I had seen an old *engang* in which her
house alone was still standing—and she applied the same diligence
to building tsetse traps for the project.

Mama Jacob finishes her work on the roof and comes down
to shake my hand. We sit in front of the house on three-legged
stools drinking *chai*, the common East African drink made of
spices, fresh milk, and tea. Mama Jacob's earlobes have been
tugged into ropy loops under their weight of decorative beads.
Another mass of beads wrapped around her neck enhances her
already impressive height. Watching us from a distance, men
fan themselves with ostrich-feather whisks. Children rush around
gathering in the animals for the evening. Cows in the middle of
the enclosure, sheep and goats off to the side. The newborn animals are led into the houses, where their bleating punctuates our
conversation.

Mama Jacob knows a lot about *entorrobo*, the Masai word for both
tsetse flies and trypanosomiasis. She understands the life history
of the fly, where it breeds, its range, and the routes one has to
travel at night to avoid it. She knows the stages of the disease and

how to dose her cattle with Novidium and other trypanocides. And now she knows how to make tsetse traps. She admits to an initial skepticism about Dransfield's project, but she and her neighbors were finally convinced of its merits. Her *engang*, she says, will buy the material and make traps even after ICIPE leaves.

"What if the project succeeds in opening up new dry-season pasture? Will there be a rush of Masai moving into the area?"

"We will have to decide among ourselves how to use the land," she says.

"And what about a future in which the Rift Valley is free of *entorrobo*?"

"We have lived with them so long, it is hard to imagine what the world will be like without tsetse."

When I next see him, Dransfield has come up to Nairobi for a meeting with his donors, and he is depressed. A team of Dutchmen has been sent out by their government to review its investments in East Africa. The Dutch have supported Dransfield in the past, but he has heard rumors of a change. Apparently they want to pull their money out of the Masai Nguruman project and redeploy it on Rusinga Island.

Several months later I get a letter from Africa indicating that the matter is still unresolved. The Flying Doctors transported the Dutchmen down to Lake Victoria to look at Rusinga Island, but on the way back to Nairobi the airplane crashed. No one was killed, but the plane was demolished, and the project leader suffered multiple fractures. The Dutch government will send out another team of reviewers before deciding whether or not to move into Luoland.

Twice a year, at the beginning and end of the long rains, Odhiambo gathers the entire staff together under a fig tree on the banks of the Masonga Wai to talk to them about "the dudu world" of insects. The meeting resembles a gathering of the clan, and ICIPE in many respects functions with the familial benevolence that characterizes personal relationships in Africa. But there is also something novel about this gathering. A generation ago there was no scientific tribe in Africa; Odhiambo was an original member. "The tropics are going to surprise us in many ways," he had said, and this meeting provides another example.

"We're an African institution, and out of Africa comes our inspiration," says Rhoda Odingo, who directs long-range planning at ICIPE. "ICIPE was conceived and born in Africa, and I think as an institution it will endure where the others — exotic enclaves of Americans or Europeans that they are — will pass from the scene. The problems we work on are ours. We know them because we live them. This is not a case of outside experts coming to give advice to Africa. It is Africa advising itself. Africa healing itself."

In our last conversation I ask Odhiambo if he is hopeful about the future of Africa. "I'm a realistic optimist, if there is such a thing," he says. "To found an institute of this type in a developing country with very slender resources and many other priorities, one has to be an optimist."

Going Lake

Why is it that I alone, among all those I knew, am still a rolling stone?

Emin Pasha

K EN MCKAYE AND I bail out his old plank boat, kick over the Seagull engine, and chug off into a pastel morning on Lake Malawi. Slipping away behind us are the coppery sands of a beach shaded by palm trees and mangoes. Above the shore rises the mountainous amphitheater of the Cape Maclear peninsula, whose green-shouldered hills tumble three thousand feet into the lake below. Domwe, Mumbo, and Thumbi islands float in front of us like emerald hatpins in a turquoise beret. To our right and left, thirty miles across the water, loom the blue mountains of the Rift Valley escarpment. They mark the line of continental drift, where one half of Africa is in the process of edging away from the other.

The lake can be treacherous with tropical storms that rush over it without warning, but today Malawi is showing its benign face as McKaye and I anchor off the islands, don our scuba gear, and prepare to drop fifty feet onto an arena of mating fish. Carrying underwater slates and a tape measure, we will spend the next two hours, or as long as our air lasts, watching fish sex. Their acrobatic performances will be scored under headings such as "courtship displays" and "number of copulations." This is part of McKaye's research into sexual selection — the process by which females choose their mates. It is McKaye's hunch that female choice is one of the driving forces behind the explosion of species in Lake Malawi.

Diving into its tropical blue waters is like falling into a blizzard of fish, a rainbow-hued, fluorescent blizzard. Purple-striped, orange-flecked, blue-spotted, green-marbled fish stream by in a luminous parade. The variety of colors alone indicates that something extraordinary has happened here. The lucky visitor has splashed into a freak of nature, an evolutionary sport in which the natural clock dictating the division of species has been speeded up.

Famous in the aquarium trade for their colors, the fish of Lake Malawi are equally famous among biologists for their diversity. Most of them belong to a single family of perchlike fish, the Cichlidae, that has split over the past million years into as many as a thousand different species in this one body of water alone. Malawi is the most species-rich lake in the world, with more different types of fish than exist in the Atlantic Ocean from Greenland to Brazil, and virtually all of them are endemic, existing here and nowhere else.

Cichlids have learned to survive in this hothouse environment through a remarkable array of adaptations. The males are highly aggressive, territorial fish who spend their days building nests, courting, and fighting. The females, with one exception, are mouth brooders. Their eggs are fertilized and hatched in the female's mouth, which is also where the fry are guarded until they are old enough to be dropped off in communal nurseries, where they school by the millions. Cichlids dance when courting. They mate in fanciful sand castles built on the bottom of the lake. They tend algae gardens or, when food is in short supply, switch to eating zooplankton or each other.

The process by which species evolve to fill an ever-expanding number of ecological niches is known as explosive radiation, and Lake Malawi exemplifies the phenomenon at its most intense. In the process of evolving, cichlids have adopted virtually every conceivable form of fish behavior, which makes the lake an encyclopedic text for studying the mechanisms of evolution. In recognition of this fact, part of Lake Malawi has been declared the world's first freshwater national park.

"Cichlids do everything but fly," says McKaye. "And who knows. If we stick around long enough, we'll probably find one that does."

In what must rank as a peak experience in biological voyeurism, we are headed for the lake's largest natural mating arena, a two-mile-long cichlid fortress of sand castles defended by fifty thousand males dressed in brilliant blue. "It's a sexual free-for-all out there," says McKaye. "One big orgy."

We jump in the water and clear our regulators with a burst of compressed air. Our descent will lead us through several of the main attractions in the City of Cichlidae. First come the rock faces covered with mbuna, the small, brightly colored fish prized by hobbyists. Sunlight rakes through the water to illuminate a natural aquarium filled with blue zebras, orange morphs, red tops, and golds nibbling algae off the rocks and defending their territories with aggressive darts at passing strangers. McKaye directs my attention to an upside-down fish, one of several species in the lake with reverse coloration—light on top, dark on bottom—that flips over for surprise attacks. We pass a beak-nosed fish that can hunt around corners, and then stop to watch another mbuna, whose Latin name translates as "fat lips," wedge its gasket mouth over a crevice and suck out a meal.

Fin biters and scale scrapers—fish that survive by dining on their neighbors' body parts—nip at my legs. I turn for a moment to float on my back. The water above me all the way to the surface is filled with flocks of silvery utaka, small zooplankton-feeding fish that are a staple food from the lake. Scattered among the utaka are thousands of translucent mbuna females waiting to drop down the water column and mate with the brightly colored males below.

Out from the rocks floats a skirt of aquatic plants and grasses that marks a shift into another cichlid neighborhood. Here most of the residents look like drifting pieces of vegetation. I give way to a needle-nosed fish whose slender body makes it hard to see head-on. A *Cyrtocara compressiceps*, commonly known as the Malawi eye plucker, this fish was once thought to specialize in nipping out the eyeballs of its compatriots. But in the only example I know of a Lake Malawi fish story being less fabulous than first reported, recent findings indicate that the eye plucker is actually a baby eater who consumes all, and not just the eyeballs, of its fellow fish.

McKaye holds his underwater slate up to my face plate. "Play Dead Fish," it says, as he redirects my attention to a mottled brown and white fish in the process of falling into the weeds and covering itself with sand. This is *Cyrtocara livingstonii*, a death-feigning fish that disguises itself as a rotting corpse before leaping up to attack its prey.

In clearings among the weeds, brooding females of various species hang low in the water, hoping to avoid mouth rammers. Mouth rammers specialize in pedophagy. They attack a pregnant female, knock the eggs or fry out of her mouth, and eat them. As I watch a pedophage sculling over a female, he zips at his prey for a head-on collision. To defend herself, the female ducks her head and suffers a glancing blow. As gruesome as the practice may be, mouth ramming has been developed by three different species in Lake Malawi, thereby providing a perfect example of convergent evolution. The niche existed; three types of fish volunteered to fill it. In a neat twist to the story, each mouth-ramming species has developed a different kind of jaw. One projects like a racing prow, one opens into a basket, and the third is shaped like a pike. Why is this? Because each pedophage specializes in attacking females from a different direction: above, below, or straight on.

Beyond the weed beds we descend into the pockmarked terrain of the sand-dwelling cichlids. This group comprises a hundred species divided by local fishermen into two varieties—utaka, or plankton eaters, and chisawasawa, or bottom feeders, which are good at plowing up insects and larvae. Twice yearly, in underwater migrations as spectacular as any across the Serengeti Plain, these fish flock inshore by the millions to breed in the lake's shallow water. The males set to work building nests, huge sand castles that are comparable to bird bowers or display sites, as their sole function is to attract females for sex. After mating, the females swim off to tend their young elsewhere. Because each species of fish builds a different-shaped nest, the lake bottom is trenched and mounded into a fantastic array of craters and cones. Pits two feet deep and ten feet across lie next to towering volcanoes seven feet in diameter. On top of the towers and down in the pits sit little beds of sand being fussed over by nervous males waiting for a date.

McKaye and I have entered a neighborhood of fish with blue heads and yellow dorsal fins. These are the flashy colors the males have adopted for the mating season. For the two weeks he endures in an arena, a male cichlid will spend most of his life as a living dump truck, hauling sand in his mouth to build a Pharaonic construction project that has to be defended from intruders on the average of once every twenty seconds. His six months' supply of fat will be exhausted in work and anxiety before another male supplants him as king of the mountain or lord of the pit.

Fish sex is polymorphous and promiscuous, but there doesn't seem to be much pleasure in it. *Arena* aptly describes these cichlid mating grounds. Courtship is a public display, with a lot of bystanders wanting to get in on the act. While the females parade overhead, the males below fan their dorsals and wiggle the egg spots on their anal fins. These brilliant patches of color near the sperm vent are thought to serve as a kind of sexual target. When all goes well, the female will do a little circle dance with the male and lay three or four eggs in his nest. The eggs remain there only long enough for her to turn, scoop them into her mouth, and turn again to have them fertilized. As the world's first vertebrates, fish must be credited with the invention of oral sex. At morning's end, a female's mouth will pucker with eggs and sperm from a dozen different males.

More often than not, though, fish sex ends in *labia interrupta*. The male gets distracted by having to shoot up the water column and attack nest darters—fish that specialize in stealing eggs before the female has pouched them into her mouth. He hurries back to find his partner flirting in his neighbor's nest. There is more fanning and tail wiggling, but she seems a hopeless tease, nest hopping only to mooch insect larvae out of their beds. Worse yet, "she" might be a sneaky male masquerading as a female by turning off his mating colors. A disguised male will climb into a nest to eat eggs or steal copulations of his own. Meanwhile catfish and other predators lurking in the nearby rocks are hoping to pick off distracted cichlids caught in flagrante delicto. Nest darting, mouth ramming, wife swapping, hermaphroditism, sudden death—this is surely an exciting yet precarious moment in a fish's life.

Because of the lake's evolutionary importance, ninety-four square kilometers, including inland waters, twelve islands at the southern end, three mainland forest reserves, and much of the Cape Maclear peninsula and its bay, were established in 1980 as the Lake Malawi National Park. Four years later the park joined other African treasures, like the Serengeti Plain and Mount Kilimanjaro, in being listed as a UNESCO World Heritage site. The ninth largest and fourth deepest lake in the world, Malawi is actually an inundated slice of the Great Rift Valley, which stretches the length of Africa from the Red Sea to the Zambezi River. The three-hundred-and-sixty-mile-long lake is bordered by Tanzania and Mozambique to the north and east, although most of it lies within Malawi, a land-locked, densely settled nation that depends for its survival on this inland sea. All the paper money in the country is etched with pictures of fishermen casting nets into the lake, and two thirds of the nation's animal protein comes from these abundant waters.

David Livingstone "discovered" Lake Malawi in 1859, when he named Cape Maclear for an astronomer friend. The Portuguese trader Gaspar Bocarro actually beat Livingstone to the lake by two hundred and fifty years, and another Portuguese explorer, Candido de Costa Cardosa, knew the lake well enough to sketch a map of it in Livingstone's notebook. Livingstone returned the favor by later denying that de Costa had ever been anywhere near Lake Malawi; his map was of some other body of water, said the doctor. But while striving to claim the lake as his own, Livingstone confessed in his journal, "Some of the brethren do not hesitate to tell the natives that my object is to obtain the applause of men. This bothers me, for sometimes I suspect my own motives."

The sheltered bay and forested hills edging Cape Maclear provided the original site for the Livingstonia Mission, which hoped to establish the lake as the colonial gateway for settlers moving up the Zambezi River into the heart of Africa. In the five years it operated at Cape Maclear, the mission generated one "convert to calico" and five ministerial graves. The bay also served briefly in the 1950s as a stopover for the Sunderland Cape-to-Cairo flying boats on their five-day trip up the continent. Now that these colonial intrusions have come and gone in the short space of a hundred years, what endures at Cape Maclear is a fishing village of thatch-roofed houses.

Unless one arrives by boat, the journey to this remote part of the world requires a sturdy vehicle capable of crossing the Dedza Mountains and dropping down the Rift Valley escarpment to the lake below. A two-lane dirt track cuts off the main road to wind for fifteen miles through a range of granitic hills before ending on the beach at Cape Maclear. Most of the peninsula is a forest reserve filled with the great fluted trunks of baobabs and the rounded crowns of star chestnuts, wild figs, and African ebony.

Near its end the road opens onto maize and rice fields dotted with little platforms on stilts. Here children sit guarding the crops from baboons, while offshore sparkles a glorious bay protected by two headlands and three islands quilted in tropical green.

To the right along the beach stretch the mud and wattle houses of the village. To the left lie the whitewashed huts of the former Golden Sands Holiday Camp and Bar, which currently serves as local headquarters for the national park. It costs twelve kwacha, about five dollars, a night for a cottage at the Golden Sands, or you can pitch your tent on the beach for a dollar. There are plans to build an interpretive center at the Golden Sands, but for the moment the park welcomes its few visitors—overland travelers from Europe and fish freaks from around the world—with nothing more than a lot of cichlids to stare at. Given its turquoise coves and equatorial light, the scene could be Caribbean, except for the African fish eagles standing sentinel in the acacias and the occasional crocodile beaching to sun itself on the sand.

When Kenneth Robert McKaye first arrived on the shores of Lake Malawi in 1977, fulfilling a lifelong dream amalgamated out of Jacques-Yves Cousteau movies, Alan Moorehead's book on the discovery of the White Nile, and Fryer and Iles's classic work *The Cichlid Fishes of the Great Lakes of Africa*, he got depressed. Lake Malawi was everything he imagined, and more. "I was overwhelmed by the system. No one knew the names of the fish, other than the common ones or the species exported in the aquarium trade, and I had only black and white photographs to work from. So I took a deep breath and said, 'McKaye, all you can do is handle one fish at a time. Pick a species and settle down and learn everything you can about it.'"

McKaye is an intellectual live wire who delights in jumping up every morning to ask himself two questions. "How did so many species come into being? How do they manage to coexist? There isn't a single problem in vertebrate behavior you can't study with cichlids," he says. "Whatever the year's hot topic, from altruism to aggression, these fish are out there doing it."

Newly married for the third time and a father for the first, McKaye is a brown-haired, mustachioed extrovert in his early forties. He wears spectacles that go smoky in the sunlight, and his medium frame is starting to plump out around the middle. "I'm like the Malawians," he jokes. "They all get fat when they're successful." His most distinctive feature is his voice, self-assured, resonant, emphatic, *informed*, with a nervous laugh catching up the end of his sentences.

While he can be quite charming and a wonderful friend, it must be said that McKaye is an aggressive, highly territorial male who bears more than a passing resemblance to the fish he studies. In the process of becoming "Mr. Cichlid," he has developed into a scrappy character adept at "taking out the opposition." He has a lot of enemies. Many people in Malawi have enemies, or are afraid of having enemies, but McKaye has more than most.

He acquired them right from the start, when he hit the lake with the vigor of an introduced species. The old colonial service chaps had divided Lake Malawi into concessions, with entire habitats reserved for biologists who might publish a paper once every ten years. McKaye embarrassed the sleepy club of Lake Malawi ichthyologists by doing enough research to publish ten papers a year. He hung a shingle in front of his house and appointed himself director of the newly established Cape Maclear Research Station. He began accumulating fish tanks, boats, students, scuba gear, and enough African assistants to keep the operation going year-round.

McKaye then kicked himself upstairs into academic policymaking. He began designing fisheries programs, doctoral exchanges, and university links among all the front-line states facing South Africa. Gifted at making his enthusiasm contagious, he worked his spell on administrators who came to visit him in Malawi. Within hours they would doff their ties and bureaucratic moorings and join him in thinking that the waters of this tropical hideaway are actually the most serious evolutionary laboratory in the world.

To be fair, it must be said that McKaye has a lot of enemies everywhere, not just in Malawi. He first got into trouble as a young professor of biology at Yale, where he sported long hair and sided with the students in condemning "police riots" at demonstrations against South Africa. But it was mainly his ideas that got him in trouble. He was telling fish stories from faraway places about species that did not behave according to classic models. The models have since been changed, but McKaye in the meantime suffered his colleagues' disbelief. "These fish haven't read the textbooks," he says. "That's what makes them interesting."

Ken McKaye was floating around the world on a boat that doubled as a Chapman College classroom when he stuck his head underwater off Ceylon and marveled for the first time at the wonders of a tropical reef. Ecstatic after this initial experience with snorkeling, he wanted to drop out of college and travel around the globe. Back in San Francisco, his mother said she would raise his allowance if he transferred to the University of California at Berkeley. Avoiding the draft clinched her argument.

McKaye studied biochemistry, got bored, and was ready to drop out again when George Barlow, one of his professors, convinced him to go on to graduate work in zoology. Barlow wanted him to study pheromones—the smells fish use to recognize their young. McKaye was more interested, though, in evolutionary ecology and field studies. "These guys were treating fish like black boxes. Experiments are OK and often quite helpful, but you want to generate your hypotheses from observations made in the field." To keep his student happy, Barlow took him scuba diving in the South Pacific and in the volcanic lakes of Central America. On one of these trips McKaye slipped away to spend the rest of his graduate career studying cichlid fish in Jiloá, a crater lake on the Pacific side of Nicaragua.

"I'm a grandson of Konrad Lorenz," McKaye says of his academic lineage. Lorenz based his theories about our innate tendency toward aggression on the study of cichlid fish, which have proved to be good subjects for laboratory experiments. Following Lorenz's example, George Barlow had spent most of his academic career putting fish in tanks and running experiments on them. One of his better-known papers discussed the "gold effect," or the pros and cons of being a gold fish. It described a Central American cichlid that comes in two color morphs, or varieties. Most of the fish are gray, but one out of five, later in life, turns gold. What are the advantages of being a gold fish? You win more fights. What are the disadvantages? You get picked off more easily by predators.

While studying fish communities in Lake Jiloá, McKaye accidentally developed a theory that got him back in Barlow's good graces. For months he had been bewildered by three fish species — two little fish that breed over rocks and a larger species that breeds over sand — whose interactions seemed completely inexplicable. One of the little fish, which McKaye called helpers, tends the young of the big fish. When they are fully grown, the big fish turn around and eat the helper fish.

Why would a fish help another fish that repays the favor by eating it? As he was mulling over this question, McKaye remembered that the big fish also eats the other little fish on the rocks. It picks them out of holes that are the breeding sites for both the helper fish and its competitor. "It's like befriending the bully on the block," he says, explaining the strategy of the helper fish. "You hope he'll defend you, even if once in a while the strategy backfires and you end up with a fat lip."

This apparent case of altruism is actually an example of one fish investing in a "delayed return benefit" from another. Sociobiologists, whose theories are based on the idea that an animal's biological self-interest governs its social interactions, found great significance in McKaye's triangulated relationship. Sociobiology now dominates the zoological sciences in England and the United States, but when it was fighting for acceptance in the 1970s, the story of the helper fish was considered a crucial piece of evidence.

McKaye's colleagues at Yale were skeptical, however. They could not imagine a fish displaying such Machiavellian genius. As a prelude to firing him with a golden handshake, they gave McKaye a prestigious faculty fellowship that included a year's leave on full salary. He put this together with a grant from the National Science Foundation and disappeared into Africa for fifteen months. When he embarked on this first trip in 1977, he had no idea that Lake Malawi would become the lodestar experience of his life. McKaye was beginning the process known to Malawians as "going lake."

Going lake is like a love affair that one can neither resolve nor quit. It involves an attraction, sometimes fatal, for this body of water that outshines the Mediterranean yet storms with the ferocity of the North Sea. David Livingstone went lake. After his hopes of using the Zambezi River as an artery into the interior of Africa were dashed on the rapids at Cahora Bassa, he turned north to

discover the lake toward whose shores he would gravitate for the
remaining thirteen years of his life. He wrote home to say he had
found the land of Canaan, whose sweet waters were perfect for
nurturing the twin seeds of Christianity and commerce. Livingstone died trying to map Lake Malawi into the river systems that
feed the Nile. His belated successors are intent on mapping it into
the behavioral systems that feed evolution.

Lake Malawi charms you. The waves that lap like ocean surf on
the mango-studded beaches have lulled more than one visitor into
thinking it was paradise regained. The dream is sometimes sus-
tained with the help of local herbs. Rolled in paper and smoked,
they are reported to have the highest resin content in the world.
Going lake also involves a touch of madness, with people running
amok and doing great damage to themselves and others.

We know from the cave paintings they left behind that the area
was once settled by Khoisan Bushmen stopping off on their way
from North Africa to the Kalahari Desert. They spent a pleasant
two thousand years camped on the shores of Lake Malawi until
the Bantu arrived to annihilate them sometime after the birth of
Christ. The black tribes that emerged from the Congo Basin were
known collectively as the Maravi, from which the word *malawi* is
derived. Technically spelled with a diacritical mark over the *ŵ*,
which gives it the sound of a *v, malaŵi* means "flame." It is unknown
whether this refers to the quality of light emanating from the lake
or the depradations wrought in pacifying its shores.

The next Malawian invasion came in the 1820s during the *mfecane*, the great explosion of tribal war bands propelled out of Zu-
luland by Chief Shaka. On their march north, the Zulu Ngoni
wreaked such havoc that the local population took to living in
mountain caves or in huts raised over the lake on stilts. At the
same time the Maravi were being carried off in the slave trade to
Oriental harems or sugar plantations in Brazil. Even though four
out of five captives died on their way to the coast, twenty thousand
slaves a year were shipped from Zanzibar alone.

When Livingstone discovered Lake Malawi, which he knew as
Lake Nyassa, in 1859, he was appalled at the bloody free-for-all
of Arabs, Portuguese, Ngoni, and Maravi all preying on each other.
The beaches were "literally strewed with human skeletons and

putrid bodies," he wrote in his *Narrative of an Expedition to the Zambesi and Its Tributaries*. "The many skeletons we have seen among the rocks and woods, by the little pools, and along the paths of the wilderness, attest the awful sacrifice of human life."

He had already walked across the continent from the Atlantic to the Indian Ocean and made numerous junkets up and down the Zambezi, but in Malawi Livingstone was robbed for the first time on his African travels. He lost the calico trade goods he used as money, and a second nighttime visit from the Ngoni reduced him to wandering in his underwear. As he wrote to his friend Roderick Murchison after the Zambezi expedition and its Malawian coda, "This is the first time I ever returned without accomplishing all I set out to do." So he went back.

Among other Europeans who have gone lake was McKaye's predecessor at Cape Maclear, a fish exporter named Peter Davies. Davies popularized Malawi cichlids in the aquarium trade and made them all the rage in fish stores from Berlin to Tokyo. To get live fish out of the interior of Africa, he transported them in plastic bags full of water, oxygen, and tranquilizers. He was also very adept at treating fish with hormones to brighten them into their breeding colors at any time of the year.

Davies was responsible for conducting an important, if unorthodox, experiment in Lake Malawi. Some of the more remarkable, and thus more expensive, specimens he sold came from the area around Likoma Island in the middle of the lake. Davies thought he would save himself the trip out to Likoma by introducing these fish into the waters off Cape Maclear and breeding them locally. Inserting a species into a new habitat is a dangerous step. For all he knew, the introduced fish might wipe out the locals and thereby erase a million years of evolutionary history.

Davies dumped his exotics onto a shallow reef known as the Aquarium, which was already packed with dozens of mbuna species fighting over every morsel of zooplankton and every inch of breeding ground. What happened? "You might have expected displacement of one species by another," says McKaye. "But instead we got a super-dense environment." Explosive radiation exploded again. All the latecomers found their own niches and developed their own micro-specialities. Davies's experiment failed in only one regard: it established no outer limit to the evolutionary plasticity of cichlid fish.

The road out to Cape Maclear was awash in mud during the rainy season, and McKaye thought he had been condemned to the end of the world when in 1977 the Malawi government gave him Davies's old house to live in. The house had been emptied of everything, including the generator and electrical wiring. There was no table, no chair. There was no place to buy food and nothing to eat except the fish McKaye was already observing, collecting, dissecting, and pickling. He realized from the start that to comprehend the larger system of a lake with three hundred and fifty described species and twice as many undescribed, he would need some help. The bulk of the research ultimately had to be done by Malawian divers, biologists, taxonomists, and professors running their own fisheries program. McKaye in the meantime was aided by graduate students from Yale and Duke, where he taught before moving to the University of Maryland. Some of his students had a good eye for fish and were excited about working in Lake Malawi. But none of them went lake. As the months passed, they invariably got nervous about being stranded in a tropical paradise with someone who had no intention of leaving.

"I've married an African," McKaye announced to me one day over the telephone. His new wife's grandparents had followed Cecil Rhodes across the Zambezi River in an ox cart. White skin aside, Beverly already *was* lake.

A couple of years ago McKaye was lucky enough to find another partner worthy of his obsession. If McKaye is a Type A personality, Jay Stauffer merits an A plus. A professor of fisheries science at Pennsylvania State University, Stauffer at age thirty-six has published so much that he abbreviates his résumé, listing only three of nine books, five of eighteen book chapters, and twenty-one of seventy-seven journal articles. Stauffer was recently in a car crash that put him in a coma for twelve days. He came out of it talking about fish. He keeps ten thousand pickled cichlids in jars in his office. "Why do you need so many?" I ask him. "Because one might be different," he says.

Stauffer is a taxonomist, one of the people responsible for sorting out and naming the twenty to forty thousand fish species that exist in the world. As McKaye recounts their first meeting, "This speedy little guy came into my office and asked me, very earnestly, if it's possible to go to Lake Malawi and describe *one* new species. There are hardly any unnamed fish in North America, and all his life he's dreamed of finding one. As a kind of test, I set him to work sorting through specimens pickled in formalin. I expected to come back in three hours and find a whole bunch of fish pushed into a pile with a question mark over them. Instead, he did the job in one hour, and everything was correctly sorted, except for the five questionable species I was already thinking of renaming. After that I took him out to lunch and treated him with a hell of a lot more respect."

"I knew it was one of the biological wonders of the world," says Stauffer of Lake Malawi, which he had wanted to visit ever since reading about it in seventh grade. "It was something I had to see before I died. But I was amazed on first visiting the lake in 1983, when I discovered that half the fish pulled up in every trawl are unnamed species."

Besides the cichlids endemic to Lake Malawi, another three to five thousand cichlid species can be found on the Indian subcontinent and throughout Africa and the Americas. Cichlids, in fact, provide a nice bit of biological proof for the theory of continental drift. Their range is that of Gondwanaland, the Mesozoic land mass that broke up and collided on opposite sides of the globe to form the Himalayas and the Andes.

In the Americas cichlids naturally occur as far north as the Rio Grande, but they are currently expanding their range throughout the southeastern United States. Tilapian cichlids now comprise half the biomass in the canals of Dade County, Florida. Introduced into the bass fishing lakes of Florida, sometimes accidentally, cichlids can take over a body of water in three years. Stauffer was recently amazed to discover blue tilapia as far north as the Susquehanna River in Pennsylvania, where they survive by overwintering in thermal outfalls from power plants.

One of the more frustrating conversations of my life is provoked when I ask McKaye and Stauffer, "What is a cichlid?" The world's leading experts on cichlid morphology and behavior should know the answer. But they have only the foggiest idea of what makes a cichlid a cichlid, and every time one of them proposes a criterion, the other bats it down with a counterexample. The largest cichlid, from Lake Tanganyika, weighs twenty pounds, while the smallest, collected in the Congo River, is no bigger than a fingernail. The type specimen for the family is a South American cichlid different from all the others, and the definitive paper on the subject defines the family by its negative attributes: a cichlid is not a trout.

When I push him, Stauffer launches into a textbook description of the family. "You have two major types of cichlids in Africa: haplochromine and tilapian. They differ in one bone, which in the haplochromines is fused. The tilapians are divided into three groups. One consists of bottom spawners, where both males and females tend the young. The other two are made up of mouth brooders. Females tend the young in one group, and males in the other.

"Most of the cichlid genera are rubbish," McKaye interjects. "Ten years from now, when we get things sorted out, at least you'll be able to tell the fish apart."

Stauffer begins again. "According to one theory, cichlids are related to wrasses and surfperches, which makes them closer to marine forms than other freshwater fish."

"But they're not like wrasses and surfperches," says McKaye. "Cichlids have only one nostril on each side of their head."

"So do some other fish," says Stauffer, before shrugging his shoulders and giving up. "I wouldn't defend that cichlids are a good family."

More confused than when I began, I get the idea that cichlids have only one unique characteristic, although this alone is good enough to make them evolutionary high flyers. Cichlids have a fused pharyngeal bone. It doesn't sound like much, but at the back of their mouths is a triangular, tooth-bearing structure that functions like a second set of jaws. Protruding from the bone are grinders that come in every size and shape imaginable, depending on whether the fish specializes in eating snails or zooplankton. Imagine that you had teeth on your vocal cords. What would be the evolutionary significance of this second jaw? Think of all the things you could do with your face if it didn't have to chew your dinner.

Taking a break from observing fish sex, McKaye and I spend a week helping Stauffer with his Lake Malawi fish collections. Since his auto accident, Stauffer has been forbidden to dive, and he wants us to gather the holotypes and paratypes of new species. One fish deposited in a reputable museum and mentioned in print is technically all one needs to describe a cichlid species. But Stauffer likes to work with hundreds of fish, and spread them among different museums. This avoids taxonomic headaches like the one caused when a unique collection of cichlids was bombed in Berlin during the Second World War.

McKaye and I work underwater chasing fish into mist nets, where they hang in the green filament like Christmas ornaments. Transferred to mesh bags and hauled to the surface for photographs and color notes, these specimens are beginning the long journey that leads from Lake Malawi to the Smithsonian Institution's cichlid collection. They will be flown to Washington, D.C., by diplomatic pouch and undergo months of comparative analysis to verify what looks to Stauffer like ten new species. "We got ten in a week," he gloats, "even though you guys took two days off just to stare at the damn things."

While we swim below, Stauffer sits in the boat writing. The color of a fish out of water fades in minutes, and by the time they land on gray metal shelves in Washington, these cichlids will be nothing more than bleached cadavers floating face up in jars full of preservative. Here are the heraldic notes for a gold fish, *Pseudotropheus barlowi*, that McKaye named for his Berkeley professor. "Head gold with green percular spot; anterior with faint blue flecks on gold ground coloration. Dorsal fin spines and rays gold; membranes pale blue with gold lappets."

One day Stauffer gives us a scare. We have been pulling up lots of little fish in the *Lethrinops lituris* group of round-nosed, sand-grubbing cichlids. There are at least nine *Lethrinops lituris* species, although only five have been described. Now that the five type specimens have gone pasty white in the British Museum, it is hard to know which fish belongs to what name. McKaye and Stauffer are in the midst of sorting out these family relationships when we start collecting two kinds of *lituris* that are identical except for the color of their throats. One is yellow, the other orange.

"Two species," Stauffer declares.

"Hold it," says McKaye. "As far as I know, these fish build similar nests, and they interbreed." He is nervous about having ten years of data on *lituris* courtship rituals disqualified because he confused one species with another. "That's the problem with these systematists," he says. "They can wipe out your data by telling you you got the wrong fish." For as long as they have known each other, he and Stauffer have waged a friendly war over the criteria for splitting genera into species. Stauffer has the Biblical urge to divide and name. McKaye inclines toward union.

"I came here figuring I'd solve the problem of Lake Malawi by lumping species," McKaye says. "Theoretically there couldn't be that many species in one body of water. I thought it was an artifact of systematists wanting to make a name for themselves. But then I studied the fish and saw they were reproductively isolated. If I started out in this profession as a lumper, cichlids have turned me into a splitter."

To settle the *lituris* question, we anchor over a local reef and drop down its spires onto an arena of mating cichlids. We slow our descent to watch gold mbuna darting over the rocks. We scare an enormous catfish out of a cave and pass electric mormyrids hanging like wraiths in the grottoes. McKaye scribbles on his plastic slate, "$100 fish," and I turn to stare at the pearly white mane of a collector's gem. Swimming out over the sand, we set to work staking and measuring the arena.

One of the nine *lituris* species builds the tallest of Lake Malawi's volcanic nests, while our little orange- and yellow-throated friends build the shortest. We find a school of them fussing over shallow bowls of sand scooped off the bottom. The sociobiologist Sarah Hrdy, who studied hanuman monkeys in India, described her field work as "similar to watching a soap opera. To get anything out of it, you had to know who was sleeping with whom." Long before he can generate a computer analysis of the data, it is obvious to McKaye that orange- and yellow-throated *lituris* are sleeping indiscriminately with each other.

Back on the surface he crows to Stauffer, "Behavior wins out again! We'll give you two color morphs, but not two species."

Even Stauffer is forced to admit that behavior has to be included with morphology when it comes to describing cichlid species in Lake Malawi. "This is heretical to systematists," he says, referring to his colleagues who work exclusively on pickled fish. "They want to be able to pull a fish out of a jar a hundred years from now and measure it out as a species. But there is no way you can put behavior in a jar."

"What's in a name?" says McKaye, reflecting on Stauffer's taxonomic passion. "Shakespeare's question becomes interesting when you try to figure out the underlying mechanisms by which these fish are speciating." The traditional explanation — that new species arise only when populations are geographically isolated from each other — is insufficient for Lake Malawi. Here a single environment may be saturated with dozens of closely related, but reproductively isolated, communities of fish. The picture is further complicated by the fact that these species are morphologically identical.

"You can't tell one of the nine *lituris* species from another when it's pickled," says McKaye. "You have to go look at their behavior. Females in one species will mate only with big-nested males. Females in another species want males with small nests, but centrally located. This is a female-driven system where runaway sexual selection appears to be the mechanism causing speciation."

If you think of fish behaving like birds, then the sex life of cichlids and its evolutionary implications will be easier to understand. This is a "female-driven system" because it is the females who choose to mate with males who have big nests or central locations. "Runaway sexual selection" refers to the fact that female choice has produced an amazing array of anatomical and behavioral adaptations. The final piece of the puzzle concerns speculation about whether something as subtle as female preference — for gold males or blue, tall nests or wide — can be responsible for splitting one species off from another.

The idea that closely related species can evolve and occupy the same geographical area without interbreeding is known as sympatric speciation. The concept is heretical to many biologists, who insist that species must develop allopatrically, that is, in geographical isolation from each other. "I no more believe in sympatric speciation than I do in UFOs and ESP," McKaye was told by the chairman of his promotion committee at Yale. But the evidence from Lake Malawi has convinced most evolutionary theorists to accept the possibility of sympatric speciation.

Genetically plastic, cichlids are capable of producing morphs ranging in color from yellow to black. If color morphs choose to mate assortatively, that is, yellow with yellow and black with black, then what started as a single community might evolve over time into two sexually isolated species. Why would fish mate assortatively according to color and other characteristics? "Organisms specialize to get through a bottleneck," says Stauffer. "Scale eating and fin biting must have evolved when times were tough." Whether speciation takes place through the preferential mating of color morphs, or female choice for one kind of courtship display over another, or the dictates of an ecological crunch, the explosion of species in Lake Malawi remains a fascinating conundrum.

It is thought to take at least ten thousand years for a new species to evolve, but the process may be faster in Lake Malawi. How fast no one knows. Jumping into a lake replete with a thousand species of fish gives me the feeling that evolution is taking place right in front of my eyes. From one day to the next I expect to find new varieties selectively mated and established in niches of their own. Suddenly fish with yellow throats or an extra inch of sand on their nests will refuse to mate with orange-throated or short-nested fish. Voilà, a new species will have come into being, not by striking out into virgin territory, but by exercising their power to choose.

As in other tropical idylls, the calm at Cape Maclear may be deceptive. The fanciest boat on the lake is a trawler stuffed with computers and a suite of air guns and hydrophones designed to generate acoustical cross sections of the lake bottom. Costing a million and a half dollars a year to run, the boat is financed by a consortium of oil companies hoping to strike it rich in Malawi and Africa's other Rift Valley lakes.

In the meantime, fish yields from Malawi are declining. Outside the park and even within it, there are signs of overfishing. To solve the problem, various ichthyologists are lobbying for the introduction of exotic species into the lake. They are not dissuaded by the fact that similar introductions into Lake Victoria have met with disastrous consequences. Victoria once supported a booming cichlid population, until the Nile perch, a predatory fish pleasing to European anglers, was introduced into the lake in 1960. Since then many of the commercially important cichlid species have disappeared, and the local fishing industry has collapsed.

Wanting to verify McKaye's claim that Lake Malawi is being overfished—an assertion that earned him a fresh raft of enemies in the Malawi fisheries department—I drive down the coast to Mangochi and invite myself aboard the *Crystal Lake*, a fifty-two-foot stern trawler that is run, like the other big boats on Malawi, by the government. A tidy craft with a patina of good use, the *Crystal Lake* was built in 1972 by John Harker Shipyards of Knottingley, England, broken into pieces, and reassembled in Africa a year later. The captain, a stocky man in bare feet with two wide scars on his chest, welcomes me aboard and gives me a tour of the wheelhouse, where the Wesmar SS 150 scanning sonar and most of the other navigational equipment are out of service for lack of spare parts.

We cruise for an hour to the north, drop our nets at seven A.M. sharp, and then settle for the next three hours into a midwater trawl across the southeastern arm of the lake. The day's quarry is a tilapian cichlid known as chambo. Grilled over an open fire, this firm, white-bodied fish is one of the country's great delicacies. McKaye and I have seen a lot of chambo breeding inshore, which means the open and closed seasons for chambo fishing in Malawi are unrelated to the species' reproductive schedule. The crew lights a fire in a metal drum on the rear deck. We breakfast on tea and bread and roasted corn. The engine drones and the boat falls into somnolence. Sailors slump against the gunwales. The captain ties up the wheel with a piece of line. The launch master and engineer snooze in the wheelhouse.

They wake to the noise of a Furano echo sounder scratching out a message from the deep. Scrolling down the paper are thick black spikes indicating schools of ndunduma, a type of freshwater minnow. Chambo often swim with ndunduma, and soon we get the light gray blips of what looks like a large school of cichlids. Having crossed the lake toward a marsh on the eastern shore, we turn north to run along the Mozambican coast.

The captain orders the nets raised. Crew members feed the lines onto metal drums and wait with shovels and pitchforks to clear the decks. Unfortunately, the decks need no clearing. I walk to the stern to see a dozen fish flopping in the nets. This is the total catch. A box of chambo with a couple of small catfish thrown in for good measure. That this is not unusual is revealed by the captain's log, which shows daily catches of one to a dozen boxes of fish on a ship with eleven crew members and a fuel consumption of ninety gallons a day.

The men grab a handful of chambo, split them down the middle, gut them, and lay them over the fire like flattened butterflies. We have worked up an appetite after four hours on the water. Grilled with a sprinkling of salt and eaten with our bare fingers, the fish make a splendid meal.

"To figure out what's going on in Lake Malawi," says McKaye, "you can't rely on northern academics doing research on their summer vacations." McKaye and Stauffer have augmented their own efforts by establishing a fisheries program at the University of Malawi. The program's initial experiments, conducted in fish ponds at Bunda College, the university's agricultural branch, are already producing surprising results.

McKaye likes to tell the following story as an example of basic research paying off in unexpected ways. A few years ago he and a colleague were studying cichlid behavior when he suddenly realized that half a dozen species of cichlids in Lake Malawi eat snails. They like them so much that completely absent from the lake's open waters are the thin-shelled *Bulinus* species responsible for spreading bilharzia. Could this be why Lake Malawi is virtually free of the disease? Could cichlids offer a means to control it? The United States Agency for International Development thought McKaye's hunch good enough to give him $140,000 to research the answer.

Bilharzia, or schistosomiasis, is a wasting disease caused by the invasion into the bloodstream of flatworms that copulate and deposit their eggs in human tissue. A couple of worms living in their host's veins can produce thirty thousand eggs a day. These eggs pass through the walls of the bladder and the intestinal tract, which results in bleeding and anemia, or they find their way into organs such as the liver and lungs, which are eventually destroyed. In one particularly nasty form of the disease the eggs mass in the central nervous system and produce epileptic seizures. Medical doctors hoping to cure schistosomiasis have been disappointed in their search for a magic bullet, and all the current drug therapies are highly toxic. Two hundred and fifty million people are debilitated by the disease, which is joining malaria as a major parasitical scourge of the tropics, and the problem grows worse each year.

Of the twenty snail-eating species of fish in Lake Malawi, four are real gluttons. McKaye and Stauffer chose the pug-nosed *Cyrtocara placodon* to be collected in block nets and transported up the escarpment in fifty-gallon drums. They stocked a fish pond at Bunda College with several thousand snails, tossed in a handful of *placodon*, and waited two weeks to see what would happen. The day the pond is to be emptied, McKaye and I drive up to take a look. We slide around the highlands on dirt roads washed by torrential rains and drive through fords so deep that the water rises over the floorboards.

The sun has reappeared by the time we reach the college, an hour's drive from the Malawian capital at Lilongwe. The fish ponds are off to one side of the campus, out beyond the wood lots and maize fields. An experiment like this has to be run in ponds with weeds and in ponds without weeds, with fish and without fish, and so on. This is a laborious process, considering the number of hours required to seine, drain, screen, and restock a pond. The first of many trials is not definitive, but the results are astonishing. Twenty *placodon* in two weeks have increased their weight by twenty percent and left not a single snail to be found in the pond.

"I thought we might get something like this in two or three months," says McKaye, peering into a bucket of mud that has been screened and examined for snails. "I didn't expect a total wipeout."

"There's something funny going on," says Stauffer. "A change this drastic bothers me."

"One of two things must have happened," says McKaye. "Either the fish went into a feeding frenzy and crunched everything in sight, or the snails got up and moved."

"How's that?"

"They could have given off an alarm substance, some chemical or pheromone, that told them to split. We might have a case of galloping snails. Now all we have to do is isolate their alarm pheromones."

"Let's patent the chemical and design it into snail traps," says Stauffer. "We could make a fortune, quit our jobs, and move to Malawi."

"I'd give up looking at sex for a year if I could win a Nobel Prize for wiping out schistosomiasis."

"But would you give up *sex* for a year to win the Nobel Prize?"

"No way," says McKaye.

Back at the lake, not long after our trip to the fish ponds, McKaye and I are arrested. To be more precise, he is arrested while I am underwater looking at cichlids, but when I get to the surface, he says we are in trouble. He had gone up for air to find a boat from the fisheries department bearing down on us. The officer on board, an old friend of McKaye's, demanded to see our papers. Did we have a permit for collecting fish in the lake? McKaye actually *does* have a permit for collecting fish in the lake, but it is issued by the parks department, not the fisheries department. Such is the stuff of ministerial turf wars, and he fears this one will reverberate all the way back to the capital. He is right.

The day had begun like any other. We rise at dawn and eat a big breakfast. This is going to be a deep-water dive, down to one hundred and twenty feet, and we need the calories. We check our gear with Amos Mwale, McKaye's boatman. Masks, fins, snorkels, wet suits, regulators, weight belts, compressed air — all of which I have learned to don as easily as a second skin. McKaye swabs his ears with tektite solution, which is supposed to be a blend of ethanol and acetic and tannic acids. His mixture is actually a home brew of Malawi gin, vinegar, and tea. "It prevents ear infections," he says. "But if you ever get one, then all you have to do is drink the stuff and the pain goes away."

We heave the plank boat off the beach and rope-start the Seagull engine, which purrs like a vintage sewing machine. Heading north across the bay toward Thumbi Island, McKaye is going to show me one of his biological treasures. He has discovered a bizarre example of "interspecific brood care," so bizarre that no one in the world has ever seen anything like it. In deep-water nests, below the depth where most of the other fish in Lake Malawi can survive, catfish and cichlids collectively tend each other's young. This is comparable to elephants and mice cohabiting, or foxes and chickens. Weighing in at thirty pounds, catfish are the biggest predators in the lake, and their favorite food is cichlids.

The scenario resembles that of the helper fish in Lake Jiloá, except that in this case the mutualistic relationship involves *joint* care of the young by predator and prey, which are not only different species, but in different *families*. To span a gap this wide, intelligence has to make a huge jump over biological difference. Other examples of mutualism can be found in Lake Malawi, and they present one of its most intriguing puzzles. All the fish in an arena will join in driving off nest darters and mouth rammers. Cichlid mothers school their young in communal nurseries and protect the fry of other species in their mouths. Cichlid territoriality, schooling, and seasonal migration all exemplify a high degree of social cooperation.

Struck by the ingenuity with which they coexist in this supersaturated environment, biologists tend to wax mystical about the social skills of cichlids. Fryer and Iles attribute a kind of socialist genius to these fish, who have managed to organize themselves into a "peaceful condominium." Cichlids exemplify what V. C. Wynne-Edwards imagined when he said that "species differences could be submerged" in an association or ecological union of animals "not in competition with one another as species, but only as individuals belonging to a mixed indivisible society." One for all and all for one in the cichlidean Age of Aquarius.

"Cichlids are a highly creative family," says McKaye. "I think they're smarter than hell." But he never credits them with group *geist*, and his scenarios for altruistic behavior always have Machiavellian plots. "You scratch my back, and I'll climb on yours" is how he conceives nature working in Lake Malawi. Darwin was apparently of the same opinion when he argued that evolution proceeds by means of individuals furthering their own genetic ends. As he wrote in the *Origin of Species*, "If it could be proved that any part of the structure of any one species had been formed for the exclusive good of another species, it would annihilate my theory, for such could not have been produced by natural selection."

What Darwin posited for the structure of organisms, McKaye would also claim for their social interactions. "No mutualism unless there's something in it for me." He gets excited about catfish and cichlids tending each other's young because it looks at first like an exception to the rule. Why would a cichlid nurture a fish designed to eat it? Why would a hungry catfish pass up a meal? As McKaye asked in one of his papers, how do you put together the pieces in a puzzle made out of "selfishness, altruism, cooperation, and spitefulness"?

We anchor the boat off a conical cap of rocks falling precipitously into the lake and suit up. Diving with McKaye is a no-nonsense business: you jump in the water and drop. We are going deep, down where mermaids start singing in your ears and monsters leap for your face plate, so we keep an eye on each other. Malawi is a stratified lake deprived of oxygen in its lower depths, which means that all the life in the lake is limited to a thin band on the surface, with a biological desert below. McKaye's megafamily of catfish and cichlids is already pushing the outer limit of endurance for many of the fish in the lake.

Dropping down a sand chute, we pass through schools of mbuna and blue-headed *lituris* before coming to the huge craters of nesting chambo. These fish are skittish in the face of what looks to them like crocodiles with aqualungs. The sun disappears into golden shards glinting far overhead. The water thickens into a greenish cloud. Our breath rasps through regulators tightening under pressure. At seventy feet we come to our first catfish nest, and the scene is exactly as McKaye described it.

In a deep bowl scooped out of the sand floats a silvery catfish surrounded by a swarming ball of fry. Thousands of little fish are feeding on the trophic eggs she has produced for them to eat. When these are gone, the female switches places with her mate. The fry move to swarm under the male catfish's gill vents, which excrete larvae foraged for their dinner. The female, a whiskered behemoth bigger than her partner, circles the nest as sentry and then swims off to feed. When I look closely I see other fish circling the nest, little black-spotted cichlids. Then in the nest itself—not in the middle, but alongside the swirling ball of catfish fry—I notice hundreds of baby cichlids.

This was one of the clues that allowed McKaye to figure out

what was happening here. Cichlids, which usually hold their fry in their mouths, had released them into the nest of a predator, and the predator, instead of eating these choice morsels, had stationed them in wagon-train formation around the perimeter. McKaye conducted an experiment. He chased away the catfish parents and watched what happened. Their fry were devoured by adult cichlids. Then he noticed that the young cichlids were growing faster than normal. Being able to forage outside their mothers' mouths, under the protective gaze of a catfish, was obviously a big advantage. Finally, he looked at predation on the nests—the everyday business of fish eating fish in Lake Malawi. As one would expect, the adopted cichlids, stationed as they were at the edge of the nest, got picked off first. The arrangement for them was a trade-off. Greater return exposed them to greater risk.

The agreement is golden, as long as it endures. But at the end of every breeding season, when the little catfish are old enough to feed themselves, they invariably look around for a meal and take their first bite of cichlid. That's when the circle breaks apart and everyone scatters for cover.

McKaye is right. After getting arrested and presenting his collecting permit to the fisheries department at Monkey Bay, he is called to the capital for another round of questioning. Malawi is a small country run on Ben Franklin principles. Waste not, want not. The day I arrived in Lilongwe the treasury held eleven thousand dollars in hard currency, and the government was on the verge of closing down until the tobacco crop got sold. With no money to spend, the functionaries in Lilongwe seemed to have extra time to worry about protocol.

McKaye drives up the escarpment to the capital. He needs to check the fish ponds at Bunda College anyway. I am to follow in a couple of days, taking the bus from Monkey Bay.

The morning of my departure I get up early and help Amos inflate the Zodiac. Powered by a thirty-five-horsepower Evinrude, this small rubber boat really moves. It gets up on the plane and scoots across the lake like a hydrofoil. The sky is chrome yellow and blue, the air light and gauzy, the water translucent, with a touch of mauve. A pink cloud hustles in from the east. A plume of rain falls to the west. A breeze comes up and sets a line of whitecaps across our bow. This is not the tropical weather dreamed of by northerners — placid and calm — but something, like the lake below, that is always reinventing itself.

Fishermen cast their nets in tandem from pirogues. The sturdiest of these wooden canoes are hewn from trees cut high on Mulanje Mountain. We pass forested peninsulas edging the lake and look shoreward onto a fringe of palm trees and huts. Women come down to the beach to bathe. Behind them, under the bright green spatulate leaves of Indian almonds, sit fishermen mending their nets and playing the local version of Africa's bead game.

We round a headland into Monkey Bay and find the *Ilala* bearing down on us with a toot of its whistle. Named after the village where Livingstone died, this trim white steamer sails around the lake from south to north and back again every week. Monkey Bay is a town of weedy lots and tin-roofed sheds selling fish and canned goods. I join a dozen people waiting for the bus in front of a line of cinderblock stores. We wait an hour and longer, and then someone says this is the third week the bus has not come, and we all go home.

I find Amos on the beach loading supplies into the Zodiac. We shove off and open the throttle. The boat gets up on the plane and skips for deep water. The town disappears behind the headland, and I find myself laughing, delighted to be turned around and going for the lake.

The Voice of the Ear

We grow many trees in Africa that are of no use to Christians.

Bede Okigbo

THE AFRICAN CONTINENT is shaped like a giant ear. I have often wondered if there is something to be learned from this geographical fact, a reminder, perhaps, that Africa reveals its secrets only to those who listen.

One spring morning Doug Couper and I drive out into the fields at the International Institute of Tropical Agriculture in Nigeria. On the way we pass laboratories and ranch houses lining tree-shaded avenues with names like Tropical Crescent and Africa Drive. The surrounding hills are tidied into experimental plots, rice paddies, and fish ponds. After crossing the dam at the head of IITA's reservoir, we park in front of a stand of palm trees and tropical bushes running wild in the otherwise well-tended fields.

Couper, IITA's Scottish farm manager, tells me that several years ago local Nigerian farmers were brought in and told to cultivate this area as if it were their own. They burned off the vegetation but left the trees standing in place. They farmed their clearing for three years and then returned it to bush, where it would lie undisturbed for another seven to fifteen years, except for occasional visits to harvest kola nuts or tap the palm trees for wine.

Couper directs my attention to the neighboring fields that were cleared and planted by machine. A D8 Caterpillar tractor mounted with a tree pusher and root rake leveled the kola nut trees and oil palms at the rate of an acre an hour. Plowed and harrowed, fertilized, and sprayed with herbicides and pesticides, the land yielded three times more maize than the farmers' clearing next to it. But the figures reversed themselves in a couple of years, as the topsoil washed away, leaving hardpan and gravel. "There's nothing you can do to bring it back to life," says Couper, kicking the stones. "Soil like this isn't good for anything other than a parking lot or a tennis court."

We drive on to the green line of forest edging the horizon. Couper stops his truck, gets out, and plunges into the trees. It is twenty degrees cooler under the forest canopy. The air is thick with butterflies and the buzz of insects. At our feet the forest floor is covered with termite mounds, leaves, twigs—a veritable junk pile of organic debris. "Feel the ground," Couper says, taking a hop. "It's spongy." Dropping to his hands and knees, he roots in the soil and holds up little fingers of earth for me to examine. "These are earthworm casts. Below them lies a maze of worm channels and root channels. The soil is fluffy, with lots of breathing room. It's got what we call crumb structure."

In spite of the lush vegetation, African soils are among the poorest in the world. Made of kaolinite clays and weathered basement rock, they erode easily into laterite surfaces as hard as concrete. "When you rip out the roots and run tractors over soil like this, you destroy the crumb structure," says Couper. "Press it with a tractor tire and it stays that way forever. The soil goes static and has to be abandoned in a year or two. That's why mechanized farming in Africa has been such a miserable failure."

One of the world's experts on tropical soils is Rattan Lal, an agronomist from the Punjab region of what is now Pakistan. Lal learned the hard way that his training in soil science at Ohio State University had little to do with farming in the tropics. When he arrived at IITA in 1970, he planted a demonstration plot according to the best ag-school practices. This included plowing and harrowing three times, applying a liberal dose of fertilizer, and planting by machine.

"The night before the trustees arrived for their annual meeting, a tropical storm washed away everything in my field, including the topsoil and seeds," remembers Lal. "I thought I was going to be sacked. Obviously I had a lot to learn about soil erosion in Africa." The same scenario repeats itself daily throughout the tropics, where twenty-seven million acres are cleared each year, while another seven to twelve million acres are abandoned to erosion.

After five years of experiments and field trials, Lal confirmed that the best way to clear a tropical rain forest is by hand. Second best is with a sheer blade, a tractor-operated cutting tool that slices trees off at the ground while leaving the roots in place. The land is then burned over and planted as is, without tilling or harrowing. "The world is doing far too much plowing," he says, "and it's plowing that causes erosion. Period."

Lal and his colleagues have developed various crop cycles that keep tropical land productive without returning it to bush. A nitrogen-fixing cover crop like velvet bean, when rotated with maize and cowpeas, will supply up to fifty pounds of nitrogen per acre. IITA has bred other plants that are good for nitrogen fixation, mulch farming, and green manure, and it has developed a range of no-till systems, including agroforestry and alley cropping. Agroforestry refers to the growing of trees and crops together in the same field. The trees are useful in themselves, for food, medicines, and wood, while the leaves provide important organic matter. Like so many other new ideas for improving tropical agriculture, agroforestry and no-till farming are modified versions of what Africans have been doing for centuries.

Photographs supposedly don't lie, but the images we see of Africa in crisis seem unreal. Farmers standing in fields blasted by drought. Mothers in feeding camps sheltering hungry children. Then we hear on the nightly news that European and American farmers are suffering, too—from *over*production. Wheat farmers in Europe have trebled their yields per acre since 1960. Rice yields in Asia have doubled. The green revolution of genetically improved crops—resistant to diseases, pests, and drought—has worked its miracle around the world. Everywhere, that is, except in Africa, which stands alone in suffering a per capita decline in food production. How has a continent that was self-sufficient until the 1960s slipped so disastrously behind? And what can be done to reverse the trend?

The International Institute of Tropical Agriculture, a thousand-hectare research station built on a hill overlooking Ibadan, Nigeria, is charged with answering these questions. Established in 1967 with money from the Ford and Rockefeller foundations, and currently supported with thirty million dollars a year from the World Bank and other donors, IITA is Africa's largest research laboratory. Staffed with one hundred and fifty scientists, hundreds of student trainees, and over a thousand workers, this City on a Hill occupies a fenced-in compound complete with standby generators, water supply, hospital, and school. Local Nigerians refer to it as "little America," and other scientists working in Africa—hardy souls camped on the banks of the Niger or in Turkana cattle kraals— regard the place with some suspicion.

When the green revolution took off in the 1960s and 1970s, bringing short-stemmed, high-yielding varieties of wheat and rice to the world on a massive scale, the task of introducing similar crops into Africa fell to IITA. It was established as the third of what are now thirteen international agricultural research centers, or IARCs. Funded by the Consultative Group on International Agricultural Research, with its headquarters at the World Bank in Washington, the IARCs manage a kind of stewardship over the world's food crops. They are supposed to bring the advances of modern agricultural science to bear on the problems of feeding people in the third world, a project that initially met with great success.

While its sister institutions in Mexico and the Philippines developed new varieties of wheat, rice, and maize, IITA set to work on two problems. It would find a sustainable alternative to shifting cultivation—modern techniques that could replace slash-and-burn, bush fallow agriculture—and it would fill a gap in the IARC system by working to improve crops grown in the world's humid and subhumid tropical zones. But if IITA's conception was clear, its birth was more difficult. The Nigerian civil war slowed its opening by five years. Problems with African soils, plant diseases, and pests proved more intractable than anyone imagined. And the very concept of the IARCs, which were founded on the belief that agricultural technology could be transferred from one part of the world to another, turned out to be wrong for Africa.

IITA's strength as an international center initially proved to be its weakness. Educated primarily at land-grant universities in the United States, its scientists often knew more about farming in Iowa than Africa. They relied heavily on fertilizers and other chemical interventions. They were embarrassed by "improved" rice strains that no one wanted to eat and mechanized agricultural schemes that failed one after another. Although women grow much of the continent's food, the experts and their new technology seldom reached them. Also forgotten was the troubling fact that an increase in food production alone does nothing to solve the inequities of who gets to eat the food.

Because of the way the IARCs divide their research on the world's crops, IITA has global responsibility for certain foods, like cowpeas (also known as blackeye peas), and African regional responsibility for others, like rice. But most of its work is directed toward tropical Africa, where IITA has substations and scientists scattered across the continent. Four of the institute's five research programs focus on specific commodities: rice, maize (American corn), grain legumes (soybeans and cowpeas), and roots and tubers (including cassava, yams, and plantains). The fifth program is in resource and crop management, which covers everything from soil science to IITA's new research on women.

IITA's historic strength has been in breeding new crop varieties. The early green revolution strategy focused on redesigning plants to make them nitrogen responsive. The plants were dwarfed to prevent their falling over and to give them a higher ratio of grain to straw. Varieties with smaller canopies and upright leaves can be planted more densely. These new plant types have been as important for the first world as for the third. All the modern varieties of wheat currently grown in the United States incorporate green revolution germ.

With their double or triple yields, the improved varieties have been viewed as a global panacea. But as the African farmer knows too well, without fertilizer and pesticides these new plants often perform worse than their traditional counterparts. What matters more to African farmers than yield is a plant's stability from year to year and its resistance to the continent's superabundance of diseases and pests.

When IITA put its ear to the ground and got this message in the mid-1970s, it began pioneering the second wave of green revolution research, focusing on plant resistance. "Rather than aiming for maximum yields through large amounts of fertilizer," says

Laurence Stifel, IITA's director-general, "we should design for disease, pest, and drought resistance. These are the advances capable of benefiting everyone across the board."

Attached to IITA's research laboratories are dozens of screen houses filled with plants being assaulted by stalk-eyed flies, leafhoppers, mealybugs, and mites, while other plants are put to the test under an onslaught of weeds and viruses. For a decade scientists in IITA's maize program painstakingly infected three hundred thousand plants a year in the hope of finding one that showed resistance to maize streak virus, a disease transmitted by leafhoppers. In bad years the virus can wipe out an entire harvest. The researchers found what they were looking for in la Révolution, a variety grown on the Indian Ocean island of Réunion. After crossing it with plants from Kenya and Mexico, IITA produced streak-resistant varieties that are now widely grown across Africa.

This ten-year effort was capped in 1986 when the program won the King Baudouin Award, a biennial prize granted among the IARCs for outstanding research. The maize team is now breeding plants resistant to corn borers and *Striga,* a parasitic weed. They are also working to develop hardy varieties of green maize and other early-maturing maize. As the year's first crop, maize is crucial for sustaining people through the "hungry season" that lies between planting and harvest.

The first green revolution started ten thousand years ago when humans began domesticating wild plants. Through years of artificial selection these plants became "improved" varieties, perfectly suited to the different climates and regions in which they are grown. Modern science works its own improvements more systematically, but it still must draw on the genetic resources conserved in these traditional crops.

There is a paradox, a Catch-22, that threatens the success of modern crop breeding. As more farmers adopt improved varieties, the gene pool feeding these improvements shrinks. To hedge against its own success and maintain a kind of insurance policy on the future, IITA sends plant explorers across the continent to find and bring back rare crop varieties. It houses one of the world's largest collections of tropical germ plasm, in the form of roots, tubers, and seeds stored in refrigerated vaults or freezers or in the form of tissue cultures preserved in slow-growth media.

What it means to store germ plasm impresses itself on me one afternoon when Sang Ki Hahn, the Korean head of IITA's root, tuber, and plantain improvement program, leads me into the basement under his laboratory. Unlocking a room filled from floor to ceiling with cardboard boxes, he pokes his hand into a carton full of yams and pulls out what looks like the batting end of a Louisville slugger. "This is a very beautiful one," he says, breaking the tuber in half. "You see the firm, white body?"

Hahn's cardboard boxes hold two thousand varieties of yams and sweet potatoes, each of which, in order to be kept alive, has to be grown and harvested yearly. Crops that can be stored in seed form require less work, but to avoid mutations and loss of vigor, these too have to be regenerated every few years. At IITA this involves growing fifteen hundred kinds of soybeans, ten thousand samples of African rice, twelve thousand types of cowpeas, and ten other crop varieties.

Along with its agricultural research, IITA conducts courses in everything from weed control to statistics for a stream of international students who are taught in French, English, and Portuguese. Five thousand Africans have been trained, mostly as technicians, although ten percent of them have completed the research required for a master's degree or Ph.D. The institute also hosts numerous government officials and experts looking for solutions to Africa's food crisis. As someone checking into the IITA hotel for a conference remarked to me, "This is the Superbowl of crop research. If you want to find out about upstream technology, this is the place to come."

IITA's emphasis on resistance breeding also motivates its research on roots and tubers. The program at various times has focused on yams, sweet potatoes, cocoyams, and plantains, but its major effort has centered on the inglorious but invaluable cassava root. Cassava is the classic famine food, the fallback crop that grows in the poorest of soils without fertilizers or pesticides. Introduced into Africa from South America by slave traders in the sixteenth century, cassava today is the staple food for two hundred million Africans who inhabit the "cassava belt" that stretches across the continent from the Sahara Desert to Mozambique.

The cassava plant bulks into huge roots that can be left in the ground for up to three years. Their high cyanide content makes the roots long-lasting and resistant to animal pests. It also makes cassava lethal to humans unless the root is properly prepared. This involves soaking, squeezing, grating, pounding, and frying to remove the cyanide—a laborious process done mainly by women. The end product, though, is simplicity itself. A starchy flour to which you add water, then sauce and serve.

Sang Ki Hahn and his colleagues have worked their own humble green revolution on cassava by redesigning the plant's architecture—giving it a bigger canopy to shade out weeds—and by adding disease resistance to high-yielding varieties. IITA cassava is now grown throughout Africa, and for his success at getting the institute's improved genotypes out of the laboratory and into farmers' fields, Hahn has been made a Nigerian chief.

To complement this work in resistance breeding and to free its new varieties from dependence on pesticides, IITA has launched a major program in biological control of insects. In 1980 Hans Herren, a young Swiss scientist fresh from a postdoc at Berkeley, arrived at IITA to take up the challenge of fighting a cassava pest that was sweeping over Africa. Herren now directs a multimillion-dollar, continent-wide program aimed at enlisting good bugs to fight bad.

Cassava mealybugs and green spider mites were accidentally introduced into Africa in the early 1970s. With no natural enemies in their new home, they began spreading into the cassava belt at the rate of two hundred miles a year. They have now blanketed the continent, killing up to eighty percent of the plants in their path and causing a yearly monetary loss estimated in the hundreds of millions of dollars.

Herren was trained in the classic approach to biological control, which says that a plant's parasites will be most abundant in the region where the plant first evolved. This is also the best place to look for *parasitoids*, the good bugs that eat the bad bugs or destroy their eggs. Biological control now includes several examples of parasitoids being successfully transferred from one continent to another.

Cassava evolved on the Venezuela-Colombia border, but the plant is grown extensively throughout the Americas from the southern United States to Argentina. Over fifty species of mealybug inhabit the Americas, but Herren was looking for the particular species that had recently invaded Africa. If he could find the bug on its home ground and identify its natural predators, he might be able to introduce them into Africa as a counterforce to the mealybug plague.

Like a detective working backward from the clues to the crime, Herren flew to Tucson, bought a four-wheel-drive van, and launched himself on a yearlong quest from the Mojave Desert to Argentina. "It was like looking for a pin in a haystack," he says. Herren and a colleague finally cornered their bug in a remote valley near Asunción, Paraguay, at the southernmost limit of cassava's range. "It was bad luck that we started looking at the wrong end of the continent, but we were terribly relieved when we finally had it tracked."

A South American wasp and other mealybug predators, bred by Herren and his team at the rate of fifteen thousand insects a day, have been released by now in a dozen African countries. Already spending close to four million dollars a year, Herren anticipates expanding his program to tackle a wide range of other pests. "The genetic resources for designing better plants are becoming scarcer, and the pests are adapting more quickly. But after years of neglect following the discovery of pesticides, biological control is still wide-open with possibilities."

"Rural development tourism" is a useful term coined by Robert Chambers, a British economist who knows the subject well. The tourists include government officials, journalists, politicians, consultants. Differing widely in interests and backgrounds, "these visitors nevertheless usually have three things in common: they come from urban areas; they want to find something out; and they are short of time."

Chambers describes other biases built into rural development tourism. It takes place along highways. It encounters a disproportionate number of men, showcase projects, and speakers of foreign languages. And it occurs in dry seasons rather than wet. Accounts of the spreading Sahara, for example, owe a lot to the fact that no one visits Sahelian Africa when it rains. Penning a poem on the subject, Chambers wrote:

> The international experts' flights
> have other seasons; winter nights
> In London, Washington, and Rome
> are what drive them, in flocks, from home.

During my own visit to IITA in March—a good time to avoid mud season in the northern hemisphere while enjoying the dry season in the south—I have ample opportunity to tour the countryside with visiting dignitaries. One of these tours begins in a conference room with forty-five experts gathered from around the world to discuss the merits of a fibrous root that if eaten raw will kill you. "Cassava holds the calories we need," a UNICEF man urges from the podium, while someone else stands up to warn that "cassava has too little protein and too much cyanide to make it the answer to Africa's food crisis."

We end the morning session early so that the participants in this weeklong IITA-UNICEF cassava conference can board an air-conditioned bus for what the program describes as "a study tour of cassava utilization and processing." Outside the gates of IITA, the calm of a college campus gives way to careening traffic and mud-walled villages packed with people and animals on the move. A quarter of black Africa's population is thought to live in Nigeria, and the rolling hills of Yorubaland are one of the country's most densely settled regions. Sprouting among the houses is a wealth of oil palms, cassava, and other crops planted higgledy-piggledy in a messy landscape that used to drive colonial administrators to neurasthenia, or worse.

After a twenty-five-mile drive into Oyo State, our bus stops in front of the walled compound of the *oba*'s palace. Cassava processing is mainly women's work, but as often happens in development tourism, the first remarks of the day will be delivered by a man. We cross a courtyard and enter the *oba*'s chambers. As my eyes adjust to the darkness, I make out a long hall filled with overstuffed chairs and couches upholstered in synthetic leopard skin. Wood-grain Formica covers the walls, in which two holes have been cut for air conditioners wheezing against the midday heat.

At the far end of the room, occupying a gilt throne placed on a leopard-skin rug, sits the *oba*. Wearing a sumptuous *boubou* of white and green silk, he is attended by a seneschal waving an ostrich-feather fan. The *oba* stands, and the UNICEF men go down on bended knees. The *dobale*, the traditional greeting involving complete prostration, has been abandoned by progressive Nigerians, and even knee-bending is considered folkloric.

We are joined at the reception by a delegation of market women wearing head ties, brightly colored dresses, and extra lengths of cloth to hold the babies tied to their backs. Nigeria's domestic economy is largely run by its female traders, a fact that the *oba* acknowledges in a little speech about their importance in "manning" the markets. I turn to the woman sitting next to me to ask what the *oba* himself does for a living. "He reigns, but he doesn't rule," she informs me, in no uncertain terms.

"Now we will take a bite out of traditional foods, symbolizing friendship and unity," says the *oba*, as his assistants pass around kola nuts. After the nuts comes a glass of schnapps.

Back in the courtyard we face a group of musicians banging away on drums and gourds draped in cowrie shells. A UNICEF man steps forward with a *pourboire*. But instead of stopping, the musicians play louder and faster than ever, as one of the drummers jumps up and down, waving some crisp dollar bills over his head. We retreat to our bus and drive a few hundred yards to the next official stop, the Oyo cassava market.

Descending into a warren of sheds filled to the roof with cassava roots and vats of soaking pulp, we are hit immediately with the rank odor of cyanide, which smells like a cross between bitter almonds and rotten eggs. I dispense with the official guide and stick close to Natalie Hahn and Janet Kwatia. Hahn spends much of her time as an IITA scientist helping to organize women's cooperatives in the Ibadan countryside. "Women are the least educated, worst trained, and single most important element in African farming," she says.

Janet Kwatia is also interested in women farmers, especially in helping them obtain machines. A mechanical engineer from the Soviet Ukraine, Kwatia has lived in Ghana for fifteen years, where she specializes in designing low-horsepower and hand-driven tools useful to women. "When I first came to West Africa I was amazed by the absence of hand grinders, like the kind used by my grandmother in the Ukraine. Someone has to fill the gap between traditional processing, done by hand, and mechanical processing with expensive diesel engines and electric motors, which are invariably controlled by men. Sometimes I think the problem is not enough women mechanical engineers."

Almost on cue, Kwatia and I arrive in front of a shed filled with motor-driven grinding machines. Each machine is presided over by a man, who literally sits on top of it, while women kneel in the dust to retrieve the flour funneled out the bottom.

Turning to walk among mountains of rust-colored roots, which someone identifies as TMS 30572, an IITA variety partly responsible for a recent glut on the Nigerian cassava market, we come to another row of sheds filled with young women laboring over wood-burning stoves made from oil drums sliced in half. These women are the roasters who handle the last stage in processing *gari*, or roasted cassava meal. Kwatia remarks on the absence of ventilating hoods over the stoves and tells me that these women are paid a lot of money, because by the time they're thirty, many of them will be deaf and blind from cyanide poisoning.

We board our bus and drive back to the *oba*'s compound for lunch, which is being prepared by the Oyo Committee on Women and Development—the same ladies we met earlier at the *oba*'s reception. As the women unwrap their offerings and lay them on a long table, the meal turns into a veritable feast of traditional Nigerian cooking. We eat pounded yams wrapped in banana leaves, cassava dipped in pepper and okra sauce, fish and watermelon-seed soup, steamed cowpeas, and other delicacies, such as bush meat stews made from grasscutter rats. If there is a food crisis in Africa, it is not evident from this outburst of Nigerian hospitality.

I leave lunch early to do some development touring on my own. An hour's drive north brings me to the town of Ogbomosho. Up a dirt road past the Baptist hospital lies the Kersey Children's Home. Part of the largest Baptist mission outside the United States, the Kersey Home itself occupies a small building with no more than a dozen rooms opening onto a central courtyard. Kersey is a former orphanage forced by necessity to handle a new problem in Nigeria: twenty-two thousand children a year are brought here to be treated for malnutrition.

Walking down its corridors, I am overwhelmed by the visible signs of poverty in Africa. I see children with toothpick limbs wasting away from marasmus, which is a double dose of malnutrition from the absence of both calories and protein, and numerous cases of kwashiorkor, the protein malnutrition that results in edemic potbellies, bleached skin, wide-eyed stares, and heads covered with crinkly red hair or no hair at all. I am surprised by the utter silence among these children, until I realize they are too weak to cry.

Most of them are treated at Kersey as outpatients, but a few children are admitted with their relatives, who sleep beside them on mats. During their five- or six-week stay, the families learn about hygiene, nutrition, and an IITA-improved crop variety that Kersey promotes with evangelical fervor—soybeans.

Ruth Womack, the tidy, no-nonsense woman who founded Kersey forty years ago, describes how people's health has degenerated since she began working in Africa. "There used to be meat in the soup twice a week. You could burn the bush and collect dozens of rats and snakes. Now you're lucky to get two or three. The antelope are gone, and there also used to be more dried fish and cashews, which are high in vitamin C. People's health has deteriorated so badly that we're beginning to see kwashiorkor in adults." But most of Womack's clients are children, and the majority are girls, simply because in Nigeria males eat before females.

Womack recounts the common story of how Western companies, trying to replace breast feeding with infant formula, have aggravated malnutrition in the third world. She herself used formula, especially the kind made from soybeans, when she began her orphanage. Over a third of the babies Womack sees are lactose intolerant, which means they are allergic to milk. But after she had come to rely on it, soybean-based formula disappeared from Nigeria, along with other imported goods, at the end of the oil boom in 1983. "With a house full of babies and nothing to feed them, we were desperate. I was driving all over West Africa looking for soy milk, when someone at IITA suggested I make my own."

Womack collected recipes and seeds and planted the front lawn

at Kersey in soybeans. Then she and IITA began sending an extension worker out into the countryside to lecture a hundred
women a day on the merits of this once-exotic crop, which now
appears in markets across Oyo State. The preferred variety is a
bean known as TGX536-02D, which Womack uses at the rate of
a ton a month. "The only problem with soybeans," she says, "is
getting the seeds multiplied fast enough."

In the late 1970s researchers at IITA succeeded in breeding a
promiscuously nodulating soybean. This marvelous phrase refers
to the fact that these soybeans nodulate, or develop bacterial bumps
on their roots that assimilate nitrogen and enrich the soil directly
from the air. Most soybeans do this only after being enzymatically
treated. IITA was able to eliminate this sophisticated and costly
step by developing a variety capable of nodulating promiscuously
with the bacteria found in African soil.

"Soybeans are the lazy man's crop," an IITA breeder tells me.
"They suffer from no major diseases. They require no fertilizer,
no spray. You just sit back and grow the damn things. No wonder
American farmers aren't keen on exporting the technology."

Although IITA's work on soybeans represents one of the institute's major accomplishments, it gets little publicity, and American
farmers are one reason why. Their lobby is strong enough to have
had it written into law that not one penny of United States foreign
aid be spent on helping foreigners grow soybeans.

Another reason for IITA's reticence lies in the intricacies of the
aid business itself. I was perplexed why UNICEF would launch a
multimillion-dollar campaign to grow cassava—which contains less
than one-half percent protein, rather than soybeans, which are
forty percent protein and twenty percent oil—until Ruth Womack
initiated me into a curious debate about the causes of malnutrition.

On one side are believers in protein, and on the other, believers
in calories. Kwashiorkor, which is a Ghanaian word, used to be
defined as protein malnutrition. High-protein foods were thought
to be the cure, and plant breeders were urged to design more
protein into their crops. But this theory has been superseded by
the idea that malnutrition is caused not by a lack of protein but
by a shortage of calories: people are malnourished simply because
they are not getting enough to eat. Unlike soybeans, which are
grown only where they have recently been introduced, cassava

grows everywhere in Africa, which makes it look like a miracle crop to someone searching for calories alone.

Womack shakes her head in disbelief over UNICEF's plans for cassava. "People come to us breathing their last breaths. They need protein and they need it fast. At this point, any food in the world would be better than cassava. It keeps you alive only until something like measles or diarrhea comes along to rock the boat. And in this part of the world, there are a lot of things that rock the boat."

Hard on the cassava conference, IITA hosts another convention. This one is on alley cropping, a straight-line version of what African farmers have been doing for centuries: growing trees and crops together in the same field. By introducing new species and tinkering with the cropping cycles, IITA hopes to engineer a replacement for slash-and-burn agriculture. Instead of letting their depleted land run to bush, farmers are being urged to plant nitrogen-fixing trees in their fields, thereby growing their own fertilizer.

"We borrowed the idea from traditional farmers," says B. T. Kang, a Javanese scientist who has spent twenty years at IITA trying to find a replacement for shifting cultivation. "The trees are used for nutrient recycling, and they provide other benefits, like firewood and forage for cattle and goats. The idea is to integrate the cropping phase and fallow phase so that they take place at the same time."

After graduating from Purdue University in agronomy, Kang was hired to work at IITA by a director-general who carried a map of Africa in his pocket, since the continent was unknown to most of his prospective employees. Kang arrived at IITA in 1969 to find a chain-link fence surrounding an expanse of bush from which three thousand people had just been cleared. Several of their huts would be kept as a kind of museum, but all other traces of the former inhabitants were removed to a new village built outside the back gate.

"What am I supposed to do here?" Kang asked the director-general. His reply: "Find a permanent replacement for shifting cultivation."

Kang tackled his assignment by plowing in fertilizer. "It works quite nicely in Illinois, where you have a lot of clay in the soil, but it was a disaster in Africa. Tractors and fertilizer make tropical soils sterile. The nutrients leach out, and the soil acidifies. Land degradation is the biggest problem in Africa, and mechanized agriculture is the biggest culprit.

"We discovered the hard way that we had to find a new concept for handling African soils. So we went back to look at traditional agriculture, where the land is used for three years and left fallow for ten. This is a biological, low-input system that works quite well in suppressing weeds and maintaining soil productivity. But for every hectare in use, you need five hectares lying fallow. There's nothing wrong with the traditional system; we just don't have time or room for it."

Kang planted his first alleys in 1976, using a tree, native to Central America, called *Leucaena*. Recommended for its ability to fix nitrogen, *Leucaena* is also the fastest-growing tree in the world. On Doug Couper's "tennis court," Kang and Couper machine-planted six hectares of *Leucaena* interspersed with cowpeas and other crops. Their yields are quite impressive, but as often happens with demonstration plots, no other farmers in Africa have been able to duplicate them.

Farmers alley cropping *Leucaena* have also discovered that the leaves are toxic to animals. If they eat even small amounts, their hair falls out. The tree tends to run off and become a weed, and no one seems to have considered the danger of introducing an exotic species into Africa. No one, that is, except Bede Okigbo, IITA's former deputy director-general and one of Africa's leading botanists. Okigbo's address to the alley cropping conference dwelt on the merits of Africa's indigenous species; it served as a reminder that the continent would be well advised to look to its own resources.

The son of an Ibo farmer in eastern Nigeria, Okigbo, before his recent retirement, functioned as IITA's encyclopedic conscience. He occupied a high position in the organization not because of his administrative skills, which were seldom exercised, but because if you wanted to know anything about African plants and agriculture, Okigbo was the man to ask. He holds a doctorate in agronomy from Cornell University, but he credits his high school biology teacher with providing his best instruction in botany. "What did the man do? He took us into the forest and made us look at the trees."

"Western scientific training is really very shallow," Okigbo tells me. "It lacks the broader background of the clergyman naturalists who used to explore these questions as a hobby. Rather than gearing their knowledge to passing exams, these gentlemen were at liberty to observe everything."

Okigbo himself is known for observing everything. He speaks in the ordered paragraphs of an early *Encyclopaedia Britannica*, and his remarks are footnoted with references culled from the books and monographs that line the walls of his study. A conversation about trees in Iboland will lead Okigbo into describing how the African *elemi* produces a fruit that can be softened in water and eaten like an olive. Or the fruit can be dried in the sun and used as an *ayo* bead or for playing jacks or another African game similar to bowling. Okigbo describes pepper trees with insecticidal properties, medicinal trees, ornamental trees, trees that are good for hanging clothing out to dry, and other trees, he says, "that are of no use to Christians."

The invention of agriculture has traditionally been credited to the Near East, where the shift from food gathering to food production marked the beginning of the Neolithic revolution. But Okigbo and other botanists now think that agriculture also evolved independently in Africa. At the same time that people in Southwest Asia were settling down to village life, Africa was developing its own Fertile Crescent along the headwaters of the Niger. Here a Neolithic civilization emerged from the Stone Age to domesticate plants that are now cultivated around the world. These include millet, sorghum, African rice, cowpeas, groundnuts, yams, okra, watermelons, cotton, oil palms, sesame, tamarinds, and kola.

This abbreviated list indicates the variety of crops available to African farmers, who have always delighted in jumbling them together and growing everything at once. On a continent where crop pests are as numerous as crop varieties, mixed cropping is actually a prudent strategy. It prevents the insects that attack particular crops from breeding to high levels. The labor of harvesting is staggered, crops are produced over a longer period of time, losses in one crop can be balanced with produce from another, and the system supplies a variety of foods, to paraphrase Okigbo, that may be of no use to Christians.

"There are five hundred thousand plant species," says Okigbo. "Ten thousand are utilized by man. Two hundred are grown industrially. But only a few of these are of commercial importance. Fifteen plant species out of the half million that exist in the world give us seventy-five percent of our food."

For the past several years Okigbo has devoted himself to studying what are known as compound farms. While cultivating their outlying fields, many African farmers traditionally grow a garden around their family homes, or compounds. Unlike gardens in temperate climates, which are horizontal, these tropical gardens are planted vertically. Above the houses rise galleries of palm trees that wave over plantains, which in turn shade the spices and cocoyams planted below. "Tropical rain forests have no fewer than four stories," says Okigbo, "and the multistoried compound farm is the only agricultural system in the world that tends to mimic nature."

A recent study of compound farms in eastern Nigeria identified one hundred and forty-six species, with as many as fifty-seven grown in a single compound. "At IITA we're working at a much simpler level than the local farmer," says Okigbo. "This means we can only give him information about one or two systems, while he has to deal with something far more complex." It also means that Western scientists stand to learn a lot from African farmers.

During the IITA alley cropping conference I again find myself on a bus heading into the countryside. Sixty of us, including two interpreters with portable loudspeakers, are off for a day of what one ironic observer describes as "boys in the bush." It is true that most of us are male, and so too are the farmers we are going to visit. My fellow tourists are wearing everything from dashikis to suits, but most are dressed in khaki trousers and short-sleeved shirts.

First stop for our entourage of two buses and three cars is a technical school where the headmaster has directed his students to alley crop a small field of *Leucaena* and cowpeas. We are running late, so we are back on the bus in twenty minutes.

Second stop is a field covered with the spiky leaves of *Imperata* grass. The arrival of this tenacious weed marks the last stage before a farm is abandoned to bush, but in this case the field has been planted with *Leucaena*. "I told the chief I wanted some land near the road for an experimental plot," says Kang. "He told me he didn't have any. I drove around and saw this field and said I wanted it. 'Of course you can have *that*,' said the chief. 'It's covered with *Imperata*.' Obviously, we have to make better use of the land already cleared in Africa, rather than simply clearing more."

Back on the bus we ride through second-growth rain forest filled with oil palms and kola nut trees. Orchids bloom in the shade, but there are many clearings where the trees have been felled to make way for cassava and yams. Every few miles we come to a village of mud-walled houses shaded by useful species like locust bean and shea nut. We have long ago turned off the main road to travel down one-lane tracks barely as wide as our bus.

We park in the middle of the bush and disembark to walk single file through a field of cassava. Down a hill we come to a small stream where women are soaking sliced cassava roots in clay pots. After fermenting for three days, the lumpy chips are spread to dry on rocks along the stream. My sixty fellow tourists hop across the water and march uphill, leaving me to watch the women work. I find it odd that no one else has stopped, but then I remember that today's tour is alley cropping, not cassava.

Following the sound of the loudspeaker, I trot up the hill into fields of maize intercropped with *Leucaena*. Each plot, except for one, is presided over by a barefoot man armed with a hoe. The men stand at attention as interpreters query them on yields per hectare and other agronomic matters. At one particularly scenic spot, I notice a man's yams being trampled for a photo opportunity. A lone woman stands among the farmers, but her plot is such a mess that no one stops to look at it. She has chopped her trees to the ground to feed her goats. I see later in the official report on these alley cropping trials that her overall rating is "poor."

Its improved varieties and agricultural practices look impressive at IITA, but only a few of them have succeeded in jumping the fence and establishing themselves widely among African farmers.

"We have an enormous body of new knowledge about tropical soils and their management," an IITA administrator tells me, "but it's not putting food in people's bellies. The sorry fact is, we've had very little on-farm impact."

Responsibility for this state of affairs is ascribed to a wide range of culprits. Many are beyond IITA's control, but others reside within the fence. "Much of our research is irrelevant," an IITA crop breeder confesses in a late-night conversation. "African farmers don't have access to herbicides, pesticides, tractors. They have no way of relating to what we're doing here. Fifteen years ago we began on-farm research because the gap between us and them was so great. This gives scientists an academically acceptable way to get out and see what's happening around them. But we wouldn't need on-farm research if we used the right techniques from the start. IITA itself should be doing on-farm farming."

Agricultural research stations have existed in Europe and the United States for over a hundred years. But early researchers worked in close proximity to the farmers next door. A crop breeder in Illinois plowed the same land as everyone else in the state, and the gap between scientists and farmers was so narrow that a few Johnny Appleseed extension agents could readily spread the new technology. The fit between agricultural research and farming in Africa is obviously very different. In order to bridge the gap between research station advances and African realities, somebody has to go out and look at what actually happens to IITA crops in farmers' fields, where plant varieties and agricultural practices are more diverse than in the temperate parts of the world.

"We need to explore the problem of how our crops fit into the life of the farmer," says Laurence Stifel, IITA's director-general, or DG, as everyone calls him. "We have to understand the farm household and how responsibilities are divided between men and women, big farmers and small. This is crucial if you want to avoid technology that has a deleterious impact on women, who have suffered in the past because no one thought about them."

Another limitation on IITA's impact is the poor quality of Africa's national extension services. While the United States is laced with land-grant colleges and agricultural research stations, Africa has few of these amenities. The crucial link between IITA and its farmer clients is often provided by solitary officials stuck in provincial capitals with broken Land Rovers, or by no one at all.

"Our most fundamental problem is how to get our technology out into national systems," Stifel says. "This was the key to the green revolution. But what do you do when the national systems are functioning so poorly that no one can grow your seeds? We're not in the seed business, and we're not here to get involved in this kind of institution building, but who else is going to do it?"

It costs two hundred thousand dollars a year to maintain a senior scientist at IITA, and critics of the international research centers wonder if the money would be better spent at national stations, where five people can be employed for the price of one IITA scientist. Sang Ki Hahn maintains that African farmers are as quick to embrace new technology as those anywhere in the world. It happens, he says, "by the invisible, efficient extension service that exists by word of mouth." Bede Okigbo likes to remind people that crops such as cassava, maize, and cacao were introduced into Africa from the Americas with no extension services whatsoever. He also cautions that Africa's food crisis is one of four crises currently plaguing the continent, the other three being political instability, economic indebtedness, and environmental degradation.

While its sister institutions work singlemindedly on rice, wheat, and maize, IITA deals with a wide range of crops that are more difficult to improve. It faces other problems in the realm of consumer preferences, which vary markedly from one part of Africa to another. "It's hard to know what you're breeding for," a scientist in the maize program tells me. "East Africans won't touch yellow maize, and West Africans don't like it white. You can't satisfy all the preferences at the same time, so you have to make choices."

When we meet one morning in the middle of an experimental plot, B. B. Singh, IITA's chief cowpea breeder, offers to take me on a tour of his plants. He shows me cowpeas that creep along the ground and others that shoot up in the air and still others that do both at once. These differences in plant architecture correspond to different needs. Some farmers want cowpeas for fodder; others are looking for edible beans. Singh's assignment gets even more complicated when he has to deal with consumer preference. The Ibo like brown beans, the Hausa white, the Ghanaians red, the

East Africans tan, and the Latin Americans black. For each color there are choices between big and small, smooth and rough, and altogether Singh has twelve thousand varieties to choose from.

"I can't help the politics," is another common refrain at IITA. People tell stories about governments that encouraged the planting of improved varieties and then turned around to destroy their national markets with cheap imports and food aid. Official power has become so arbitrary in Africa that many farmers have responded by going on strike. Rather than selling their crops to state marketing boards, which are desperate to translate farm surpluses into revenue, farmers resort to parallel markets and the barter economy, or they choose not to grow any surpluses at all.

"It took us ten years to get the package together, and now we don't have anyone to sell it to," one researcher complains to me. But the longer I spend at IITA, the more I wonder if they really have their "package" together. The institute is filled with enthusiasts yelling "Eureka!" over their exploits in breeding new crops. Breakthroughs arrive with every harvest, and in Ibadan there are four harvests a year. But I begin to notice a kind of Alice-in-Wonderland effect, where one man's miracle invariably turns into someone else's flawed experiment. I keep discovering simple facts, minor problems hardly worth mentioning, that have been left out of the story.

"Yes, there's a new cowpea that can be grown in sixty days, but it takes another sixty days to cook it. And without at least four sprayings of insecticide, you don't get any cowpeas at all."

"When they were first released, our improved cassava varieties were resistant to blight and mosaic disease, but they also rotted in the ground after a year. This was a slight oversight by our breeders."

"Plantains are a fantastic source of carbohydrate. But look at this graph. The little dashes represent years in which the trees blew down."

An increasing number of people in the world do not grow the food they eat, and a decreasing amount of time is spent preparing this food. When these two trends are put together, it is not surprising that the foods themselves are in the process of changing. Down goes consumption of pounded yam, millet, and sorghum.

Up goes consumption of "faster" foods like rice and wheat. "Cassava is on the way out," someone assures me. "It's going to be replaced by wheat."

"Rice is the food of the future," someone else says.

"No," another person counters, "It's sweet potatoes. Even NASA is growing them for use in outer space."

After my initial confusion, I come to think of these disputes as healthy. IITA puts out a progressive line for public consumption, but a more skeptical view prevails inside the fence. Everyone knows the constraints on everyone else's research and is thus pushed to get beyond them. By the end of my visit, I have come to respect these scientists who are working on some of the world's most difficult problems.

I cheer for his side when an IITA plant pathologist tells me the following story. Cuban soldiers bringing untreated cassava plants into Angola have infected southern Africa with an exotic strain of cassava mosaic disease. The disease's recent spread north into Zaire could prove disastrous for a country where half the cultivated land is planted in cassava. After an emergency visit to Zaire to study the new disease and identify cassava varieties capable of resisting it, the IITA pathologist has rushed back to Nigeria to meet a team of consultants from the World Bank.

"I tell the World Bank people we're doing our best to improve African crop varieties, and I think we've done a remarkably good job, given corrupt governments and the lack of infrastructure. But they keep asking me, 'What's the impact of your research? How do you measure your impact?' I finally get angry enough to toss the question back at them. 'What's the impact of your research? You guys are going to go home and write another report on Africa that sits unread on someone's shelf. Is this impact?' "

Another problem confronting IITA is the question, "For whom is it doing its research?" Big farmers, state plantations, or African smallholders? A standard criticism of the green revolution is that it increased both production and class divisions. Big farmers got the new technology before small farmers, and they used it to consolidate their social dominance. Yields increased, but so too did the income gap between rich and poor.

Yoel Efron, the former head of IITA's maize program, has strong views on a lot of subjects, and one of them is the question of IITA's clientele. "We can't do much for the bush farmer. He already has the best available system under the circumstances. The problem isn't these guys; it's who's going to feed the people in Lagos."

"Who *is* going to feed the people in Lagos?"

"You have to develop commercial agriculture," says Efron. "It doesn't have to be large scale, but the younger generation is going to want better tools than their fathers and better technology. Africa's agricultural potential is its major treasure. If you don't have much else by way of resources, this is your base for industrialization."

"How long is that going to take?"

"Each year I hear a new target date for maize self-sufficiency. A nice word, but it's meaningless. Your needs today may have nothing to do with your needs tomorrow. Are you growing maize for human consumption, animal food, oil production? For each need, your target goes higher."

To pursue these questions further, I go to lunch one day with Laurence Stifel. Ushered into the study of his house, I find the DG wearing a white T-shirt and sweating badly. He has crawled out of bed, where he spent the morning doing paperwork and shaking through a case of malaria, or what he thought was malaria, until the tests came back negative and the ailment passed without receiving a proper name.

Stifel is an unpretentious, straight-talking Ohioan who left the number-two position at the Rockefeller Foundation to head IITA. He has a law degree and a doctorate in economics, and although he has never grown any crops outside of his family garden, there was a collective sigh of relief when he was named director-general in 1985. IITA was running in the red and overly dependent on the special projects that had come to make up nearly half its budget. It was in danger of becoming "donor driven," an ailment common to research centers in Africa that have no agendas of their own apart from the two-year scenarios scripted by their patrons.

When I ask him why he left New York for Ibadan, Stifel says, "The greatest development problem in the world is African agriculture. I couldn't find a bigger challenge." What are his ambitions for IITA? "To make it a crucial player in increasing food production in Africa."

Stifel and I spend some time talking about the inequities of access that plagued the green revolution in Asia. This is a subject he knows well, having worked for many years as an economist in the Philippines and Thailand. "Both the poor and rich have benefited from the new technology," he says. "What has increased is the inequality *between* regions. In the upland areas, far from irrigated farming, people are just as poor as they were before."

When I push him for examples of increased inequalities *within* regions, he is honest enough to supply them. "Women in Indonesia have been hurt by the new technology. The improved rice varieties are more uniform, which allows for more efficient methods of harvesting. Women formerly hired to do the work have been replaced by men from other areas, and by imported rice mills."

I ask him if he wants to go back to bed, but Stifel assures me he looks worse than he feels. We press on to talk about IITA's policy in the big-farmer-versus-small debate. An IITA board member has defined the issue for me as follows. "You'll always have the poorest of the poor, and you'll always have the filthy rich, who will get out ahead and make a profit. They can afford to take risks, while the small farmer, if he wants to put food on the table, has to be more conservative. It was never official policy, but Stifel's predecessor as DG said, 'To hell with the small farmer. If you want to improve the standard of living in Africa, you can't fool around with itsy-bitsy people who aren't going to hack it.'"

"Is there a conflict between doing research for large farmers or small farmers?" Stifel muses over lunch. "I think there is, and I think we have to make a choice. It's a question of where you're going to have the most impact on food production. The big farmers are going to get whatever they want out of us anyway. But when you look at what they've done to the soil, I have my doubts about the potential of large-scale farming in Africa."

Later, when I send him an early draft of this chapter, Stifel's handwritten comments on the manuscript say, "No one would agree that IITA's approach was geared to the big farmers, although they have clearly benefited from the research. The research was not geared to either large or small farmers—in the future it will be geared to small farmers. That's an important distinction."

Three fourths of all the people in West and Central Africa farm plots of three hectares or less, but from IITA's perspective these smallholders divide into two categories: subsistence farmers, barely providing for their own needs, and market farmers, who can produce surplus food for sale. As a "moral imperative," and to make amends for having overlooked them in the past, IITA has promised to direct part of its attention to the poorest of these farmers. What they need to feed themselves are insect-resistant, drought-tolerant crops that produce a steady yield from one year to the next without reliance on chemicals or fertilizer.

In spite of its well-meaning pronouncements, and the many instances where IITA's research does aid Africa's resource-poor farmers, the heart of its effort is directed elsewhere—toward the progressive farmers who can produce surplus crops for the market. "I don't think we should target our research on the poorest of the poor," says Stifel. "We should focus on the small farmer who makes up the vast majority and who's going to bear the brunt of responsibility for feeding people in the cities."

To choose a plant and redesign it is a political decision, and a telling example of this can be found in IITA's work on maize. While the maize program is a world leader in resistance breeding, its egalitarian advances exist side by side with the program's work in hybrid maize—a crop that stands in IITA's fields as a political lightning rod. Hybrid maize tends to be grown by big farmers and state plantations as an agro-industrial crop. Hybrids give substantially higher yields than the pure lines from which they come, but they are finicky plants requiring extra fertilizer, and their sterile seeds cannot be used the following year. The availability of fertilizer and hybrid seed often has as much to do with politics as money.

Because the subject is so hotly contested, I should mention that many small farmers in Africa grow hybrid maize. Colonial breeders in Rhodesia claimed to have been the first to hybridize maize, and average yields per acre in Zimbabwe are greater than those in Iowa. New crosses have appeared regularly in Africa since the 1930s, and by now the technology has been adopted up and down the east coast of Africa. *Dukas* in the Kenyan highlands, stocked with little more than beer and soap, will sell a good selection of hybrid seed, which is avidly planted by Kenyan smallhold farmers.

The same experience could repeat itself in West Africa, but for the moment the push to develop maize hybrids is coming from the top down. The generals running the Nigerian government want a green revolution in maize, and IITA has been asked to lead the troops. Whenever the name of IITA's chief hybrid maize breeder is mentioned, one also hears that "Kim is very tight with the generals."

Soon Kwon Kim is not a modest man. "I made the green revolution in Korea," he says. "When I saw the beautiful fields in the American corn belt, I said to myself, 'Before I die, I will make my country look like this.' "

He may not be modest about the results of his work, which he regards as a matter of public record, but Kim conducts his personal life with the humility of a Christian fulfilling his calling. "I want to become like a farmer, even my clothes, to lessen the gap between farmers and scientists," says this small man who dresses in blue jeans and a work shirt.

Kim was one of seven children born on a family farm of less than a hectare. "There was no electricity in my village. I ran oxen in the field and transplanted rice from the time I could walk. My knowledge of village life gives me patience."

He graduated from an agricultural high school in Korea and went on to the University of Hawaii, where he finished a Ph.D. in plant breeding in 1974. Kim by then was deeply involved in Saemaul Undong, the New Village Movement that would modernize Korean agriculture as fast as its industry. "When I went to Waikiki I felt sin, because I thought about the suffering farmers back in Korea. America deeply impressed me, but at the same time I knew we should not live like Americans. We had to accumulate our own experience. This is what the New Village Movement tried to do, and I think Africa needs something similar."

Returning to work for the Korean Office of Rural Development, Kim started breeding Asian-specific hybrid maize. "People told me I was crazy. 'Hybrids can't be grown in underdeveloped countries. All previous attempts have failed.' " In three years Kim developed a hybrid that yielded fifty percent more than open-pollinated varieties, and today virtually all the maize grown in Korea is hybrid. For his efforts Kim was awarded the Order of the Green Stripe and a cash prize of six and a half million Korean won, about ten thousand dollars.

Then the Nigerian generals started calling. They had called before, in 1975, but Kim turned them down to finish his work in Korea. When they called again in 1979, he accepted their offer and moved to Ibadan. If Kim could design a tropical maize hybrid, the government promised him enough support to plant fifty thousand hectares of savanna—equal to the total farmland of South Korea—in hybrid maize by 1987, and a *million* hectares by 1990. Kim met the first date right on target, and by now three private seed companies have sprung up to market IITA hybrids. One is run by a former general and president of Nigeria. Another is controlled by the local Coca-Cola and Mercedes-Benz distributor.

"People believe it's a different world over here," says Kim. "They like to think Africa should be satisfied with yields of one ton per hectare, while yields in the United States are five to six times higher than this. People condemn hybrid maize for developing countries because of 'poor infrastructure' and so on. But I believe these are excuses. World peace will never come with differences too great between rich and poor."

During their morning break, I arrange to meet Yussuf Amole and Musa Akinola. Amole is a field hand at IITA, and Akinola is a laboratory technician, but both men are also farmers. At the end of the day, like many other IITA employees, they walk home to their own fields. This gives them a double perspective on IITA technology. They know what it produces both inside and outside the fence.

Amole farms an acre of cassava and yams. Weeds are his biggest problem. He pays someone to keep them under control, which cuts his profit in half. When the stores in Ibadan have any to sell, he buys herbicides, and when pests like grasshoppers become a big problem, he buys insecticides. IITA cassava is too bushy to be intercropped with his other plants, but Amole has borrowed the idea of plastic mulch and other IITA technology for planting yams, and he likes the results.

Akinola grows cassava, yams, tomatoes, peppers, maize, and other crops on an acre and a half. He too spends a lot of time cutting bush by hand and fighting weeds. Unlike his friend, Akinola is not keen on IITA's yam technology. "Tractors make smooth fields. Farmers have rough fields. I plant my yams in October. IITA plants them in April. This is because their fields are irrigated. Their system of using plastic mulch is good only when you're growing one crop at a time, but I plant my yams and peppers together."

The peppers fetch a good price in the market, and the yams do more than provide food. When Akinola wanted to marry, he presented sixty tubers to the father of his prospective wife, and each one was supposed to be as large as a man. "We need big tubers," he says. "We can't waste our time with small IITA seed yams."

We run down a checklist of available technologies. Amole and Akinola like IITA cassava, but it was not intended to be grown with other plants. They think the maize designed for alley cropping is superb, its prime virtue being the fact that it has to be weeded only once. Like everyone else in Africa, they face a plague of mealybugs. With no apparent help from IITA's program in biological control, they do what other farmers are doing. Cut off the tops of infected plants and burn them.

Amole and Akinole give me a full list of the crops they grow, some of which have no English names. There are okras, melons, bananas, groundnuts, and cocoyams, "which are good for fighting diseases. Actually," says Akinola, "we grow many things that no one at IITA ever sees."

When it starts raining during my final week in Nigeria, I think of returning to my own garden in the north. I have part of an acre to clear and decisions to make about which kinds of beans and melons to plant. But my family won't go hungry if I make the wrong choices. The risks are greater for my friends in Ibadan, and greater still for someone worried about feeding the continent.

"We can promise no green revolutions for Africa," Laurence Stifel said in his inaugural lecture to the staff. What IITA can offer instead is "a stream of technologies that will give our national partners the means to start a quiet revolution in the villages of Africa."

As a foot soldier in this quiet revolution, Akinola appreciates what IITA is doing to put food on his table. But his praise is quiet; I have to listen for it in the voice of a farmer getting ready to plant his field. "This year I'm looking forward to trying out some different crops and new ideas," he says. "God willing, it should be a good harvest."

The Fourth World

It is not all pleasure, this exploration.

David Livingstone

HAVING SPENT many of the past fifteen years living among hungry nomads, Jeremy Swift feels more at ease than I do as we lie stretched out on a cow skin in the middle of a Turkana herders' camp high in the Loima Hills. All that protects us from the *ngoroko* cattle rustlers at large in this no man's land on the northern border between Kenya and Uganda is a circular wall of thorns and a Lee Enfield bolt-action rifle that our host has leaned against the wall of his hut, a small igloo-like structure woven from sisal and twigs. Twenty of these huts surround a central corral, where we are penned in for the night with a troop of goats, some belabored donkeys, and a herd of sobbing camels.

A dozen nomads lie with us drinking camel's milk out of a wooden bowl. The women are naked except for goatskin aprons and foot-high collars of bead necklaces around their necks. The men wear togas of brown cloth tied at the shoulder, or nothing at all. Their scalps are decorated with orange mud packs, and their chests are scarified with checkerboard patterns that tally the number of enemies killed in battle.

"If you come visit me in the Sahara," says Jeremy to the *laibon*, the camp leader who is our host for the evening, "I will give you milk from my camels. They are bigger than your camels, but because we ride them, they are not as handsome and fleshy."

"Who is taking care of your camels?" asks the *laibon*, a wiry man dressed in what looks like a miniskirt and a canvas porkpie fishing hat.

"My stock associates, my bond friends," says Jeremy, using the Turkana words for a custom practiced widely throughout the nomadic world. Livestock are lent to family members and friends in order to build up a network of alliances. Since the animals can be redeemed at a later date, these bond friendships function as an insurance policy against disaster.

"How am I going to get to the Sahara?"

"If you learned to ride your camels, they could carry you across Uganda and Sudan to the desert."

"This is very dangerous territory. Is there some other way I could get there?"

"You could fly in the TRP airplane." TRP stands for the Turkana Rehabilitation Project, a multinational relief agency formed after the great famine of 1980. At one point the TRP was feeding a third of the Turkana population. The number has been reduced since then, but the organization still effectively runs Turkana, which is the name for both the district and the people in it. Everyone laughs at the thought of the *laibon* flying off in the TRP airplane to look at camels in the Sahara.

The men lie back against their wooden stools that double as pillows, and the women return to milking their animals. "Why are you really here?" asks the *laibon*.

Jeremy explains that the government wants him to design a famine early warning system for Turkana, some way of predicting and preventing famines before they start. "Since you've been dealing with drought and famine all your lives, I've come to get your advice."

The *laibon* launches into an oral history of the ten major droughts that have killed animals and people in Turkana over the past hundred years. He rolls his *r*s and gesticulates to great effect as he describes how herders moved through the region, chasing what little rain arrived. Either through alliance or combat, they pushed their way into foreign territory. They traded animals for grain grown by their neighbors. They foraged for berries, leaves, and roots.

"The grass was sick and poisoned the cattle," he says of 1962, a drought year made worse by animal diseases. By the time he gets to 1980, the *laibon* gathers his fingers together and shakes them out for emphasis. He leans to the right and leans to the left to demonstrate how there was no pasture here and no browse there. "People starved or went to relief camps. They have not come back," he says, splashing his fingers straight toward the ground in utter disgust.

Like an economist checking for signs of inflation at the local grocery store, Jeremy queries the *laibon* on the price of maize meal and livestock. Nomads seldom live solely on the meat, milk, and blood of their animals, and the Turkana are no exception. A substantial part of their diet comes from trading animal products for grain. The price of cornmeal flour, or *posho*, is supposedly controlled by the government. But the *laibon* confirms that the price actually floats up and down with supply and demand. As drought verges on famine, the value of animals falls to zero, while the price of *posho* doubles or triples.

"You see," Jeremy says to me, "the model works." He is referring to his hypothesis that a famine is not an accident of nature, catching the world by surprise, but the end of a long process with recognizable stages and countermeasures that can be taken all along the way. After fifteen years of watching them come and go, Jeremy thinks he has pieced together a theory of famine good enough to make it predictive, which also means preventive.

Turkana is a windswept quarter of deserts and semiarid steppes lying wedged in the northwestern corner of Kenya between Lake Turkana (formerly Lake Rudolf) and the arbitrary borders of Ethiopia, Sudan, and Uganda. Sloping down from the Uganda escarpment to Lake Turkana, this arid savanna full of volcanic cinder cones and dry-wash riverbeds lies in one of the least hospitable parts of the Eastern Rift Valley. But it is home to two hundred and sixty thousand nomads, or former nomads, who survived until recently by running their herds into Ethiopia, the Sudanese plains, the Ugandan highlands, and anywhere else that grass could be found growing.

A tall Nilotic people, the Turkana are the most easterly offshoot of a number of related tribes known as the Karamajong cluster. After splitting from the primordial Karamajong some two hundred years ago, the Turkana jumped the mountain barrier into Kenya and shoved their way into territory formerly held by the Samburu and Marile. Turkanaland was one of the last areas in Africa to come under colonial control. A kind of war zone between the King's African Rifles and nomadic raiders, it was closed to outside visitors until 1960, when the worst famine in seventy years brought food aid and missionaries to the subdued Turkana.

Hungry they may be, but the area's nomads remain independent to the point of truculence. After eighteen months in the district, the anthropologist Philip Gulliver wrote, "Frankly, I never felt, with the exception of one or two cases, that I was ever entirely trusted by the Turkana amongst whom I lived. . . . At no point, except that of warfare, was I able to stir their interest. Evasions and downright lies were the common practice to the last." As the traveler John Hillaby remarked after taking a thousand-mile walk around Lake Turkana, "I was Marco Polo. But among the Turkana it seemed that I was not appreciated."

Jeremy and I had begun the day in Lodwar, the dusty village of Somali *dukas* and petrol pumps that serves as Turkana's district capital. We had driven west over a sandy track leading onto the Puch Prasir Plateau. In front of us rose the Loima Hills, and beyond this line of deep green ridges towered the ten-thousand-foot peak of Mount Moroto, which divides the Turkana from their Karamajong cousins. Mount Moroto itself is home to the Ik, a tribe of hunter-gatherers whom Colin Turnbull described in *The Mountain People* as the most depraved on earth. The Ik steal food from each other. They abandon their parents to die of exposure. They laugh with gallows humor at other people's misery. According to Turnbull, the spiritual corruption of the Ik is so great that the world would be better off without them.

When he visited the Ik, they were actually suffering from famine brought on by drought, civil war, and the loss of their traditional hunting grounds to a game reserve. Turnbull's diagnosis may have been wrong, but his prescription seems to have been followed. After a stage adaptation of *The Mountain People* closed in London, the outside world heard nothing more from the Ik.

As we ascended the Uganda escarpment, we passed various species of acacia, some with red bark, some green, some prized for their gum arabic and others for their edible leaves and fruits. Hornbills lumbered among the *Dobera glabra* trees, which are valued for their red berries. Wild sisal lined the road, and when we stopped to admire the bright red flowers of a desert rose, Kaitio Kalochoro, our guide into the Loima Hills, told us that the resin in its twigs is used for making poison-tipped arrows.

The former chief of the area, before the government sacked him on charges of aiding *ngorokos*, Kaitio is a tall, lean, elegantly fine-featured man in his early thirties. He may have winked at cattle raiding, which, after all, is a long-standing practice for re-distributing wealth among the Turkana, but the more likely reason for Kalochoro's discharge is related to the series of events that culminated in the famine of 1980. He crossed borders at will and showed himself more enterprising than the government liked.

Kaitio is the only educated son of a man who fathered sixty children with twelve wives. Kaitio himself recently married for the first time, paying a bride price of forty cattle, twenty camels, and one hundred and twenty goats, so one can imagine that his father was a very rich man. Being a chief in Turkana these days involves a lot of tax collecting for the government. It is a job worth losing. For our trip into western Turkana, Kaitio is wearing blue jeans and a T-shirt bearing the message "Officially On Leave."

After several miles of grinding uphill in first gear, we were waved to a halt by three men carrying automatic weapons. This was our first meeting with the famed Turkana *ngorokos*. They looked quite fierce, with their red togas, white ostrich-shell necklaces, and scar-ified arms. Their hair was matted with ocher and plastered on top of their heads with a band of mud. The necklaces and ocher in the hair were signs of having killed someone within the last three months. Along with firepower, the other essentials in the *ngoroko* kit include a walking stick, a stool-headrest, a bowl for grinding tobacco leaves, and a circular knife worn as a bracelet around the wrist.

Fortunately, Kaitio knew the gentlemen. They exchanged Har-lem handshakes, and the men climbed into the back seat for a lift. A short way up the mountain road the *ngorokos* jumped out and disappeared as suddenly as they had come.

"*Ejoka!*"

"*Ejok!*"

In Turkana the same words cover both arrivals and departures. Kaitio told us that his friends were bracing for a reprisal from the

Ik, who in the last few years have themselves become formidable cattle raiders. "The Ik!" Jeremy exclaimed, getting visibly excited. "I thought they died ten years ago on the London stage."

"No," said Kaitio. "The Ik are out in force somewhere ahead of us, armed and very much alive."

Spear carriers naked except for the ostrich feathers in their orange mud headdresses, women whose necks have disappeared behind multitudinous strands of beads—these are the postcard images of people who are remarkably astute at surviving in a part of the world that receives no more than a few inches of rain a year. The Turkana live on a high-protein diet of milk and blood, supplemented with grain, fruits and berries, fish from the lake, and an indigenous sorghum that can be harvested in sixty days. In the dry season, from September to March, the Turkana divide into small groups and scatter over their territory. Some go to the lake and fish. Others stay in the plain to browse their camels and goats. Everyone else heads west for eight or nine months of grazing in the mountains. Formed into *adakars*, mobile herding collectives that hold their land in common, the Turkana have traditionally arranged among themselves to save the best grassland for the driest times.

Droughts are so common in Turkana that they receive little notice until achieving the status of *eron*, which is a drought that parches the land and kills animals and people. Droughts like this arrive on average once every ten years, the latest being in 1979, when *atanayanaye*, "the broom," swept away everything in its path. Famine followed in 1980, not inevitably, but from a mix of events that illuminates how African pastoral societies get tipped from ecological balance into crisis. One of the things that *atanayanaye* may have swept away was the traditional basis of Turkana society itself.

The government denied the existence of the famine for nine months. After it belatedly acknowledged the situation, eighty-five thousand Turkana—more than a third of the population remaining in the district—came to survive on food aid. Five years later twenty-five thousand people were still enrolled in a giant public works project that showed no signs of fulfilling its mandate to "rehabilitate" the area. Turkana today is still divided into two worlds. A client population dependent on foreign aid lives in the lowlands around the lake, while in the highlands of the Uganda escarpment and the northern plains, gun-wielding tribesmen continue their pastoral traditions. If the Turkana in the lowlands present themselves as a destitute population, those still tending their herds are as truculent as ever.

To learn about the series of events that produced the famine of 1980, Jeremy and I make several trips into what he calls the "insurrection zone," territory so remote from a central government that it periodically escapes its control. After climbing the Uganda escarpment, we will venture north into the Sudanese plains and south toward the volcanoes bubbling along the shores of Lake Turkana. Our goal is to search out the *adakars* of nomads who survived *atanayanaye*. "They possess a wealth of traditional knowledge for coping with drought," Jeremy maintains. So why did famine overwhelm them in 1980?

When he recognized the first signs of drought two years before the government declared an emergency, Kaitio Kalochoro led seventeen thousand Turkana and all their animals into Uganda. Guaranteed safe passage by an alliance with the neighboring Karamajong, a united band of nomads migrated one hundred and fifty miles south to the shores of Lake Kyoga, almost within sight of the Ugandan capital of Kampala. "We bounced," says Kaitio, laughing about the three army raids they fought off during their eight months in Uganda. The Turkana returned to Kenya in April 1979 to wait for the spring rains, which never came. Their herds were already weakened by an outbreak of pneumonia, but it was politics more than drought that ultimately pushed the Turkana into famine.

With Idi Amin's government collapsing into chaos, the Karamajong raided the military armory in Moroto and carried off two thousand automatic weapons. They distributed the guns among their fellow tribesmen in Uganda and dissolved their alliance with the Turkana, who now confronted a fortified wall between themselves and a possible escape from drought in Kenya to pastureland in Uganda. Because of civil wars being fought in Ethiopia and Sudan, routes through those countries were also blocked. Thanks to the firepower now employed by cattle raiders in the region, a third to a half of the Turkana district itself, much of it prime grazing land, remains insecure and unusable to this day.

Trapped in their dry plains with no way out, the Turkana still held their valuable herds, and they could have survived the drought of 1980 were it not for the economic breakdown that is the ultimate cause of famine. In a normal year three or four out of a herd of forty cattle may be sold to buy the grain needed to supplement a diet of milk and blood. But with traders and other herders wary of buying livestock in a drought, the market for animals weakens and finally collapses. In situations such as these, Africans, even with animals remaining in their herds and food for sale in nearby markets, can starve to death.

Politicians are embarrassed by the economic terror that prices food beyond the reach of people normally able to buy it. This is one of the reasons why the government insisted there was no famine in Turkana. "No Kenyan shall die of famine," the president had announced in one of his speeches, and on its way to becoming official policy, this sentence was reinterpreted to mean, "Famine does not exist in Kenya."

A priest we met on our travels told the macabre story of what happened when he went to a local official and said, "Turkana are dying of starvation."

"Prove it," said the official.

"We produced bodies. But he still refused to believe us. There were enough other diseases and probable causes of death that famine was ruled out every time."

This went on for nine months, until the sheer volume of dead people and animals necessitated a policy switch. Reliable statistics are impossible to obtain, but witnesses report that tens of thousands of humans and up to ninety percent of the livestock died. Once the need for outside aid was acknowledged, the Turkana were effectively signed over to become the client population of the Dutch government, the European Economic Community, and the United Nations World Food Program, which united to form the Turkana Rehabilitation Project. The TRP had a double mandate: to prevent people from starving and then, in a five-year program, to "rehabilitate" the area.

Importing up to two thousand metric tons of grain a month, the TRP performed its first task with admirable efficiency. Its second assignment has proved more elusive. "As development projects go, the TRP is one of the greatest failures of all time," says one knowledgeable observer. "It's a terrible mess, a case history in how not to do food aid."

Switching from handouts to another form of aid known as food-for-work, the TRP in 1982 launched a campaign to improve rainfed agriculture in Turkana. With ideas borrowed from the Nabataeans, who developed water-harvesting techniques in the Negev Desert two thousand years ago, food-for-work teams started digging and trenching Turkana with bunds (earthen dikes for catching rainwater runoff), macrocatchments (vast plains criss-crossed with bunds), microcatchments (fields pockmarked with holes), and dozens of check dams and spate diversion systems feeding off the seasonal rivers. Work crews a thousand strong were paid at the rate of three kilos of maize for every cubic meter of earth they moved in baskets on their heads. By now so much earth has been shuffled around Turkana that many areas are pockmarked into a lunar landscape, while others resemble vast fields filled with burial mounds.

When they work, large water-harvesting schemes offer an elegant way to stretch scarce resources, but they demand a level of technical expertise and forms of social organization that the Turkana do not have. A people used to being grouped into *adakars* of a half dozen families and to shifting their plantings yearly from one small plot to another, the Turkana have no experience operating irrigation schemes built on a Pharaonic scale — especially if these schemes happen to be badly designed. When the drought momentarily gave way to heavy rains in 1982, many of the TRP bunds and river diversion systems washed away. Since then, food-for-work teams interviewed by the BBC have claimed to be just as happy tearing down old bunds as building new ones.

The TRP experience highlights another hidden cost of famine. What happens when relief projects take on a life of their own? Is it true that thousands of Turkana have been permanently displaced from the pastoral economy, or are they merely waiting for the disappearance of European food before rejoining their family herds? When to call a famine finished is in some ways as problematic as when to announce its onset.

Famines are costly, and for more reasons than the fact that they kill animals and people. Famines tie up the trucks and petroleum and resources of a country engaged in fighting them. They create destitute populations reliant on food aid—farmers without seeds and herders without herds—who may never again be able to reenter their traditional economies. But credible means to rehabilitate these people and avoid the famines of the future are themselves commodities in short supply.

It is now completely dark in our herders' camp, save for the stars overhead and a smoldering fire in front of the *laibon*'s hut. The people lying around us are barely visible, except when the flames lick up to light them in red. Jeremy tells the *laibon* he has some ideas about how Turkana can avoid famines in the future. When a drought becomes serious, the government should buy animals at a decent price, slaughter many of them, but save the best females for restocking the area at a later date.

"No one pays decent prices for animals in a drought," says the *laibon*. "If you buy them, how are you going to keep them alive any better then I do?"

"Give them fodder from outside the district."

"And who's going to keep the Pokot and the Karamajong from raiding these animals?"

"The Turkana Home Guard and the government."

"Animals are scarce and expensive after a drought. Why should I believe the government will sell me what I need to restock my herds?" Waving his arms and splashing his fingers toward the horizon, the *laibon* plays to his audience.

"Your plan sounds very good," he concludes. "But I doubt that anyone would ever do anything so sensible."

After moving for the night into the *laibon*'s sleeping hut, a small, open-roofed enclosure with sisal walls, we recline on our cow skin and wrap ourselves in blankets against the evening chill. The *laibon* disappears into the neighboring hut and returns with a Yugoslavian Mark IV automatic rifle and clip of cartridges, which he leans against our door. "Now we're ready for the Ik!" Jeremy says.

A chorus of laughter rises from the huts around us. "The Ik! The Ik! Now we're ready for the Ik!" The camels join in with chesty bellows. The goats start bleating, and even the donkeys add a wheezing bray of appreciation. "The Ik! The Ik!"

I strain to pick up sounds in the night. Twigs snapping. Pebbles rolling underfoot. But from outside the enclosure comes nothing more ominous than the chuckling of guinea fowl. The animals shuffle into somnolence. I hear Turkana whispering in their huts, exchanging confidences and giggling. I drift off to sleep, and before I know it the sun is raking my face with the quick light of an African dawn.

I look out to see Jeremy and Kaitio standing in the middle of camp wearing blankets around their shoulders. They share a bowl of warm milk with steam curling over it. Women open the thorn gates and drive the camels out to pasture. Jeremy follows in the Land Rover, which has been closed inside for the night. Soon we are heading up the valley to a second herders' camp, where the *laibon* and his wives come out to greet us. After exchanging pleasantries and a little gift of tobacco, we sit down for another chat with the world's experts on drought in Turkana.

Jeremy was in northern Mali, studying the household economies of Twareg nomads, when he encountered his first African famine, the 1973 Sahelian crisis that killed two hundred thousand people. "It was a turning point in my life," he says, "although at the time I had no way of understanding what was going on around me. The common myth about famines is that people die of starvation because there is no food. But two facts about the Sahelian famine flew in the face of the common myth. People were not dying of starvation but of measles, whooping cough, and gastroenteritis. Secondly, there was food around. The markets were filled, but no one could afford to buy what was available."

As an economist specializing in what he calls the fourth world of traditional nomadic cultures, Jeremy by now has watched the onset and aftermath of several famines. Twenty-five million pastoralists wander the driest and least hospitable parts of Africa, but their animal-based economies are becoming increasingly vulnerable to drought and other economic mishaps. It was not something he set out to learn, but Jeremy has become expert by now at identifying the stages through which nomads spiral into famine.

A fifty-year-old research fellow at the University of Sussex's Institute of Development Studies, Jeremy researches the household and market economies of nomadic pastoralists, whom he has studied in Africa, Iran, Oman, Mongolia, and other remote parts of the world. In a typical year he will advise the sultan of Oman on what to do with his nomads, vet grant applications to Band Aid and Oxfam, fire off position papers to the House of Commons, direct a development program for USAID or the World Bank, represent the Anti-Slavery Society at the United Nations, supervise graduate student theses, write scholarly articles, and think about famine. The last of these is an accidental preoccupation, not his main line of work at all, but something unavoidable when one considers the life of nomads in the second half of the twentieth century.

When I first met him in a London apartment overlooking Primrose Hill, I was surprised by the solidity and red-cheeked healthiness of the man. I was expecting to find someone lean and twiggy, with a mad desert squint, and instead there was this large, friendly chap with a mane of black hair above the wide expanse of his face. The only hint of his being an Africa hand is the bushy clothing — corduroy trousers, wool shirt, and hiking boots with Vibram soles.

It was birds that got Jeremy to Africa the first time. Born in 1939, the son of an RAF officer killed in the Second World War, he had been interested in ornithology ever since he began boarding school at the age of seven. On going up to Oxford, Jeremy planned to study zoology with Nikolaas Tinbergen, another avid birder, but was disappointed to discover that "zoology at Oxford meant the evolution of the metacarpal of a horse. No one recognized Tinbergen as the father of the modern science of animal behavior. He was just a funny Dutchman in a room full of sticklebacks. I got confused at Oxford and changed my subject several times before taking a degree in English literature."

Jeremy returned to birds when he took a job in the Camargue region of France with the International Wildfowl Research Bureau. Part of his work involved counting ducks in Europe as far east as Turkey. "It was a golden period in my life, but the Camargue was too remote," he says, explaining why he left to go to work for the United Nations Food and Agricultural Organization in Rome. "The FAO had just established a program in wildlife conservation and national parks. As one of two officers in the program, I was supposed to handle the non-English-speaking world, and I chose West Africa as the place that interested me most."

On his first African visit, to Chad in 1966, Jeremy found thirteen kilometers of paved road in the country, and eleven of those kilometers were the airport. He also found a remarkable concentration of elephants and antelope on the southern edge of the desert — and nomads. "It was an extraordinary leap from counting ducks in Greece, and I knew I had found the subject for a life's work.

"It was on one of these early trips to Africa that I began to get worried about nomads being thrown off the land to establish national parks. The FAO were more interested in animals than people, which struck me as a contradiction, and I personally couldn't see the benefit of aggressive Frenchmen shooting nomads who transgressed park boundaries." Jeremy quit to go back to school and study economics.

Following a year of course work, the thirty-two-year-old graduate student in development economics at the University of Sussex left his wife and year-old daughter in England to spend thirteen months in Africa living among the Twareg. "I must be one of the few economists in the world who did his Ph.D. research sitting in a tent in the middle of the desert."

Jeremy had read a book on the seven main confederations of the Twareg. The book gave detailed information on six of them, but the seventh, the Kel Adrar group in the Adrar n Iforas Mountains of northern Mali, was completely unknown. "That's the tribe for me," he said, before traveling to Mali and getting government clearance to research the Kel Adrar. "I then flew north to the district capital at Gao, where the governor told me my pieces of paper were worthless. The Adrar n Iforas lay in a military district that was closed to outsiders. He couldn't elaborate, because it was top secret, but the area also held several prisons for political prisoners.

"Because I was in my thirties and not my twenties, I visited the governor's office every day, camped in front of his door, banged on his desk when admitted, and refused to be turned away. I'd gone to a lot of trouble to get there, and I was damned if I was going to go home with nothing to show for it." By noon on a typical day the temperature pushed over 113 degrees Fahrenheit, and Jeremy was planning to travel two hundred miles north into an even hotter part of the desert.

After two weeks the governor gave in. Jeremy hitchhiked out of town with the Malian soldier who was sent to accompany him as spy, escort, cultural informant, and, only accidentally, as a friend. "This was a very remote part of the world, and all my subsequent trips to the desert have seemed quite civilized by comparison."

The Kel Adrar Twareg greeted him as an ally, mistaking Swift for a Frenchman returning from the colonial days. "Then they realized I was in no better odor with the government than they were." The Twareg had recently fought a civil war against Malian troops, whom they could have beaten had it not been for the Russian helicopters that turned the Adrar n Iforas into a free-fire zone. A lot of nomads accustomed to fighting their enemies from the backs of camels had died in the war.

"The Twareg gave me a sheepskin tent and a slave girl to roll the flaps up and down. It was unbelievably hot," says Jeremy, who set to work recording the economic activity of two hundred people living in thirty tents. He spent nine months camped in the desert, with a break in the middle when he was thrown out of the country for accidentally walking too close to one of the secret prisons. "Since no one could tell me that it *was* a prison, the reason for my expulsion remained a mystery until much later."

Jeremy spent a lot of time devising strategies for interviewing nomads, and one of his most successful techniques is based on a modified version of *ayo*, the bead game played throughout West Africa. The eight holes in the ground on each side of the "board" represent a camp's most significant problems. When people are asked to rank the importance of various issues, they engage in heated discussions about how many cow-dung beads should go in each cup. "Face-to-face interviews never produce discussions like this, although it's exactly the kind of exchange you're looking for."

When Jeremy returned to visit his Twareg friends the following year, in 1973, he found some of them dead and everyone else in a very bad way. "Part of my research involved household economics. So I knew what they were eating, the price at which they were selling their animals, and so on. People were eating only once every two days, and I said to myself, 'What's going on here? This can't be true.'

"I had no model for understanding what was happening around me. Famine was something that occurred in India and Bangladesh and China. Before the news broke in 1973, no one had heard of any recent famines in Africa. In fact there had been famines in the Sahel in 1913 and 1942. But in the first instance the French were busy colonizing West Africa, instituting slave labor and otherwise disrupting the region, and in the second instance a world at war was too busy to notice."

Jeremy quickly realized that he had walked into the middle of a famine, but it was not the kind of famine he had ever heard of before. Technically, people were dying of flu and measles, not hunger. There was no shortage of food for sale in Gao and Kidal; what *was* in short supply was money to buy the food.

"I spent a lot of time taking sick nomads to the hospital, and I dispensed a large part of my research council grant on feeding people. I knew the Twareg wouldn't appreciate my handing out food, so I arranged various feasts and competitions. An *amzad* player would come from a neighboring camp to sing, or children would narrate the elaborate stories they know about mythical animals. Five camps of two hundred and fifty people might be gathered for one of these feasts, but I knew there were another twenty-five thousand Twaregs starving in the mountains around us.

"I was even more confused and bewildered when I tried to alert the outside world. The Malian government said that as a matter of policy there could be no famine. The United Nations said they were prepared to believe me, but they couldn't act over the objections of Mali. The FAO said that what I was describing didn't sound to them like famine. They were only concerned about shortfalls in grain supplies and making up the difference." Only when *Le Monde* later published a series of articles accusing Mali of practicing genocide against the Twareg did the world acknowledge there was famine in the Sahel.

*

"Famine is often associated with drought, but drought alone is not responsible for famines. Civil wars or collapsing markets are often the more immediate causes. When I got back from Africa, some of us began composing our ideas. Those of us who were serious about the issue already understood the theory of famine by the time Sen's book appeared."

The new evidence on how famines actually kill people was synthesized in a landmark book published in 1981 by Amartya Sen, a professor of political economy at Oxford. Called *Poverty and Famines: An Essay on Entitlement and Deprivation*, the book argues that famines are not caused by natural disasters such as droughts, which produce shortfalls in the total availability of food. They result instead from the kind of social collapse that makes people's assets or labor worthless. "Some of the worst famines have taken place with no significant decline in food availability per head," explained Sen, who proposed that we think about famine not "in terms of what *exists*," but rather "in terms of who can *command* what exists."

Sen's argument flies in the face of our everyday myths about famine, but there is ample evidence to support it. During the great Bengal famine of 1943, in which three million people died, more rice and wheat were available than in the preceding year. Grain was exported from Welo Province during the Ethiopian famine of 1973, and no countrywide shortage of food was registered that year in Ethiopia, or in most of the West African Sahelian countries that also suffered famine. "Droughts may not be avoidable," wrote Sen, "but their consequences are."

What Swift discovered from his own observations is that famines in Sahelian Africa unfold in a recognizable pattern. Rather than freaks of nature, accidental and unforeseen, they announce their onset six months to a year in advance. A warning comes when the price of livestock drops in relation to grain. Meat provides what nutritionists call expensive calories. By weight, a sack of maize holds five times more calories than the same amount of meat from a range-fed cow. People are willing to trade grain for animals and eat high off the food chain when times are good, but they switch to more efficient calories when times are bad.

"If a nomad gets less than double the number of calories when he exchanges meat or milk for cereals, then he is entering a famine, and if he has to start eating his own animals, then he's really in trouble. It's like a caviar fisherman eating caviar. Eating caviar is not an efficient business."

The only good news about the orderliness of famines lies in the possibility of devising measures to break the spiral. "What you need is an index number, the price of animals over grain, that would allow you to monitor the declining ability of people to feed themselves. Once the number reaches a certain point, you call in emergency food stocks and set up a series of responses." While rock stars solicit food aid on global TV, and governments rush from crisis to crisis, the new theoreticians of famine think it would be more sensible to stop famines before they start.

Jeremy verifies during our travels in Turkana that his shopping list of famine indicators works the same here as elsewhere in pastoral Africa. A year to six months in advance of famine, the price of animals begins to drop. Forced to trade more animals for less grain, pastoralists begin selling reproductive females and heifers, the stock most important for maintaining their herds. They also begin selling their jewelry, blankets, and household items. Migration patterns shift. Herdsmen abandon their usual seasonal pastures and spread farther afield. Women, children, and old people leave the countryside to cluster in towns. Those remaining in the bush rely increasingly on roots, berries, and other famine foods. Respiratory diseases and malaria spread through the population. The crisis peaks with outbreaks of cholera and measles, and then the epidemics arrive that account for most of the deaths in a famine.

An ideal famine early-warning system would track data from all sectors of the economy. It would follow livestock marketing, including prices and age and sex of animals for sale. It would accumulate information on agrometeorology and plant production. And it would get a fix on the problem from outer space, with global weather forecasts and satellite photos of the distribution of animals and herding camps. But as useful as satellite photographs may be, Jeremy is suspicious of high-tech solutions to African problems. "I'm keen to get away from people's dependence on government. I'd like to see pastoralists given the means to cope for themselves." This is why his Turkana early-warning system will start on the ground with what people already know. But even this apparently simple idea is not so simple when it comes to Turkana.

Jeremy and I were in Nairobi, introducing ourselves around town and getting ready to travel north, when we met a Norwegian anthropologist who had spent three years in Lodwar and knew the district well. After we invited him to dinner, the Norwegian informed us that none of Swift's theory would stand the test of Turkana. The man was wrong, but at the time the news was rather disconcerting.

"What about fluctuations in the relative price of grain and livestock?"

"No go," said the Norwegian. "Even if the EEC hadn't screwed up the local economy by dumping surplus food in Turkana, there are two problems with your model. Grain prices are fixed by the government, and there's a quarantine on selling livestock out of the district because of foot-and-mouth disease."

"How about monitoring charcoal sales as an early warning indicator?"

"There's a ban on selling charcoal. The president thinks it wastes too many trees."

"My God. No wonder these people are living off food aid. They can't sell their cattle, and they can't sell their charcoal." Jeremy tried a new line of questioning. "How about development in the region? Is the government doing anything effective?"

"The government in Turkana is nothing but an instrument of repression," said the Norwegian. "It's irrelevant to the Turkana."

"Is there some way development could be linked to indigenous social groupings?"

"People claim there are territorial units in Turkana, but I've never seen one. There's no way you can keep anyone in or out. You know what they say about the Turkana? The only social structure they have is for raiding and war. It's not true, but no one knows yet what the rest of the structure is."

"How useful is the nutritional data gathered by the Catholic Relief Services at their feeding centers?"

"The CRS clientele are washouts," said the Norwegian. "They're urbanites who won't tell you a damn thing about conditions in the countryside."

"How about aerial data on ground cover and browse?"

"The fly boys have never been able to distinguish noise from signal."

"OK," said Jeremy. "What do *you* suggest for an early warning system?"

"*Fingerspitzengefühl*. The best monitoring system is the tingling you get in the tips of your fingers. It's like a mechanic holding a wrench. Either the tool is good, or it's shit."

"Nomads are bred to disaster," says Jeremy. "They have to be opportunistic. They look out for their chance and grab it. That's why I like them."

A third of the earth's land surface is desert or semiarid scrub, but this otherwise unpromising terrain is home to forty million nomadic pastoralists with animal-based economies. They survive in the wilder parts of Asia, the Americas, and Australia, but more than half the world's pastoralists live in Africa. Most have been pushed by now into marginal environments where their share of available resources is scanty and unreliable.

Nomads occupy the nether reaches and boundary areas of modern states. "As one moves away from the dominant center of a society, there are successive geographical and political zones that pass from full control to another band of territory that periodically escapes from the central government. These areas are the traditional niche of pastoralism," wrote Jeremy in one of his articles. But these escapes "become less and less easy to make as the technology of control is developed."

The rise of nation-states has weakened the most successful nomad strategy for survival—their ability to move hundreds and sometimes thousands of miles a year in search of water and pasture for their animals. Two theories explain the decline of nomadism as a way of life. According to the first, nomads are accidental victims of the industrial revolution. The world got integrated in ways that left no room for hunter-gatherers, nomads, and other footloose types. The second theory sees their demise as the result of a conscious policy to sedentarize a mobile and threatening population.

Colonial governments throughout Africa adopted a head tax on livestock. Even when it produced less revenue than the cost of collecting it, often by force, the tax was thought to have a salutary effect. It let the nomads know who was boss. It forced them to participate in the market economy. And it encouraged the removal of animals from rangeland that was thought to be dangerously overgrazed.

Ever since the American anthropologist Melville Herskovits coined the term "cattle complex" in 1926, the nomadic pastoralists of Africa have been diagnosed as suffering from a fetishistic relationship to their animals that drives them to accumulate ever-increasing numbers of livestock. From the perspective of someone born in Bellefontaine, Ohio, the size of African herds seemed way out of line with what people needed to survive. This "irrational" use of animals as status symbols leads inevitably to what Garrett Hardin later described as "the tragedy of the commons." Collective grazing land will invariably be destroyed by cow-crazed individuals acting in their own self-interest.

Although it endures in popular myth, Herskovits's view has been largely discredited. He failed to make a crucial distinction between owning cattle in family herds and ranching them for profit. A nomad's family herd consists mainly of females, whose reproductive cycles are staggered to provide milk throughout the year. This supply of milk allows a large number of pastoralists to live on the land. Ranching for meat production, on the other hand, requires selling both male and female animals from herds that support fewer people on the land. The sale of stock from commercial ranches may add to a country's gross national product, but it also adds to the number of displaced nomads surviving on food aid.

"Herd accumulation has nothing to do with irrational prestige or an unhealthy love of cows, although both these things may appear as psychological rationalization and reinforcement of the underlying economic strategy," Jeremy wrote a few years ago. "Among other virtues, large herds enable food to be stored on the hoof and make it possible for a network of reciprocal gifts and loans of animals to be set up between families, which serves as insurance against individual disaster."

*

Central governments are terrified of the highly mobile, well-armed tribesmen wandering within their borders. "The idea of settling nomads comes in phases," says Jeremy, "and I'm afraid we're back in one of them." Sedentarizing nomads ignores the fact that they employ their marginal resources better than anyone else could. Nomads have lower birthrates than their settled neighbors. Their family herds support more people on the land than do commercial ranches. Nomads make few demands on the state, and they practice the kind of self-sufficiency that any enlightened government should want to encourage. If the logic of this argument seems clear, Jeremy is always surprised by the number of people who find it crazy or downright subversive.

At a Nairobi conference in 1977, the United Nations Environmental Program launched a multibillion-dollar fight against desertification, primarily in Sahelian Africa. Several years later Jeremy was summoned to Nairobi as one of five consultants hired to evaluate UNEP's progress. Originally only four consultants had been hired, until someone noticed a gap in their collective expertise. "They called me in to cover the human dimension. I was standing in globally for nomads from Mauritania to Mongolia.

"The first thing we did as reviewers was to question the very concept of 'desertification.' There is no doubt that environmental degradation has taken place, usually around settlements, boreholes, and other examples of 'progress.' Pastoralists who have maintained a balance for hundreds, if not thousands, of years between their livestock and highly variable conditions are not the people to blame. If anything, they know more about range management, browsing loads, and carrying capacity than the technical 'experts' called in to advise them."

In their final report, which was not written by the reviewers themselves, Jeremy's sentiments were reinterpreted as a call for more big UN projects.

Rather than settling nomads, Jeremy argues for an entirely different approach based on keeping nomadic societies intact by "drought-proofing" them against disaster. As senior social scientist on two multimillion-dollar aid projects in Sahelian Africa — one financed by the International Livestock Center for Africa, based in Addis Ababa, and the other by the United States Agency for

International Development—Swift has worked to get his ideas adopted as mainstream policy. Both projects ultimately failed, but Jeremy considers them exemplary failures that hold the promise of something better.

For several years in the early 1980s he was "working like a maniac running five research sites in Mali and three in Niger." After a thorough study of its economy, conducted by ten full-time researchers, Jeremy recommended turning control of Mali's Sahelian grassland over to "agro-pastoral units," or cooperatives of local farmers and herders. "The government was terrified at the thought of creating another power group, especially one that would comprise eighty percent of the population. The idea was opposed by wealthy Fulani, and the World Bank finally decided to channel its money through livestock merchants in Mopti, which is the opposite of development. All told, it was a fantastically unsuccessful piece of work, with not a single proposal adopted by anyone who had solicited them."

Jeremy's USAID project among the Wodaabe and Twareg pastoralists of Niger met, at least initially, with more success. "The basic principle is that you want to develop from the bottom up via some form of pastoral association, not from the top down by means of expanding the bureaucracy. I think development is about reaching poor people and giving them control over their means of production. Land, capital, labor should all be in the hands of rural producers.

"There's a large supply of cash and salable assets in the pastoral economy. The market value of a family herd can range from ten to twenty thousand dollars, and it has an enviable growth rate of fifteen percent a year. But what these people desperately need are banking, insurance, and credit schemes to see them through the tight spots. The first thing I looked at in Niger was establishing credit for herders.

"Everyone told me, 'You can't run a banking scheme among illiterate pastoralists.' But it worked quite nicely with nonliterate forms of accounting, using pictures. Then they said, 'You can't give money to nomads. They'll take it and disappear.' But most of them repaid at a high rate of interest and on time."

In their heyday the Niger cooperatives had three hundred nomadic families working together to organize cereal stocks, credit programs, and primary health care for people and animals. "I wanted to negotiate them through the next drought. That was going to be the real test."

The project was so successful that USAID raised its stake from five to twenty million dollars. Outside reviewers described it as "the only livestock project working in Africa. This is one sector of the economy that invites disasters." But a new team of Americans, with ideas of its own, was hired to run phase two of the project. Jeremy moved on to other assignments, the experiment disintegrated, and before long the reviewers were saying, "Close it down."

"Do you ever suffer from despair?" I ask him one day.

"Yes," Jeremy says. "That's when I retreat to the study of history and banking systems. But it never lasts very long. There's a cumulative nature to these projects. Things move and change, rather than sliding back to the status quo. Not all twenty million dollars goes down a black hole. Something that worked is in the consciousness of people and governments. It's part of their collective experience. Ideas have a way of going underground and resurfacing."

Familiar with the realpolitik of third world development, Jeremy still finds himself capable of outrage. "It's a scandal that people are dying of famine in Africa today, given the amount of money and technical expertise that have poured into the continent. Everyone is disappointed by the failure of this colossal investment, most of which has gone into white elephants. There is something mad in this system."

At one point I quiz him on development economics. "How do you characterize this hybrid field with so many failures to its credit?"

"Development economics is a very messy business," he admits. "Production systems are like spiders' webs in their complexity. They are tight-knit and intricate mechanisms made out of hundreds of interwoven strands. It's hard to focus on all the strands at once, but that's what you have to do if you want to understand how the thing works. The cutting edge of research in areas like this is done by people who combine anthropology, ecology, and economics. A pure economist or a pure ecologist, if you could find one, would offer very little of use."

Given the hybrid nature of his profession, does Jeremy think of himself as a scientist? "Yes," he says, "in that the work involves testing hypotheses. Does the model hold up in the real world? How good is it as a predictive device?

"People tend to make their reputations in Africa in one narrow area. The model for their research comes from physics and is basically reductionist. But this isolation of elements in the hope of finding one item capable of improvement doesn't work. You have to move forward on all fronts at once. The real challenge is to relate the detail of the mechanism to these larger, more amorphous systems, and to do this, you have to listen very carefully to what farmers and herders say."

For our next consultation with the world's experts on famine, Jeremy and I travel north of Lake Turkana. Our trip begins with a drive along the shore of this Rift Valley lake, which has been known at various times in its history as Rudolf, Aman, and the Jade Sea. When we first spy it over the horizon, the lake looks like a turquoise mirage. It owes its distinctive color to an algae bloom that rises and falls throughout the course of the day. Because it has no outlet, Lake Turkana is slowly thickening into a soda soup. This gives it a slightly soapy feel, which in no way detracts from the pleasure of an afternoon swim. The bottom is sandy, the water warm yet refreshing. There are no crocodiles in sight, but the thought of them adds to the delicious tingling in my toes.

Lake Turkana entered the annals of African exploration in 1888 when Austrian Count Teleki von Szek, accompanied by two hundred porters and his plodding yet faithful biographer, Lieutenant Ludwig von Höhnel, arrived at its shores dehydrated and half dead. As von Höhnel explained in a two-volume work on the subject, Teleki "named the sheet of water, set like a pearl of great price in the wonderful landscape before us," after his royal master, Crown Prince Rudolf of Austria. In the same year he was having a lake named after him, Rudolf was meeting the seventeen-year-old girl with whom he would later carry out a mutual death pact.

We stop for the night in Lokitaung, a village near the north end of the lake. The following morning, after securing the police permit required for crossing the Kenya-Sudan border, we find ourselves bouncing on a grassy track into the Elemi Triangle, a piece of Sudan recently annexed by Kenya. Compared to the rest of Turkana, this looks like the Garden of Eden. A storm in the middle of the night, which drenched me before I was conscious enough to pick up my sleeping bag and run for cover, has greened the rolling savanna. To our right we look over the Omo River into the mountains of southern Ethiopia. To our left rises another range of mountains that we will eventually climb before circling back into Turkana.

Eleven of us have squeezed into the Land Rover, which proves a goodly crew for pushing our vehicle out of flooded rivers. Included among us are Meiyen Makario, our guide, whose *adakar* we are going to visit. Meiyen's brother and half brother and the half brother's wife and two children and some cousins have also come along for the ride. The law of the road in Africa begins with an abhorrence of vacuums. If there is empty space in a vehicle it will be filled, and filled again, until the driver pleads for mercy on behalf of his leaf springs.

We spend the day fording rivers and digging ourselves out of mud holes until the sun drops at six o'clock with tropical promptness. Meiyen informs us that we have entered Marile country. This is not good news. Testicles play a large role in Marile initiation ceremonies, and young warriors have to produce evidence of successful raids before they can choose a bride. The Marile run around naked and paint themselves white. The Turkana run around naked and paint themselves red. "This is clearly a case of divergent evolution," says Jeremy. "It prevents them from bumping into each other in the dark."

As night settles over us, the Turkana sitting next to me look distinctly worried. Our track disappears into an expanse of thorn bush. Meiyen has fallen silent, and Edipal, his brother, crouches on the tailgate and listens for noises in the night. We are looking for nomadic pastoralists who could be anywhere in the triangle, and it has been three months since Meiyen and Edipal last saw their *adakar*. Along with the usual anxieties involved in going home, nomads also have to wonder where home might be.

Branches go *thwop* against the windscreen, and thorns scrape the sides of the vehicle like fingernails on a chalkboard. Meiyen raises his hand. We stop the car. He has spotted a campfire in the hills above us, and he sends Edipal running up the mountain to see if the fire belongs to friend or foe. We switch off the ignition and sit in the dark listening for the snap of twigs.

Edipal trots back with good news. They are friends, and they know where to send us. We make a hard right toward the Omo, heading straight for Marile country. We stop the car every few minutes so Edipal can jump out and listen. With the onset of the spring rains and a new flow of milk, dancing season has started. We are trying to pick up the sound of singing. When we hear it, we kill our headlights and drive by ear, until we come to a circle of boys and girls yodeling on the plain.

Under the watchful eye of two youths sporting Kalashnikovs, dancers are jumping up and down, clapping their hands and chanting. One of the boys hops forward to face the girls in front of him. Holding his hands to his head, with his index fingers pointed like horns, he begins singing the virtues of his bull. It is a big bull. A strong and beautiful bull. A girl jumps forward to slap the boy-bull with her skirt and tickle him with the ostrich feather in her hair. The bull charges and scatters a group of laughing girls. Long after I have stretched out on a cow skin and given up counting stars in the Milky Way, I wake to hear the spring prom in Turkana still rocking through the night.

We breakfast on cow's milk curdled with urine and watch Turkana women at their morning toilette, which consists of greasing themselves from head to foot with a mixture of butterfat and mud. Amid the ruckus of animals being led out to pasture, a sleepy Meiyen produces a dozen men for us to interview. Our informants are decked out in tin earrings, wrist knives, lip plugs, spears, cow-skin shields, and mud hats decorated with ostrich feathers. We repair to the shade of an acacia tree, where the men recline on their wooden pillows.

Two warrior spokesmen take the floor. One is wrapped in a pink wool blanket and the other sports an ostrich feather hat. Mr. Pink Wool Blanket busies himself poking a stick in the dirt, while his friend delivers what sounds like an incendiary address. Mr. Ostrich Feather Hat sweeps the air with outstretched fingers and then moves into a two-fisted hand dive, a ten-finger shazam, a wave to the horizon in spear-throwing position, and a slap to the armpit. Mr. Pink Wool Blanket concurs with a spit.

The speech is translated as a chronology of drought in Turkana. There were years when all the cattle died of rinderpest. That was in the 1890s. This was followed by *ekwakoit* in the 1920s, and the time the Italians came in an airplane to raid Lodwar; that was during the Second World War. Another time airplanes came and dropped *posho* and fish from the sky. This was in the 1950s, when Turkana was a military zone closed to outsiders. Then there was the drought when everyone went to feeding camps for the first time. That was 1961. Then in 1970 came the cholera epidemic, and in 1980 there was *atanayanaye*, "the broom." This is the basic story in Turkana. A killing drought arrives once every ten years to sweep a lot of people and animals off the plain.

Sitting cross-legged on a mat, Jeremy begins ticking off his shopping list of items sold during a drought. What happens to the barter terms of trade for animals, beads, calabashes, goat skins, jewelry, knives, feathers? The discussion breaks off when Messrs. OFH and PWB start jabbing fingers into their open mouths. No more tobacco, no more talk. They give us the look of people too busy for this kind of thing anyway, as they get up and stroll to a neighboring tree. "Maybe they thought you were government men," says Meiyen by way of apology.

Lodwar's dusty main street is lined with cinderblock *dukas* painted in flamboyant shades of pink and green. Cans of South African butter and boxes of Uncle Ben's rice and Lever Brothers soap powder are sometimes in short supply, which is why, on a typical shopping day, Toyota Landcruisers and DAF trucks roll up and down the main street, and people lean out the window yelling "Nescafé! Nescafé!" until a Somali storekeeper comes running with the goods.

Lodwar sits in the middle of a thorn-bush plain humped with volcanic cinder cones. It receives about six inches of rain a year, and the town has another sporadic source of water in the Turkwel River, which rises in the Kenyan highlands. One evening I strolled along the dry bottom of this seasonal stream, but the next day, had I attempted the same feat, I would have been walking under five feet of water. I find it hard to believe that Lodwar is home to six thousand people until I survey it from above in the TRP airplane. I make out the shady compound reserved for Lodwar's fifty expatriates and the tin roofs of the *dukas*, and then I see, stretching along the banks of the Turkwel, grass huts by the thousands tumbling out into the surrounding bush.

The huts give way to a scaly landscape marked with the circles of abandoned corrals. Sutured across these sunburned terraces are forests that hug the rivers and give Turkana its only hint of greenery. We fly west to the Loima Hills and dip over the sawtoothed escarpment that marks the boundary of defensible Kenya. We then turn north to look at a food-for-work project that has dug three hundred thousand holes for tree planting. A spate of water from a storm over the mountains has snaked its way into the sandy plain, but the nearby project is bone dry.

The central watering hole in Lodwar is a bar called the Turkwel Lodge, where Jeremy and I quaff too many Tusker beers while interviewing local informants. Each conversation turns up a crucial bit of knowledge. A Dutch forester, for example, tells us about the hierarchy of famine foods. As hot and windy and rainless as it may be, Turkana has a high water table that supports a wealth of trees. The berries of toothbrush trees and the fruits and seeds of desert dates, acacias, tamarinds, and jujubes are all avidly foraged. The fruits of *Balanites pedicellaris*, on the other hand, are poisonous unless boiled for twelve hours. In a land short of water and firewood, to find people eating *Balanites* seeds is a sign of very bad times indeed.

A local doctor tells us that most of the Turkana children living on food aid are malnourished, while the children in the bush are not. "It's obvious," he says, "that the more animals you keep, the better off you are. We have to have this kind of information to throw in the face of people in Nairobi who want to settle the pastoralists."

Before visiting the Turkwel, Jeremy and I had walked up to Capitol Hill to make the round of government officials swatting flies in their offices. Capitol Hill is a collection of concrete cells perched on a nipple of land overlooking Lodwar. Displayed here is the bent propeller of the Italian plane that attacked Turkana in the Second World War. Two stories are told about the plane's demise. Either it was shot down in brave defense of the territory, or it ran out of fuel and crashed.

On Capitol Hill we meet an Irish rancher who is trying to build

ngoroko-proof holding pens and animal markets in southern Turkana. He describes how the Turkana smuggle their cattle out of
the district through Uganda to avoid medical quarantines and
barter them for grain and other commodities. "The bartering completely foxes me," he says. "I can't keep track of it, and I bet the
Turks get hoodwinked by it as well."

"You mean no one has studied cattle markets as the Turkana
see them?" Jeremy asks.

"Not that I know of," says the rancher. "We're just going to start
afresh and work out a system by trial and error."

Sitting behind two empty desks positioned back to back, the
district veterinary officer describes how his latest vaccination campaign against rinderpest has done a good job of attracting both
cattle and bandits. "It happens quite frequently here," says the
soft-spoken Kenyan, who is missing his front teeth.

"What do you think about building animal markets in the district?"

"I would suggest putting the holding pens anywhere but in
southern Turkana. This is where the Pokot like to raid."

We find the district agricultural officer sitting in a large room
with paint flaking off the walls. This Kenyan is also missing his
front teeth. As he talks to us, the DAO squirms in his chair and
looks down at the floor like a schoolboy dying for recess.

"All the big water-harvesting projects washed away in the No-
vember rains," he says. "The TRP likes big schemes because they
need something to do with their labor force, but we have no way
to maintain these structures, nor have we sorted out who should
be allowed to use them. Irrigation is not the solution to Turkana's
problems. Irrigation is expensive, and it doesn't support a lot of
people."

Jeremy starts him squirming again with another question. The
man continues, "Traditional agriculture in the district depends
entirely on broadcasting seed in low-lying areas along the rivers.
In the midst of all this food-for-work, nothing is being done to
improve traditional agriculture, and the gene pool for the local
sixty-day sorghum has unfortunately been polluted by slower-
growing varieties given as food aid. We've seen a lot of big people
come with many ideas, and it's all a bit confusing."

The offices of NORAD, the Norwegian aid agency, with their

pine paneling and blond desks, feel like a breath of the north woods. The Norwegians have been embarrassed by some bad investments in Turkana. They spent two million dollars on a fish-freezing plant that never froze a fish and another twenty million dollars on a road connecting the plant to the Nairobi highway. Far from being apologetic, the agency's acting director is undeterred in his enthusiasm for big projects. "We built another fish-freezing plant just like it in southwestern India. It never worked either. Development aid as a profession is only twenty years old. You have to expect we'll make a lot of mistakes before we get it right."

A British forester in a neighboring office is not so sanguine. "There are twenty-five thousand people in the district planting trees or watering them to keep them alive. But almost all the trees are exotic species, like *Prosopis chilensis*. I've seen some *Prosopis* thirty years old, but most of them die out in five. If you want my honest opinion, the food-for-work program should be phased out immediately. I know the Europeans are sitting on mountains of butter and lakes of wine, but dumping excess food in Turkana just won't do. We're going to have to find some other way to keep the farmers of Europe rich."

Our final interview is with the director of the Turkana Rehabilitation Project, a burly Dutchman who runs clinics, feeding centers, and a trucking company that hauls two thousand tons of food a month from the Indian Ocean port of Mombasa. "We're screwing it back to six hundred tons," says the Dutchman, who uses his food to finance earth-moving projects all across Turkana. His barter economy of food-for-work has become the local gold standard, and the price of everything in the district is now quoted in food. A Kalashnikov AK-47 with a thousand rounds of ammunition, for example, is worth one bag of *posho*.

Like a visiting accountant, Jeremy spends a lot of time popping his tortoiseshell glasses on and off while inquiring into the TRP's budget. Then he asks, "Why do you pay people with food, rather than money?"

"They'd be exploited by unscrupulous shopkeepers if we paid in cash. People wouldn't get the same value for money."

"What about price controls?"

"No trader in his right mind sells at the controlled price. There's no doubt that the black market price of food goes up in a famine."

The Dutchman says he is doing his best to reduce the number of people on the dole. He sounds almost reflective when he admits, "The magnitude of the project and number of people involved are frightening. How are we ever going to extricate ourselves?"

Jeremy suggests that some "action-oriented" research might be called for. It would help to know what the Turkana would spend their money on, if they had any, and what they would eat, if not for EEC grain.

"When it comes to writing up your final report," says the director, "don't leave out logistics and infrastructure. That's the stuff that makes you or breaks you. But it's always overlooked by airy-fairy researchers."

Jeremy assures him there is nothing airy-fairy in his regard for logistics.

"The intellectual plays a dicey role in this business," Jeremy tells me over a beer at the Turkwel. "When it comes to writing my final report, if I say, 'You guys have made a mess of things, while I've got the secret to a brilliant famine plan,' that will antagonize everyone, and it won't be helpful. Instead, they should perceive my plan as completely unoriginal. It should look to them as if I've merely pulled together ideas they've already thought of.

"People are suspicious of intellectuals coming in and 'solving' all their problems in two weeks, and there is something to be said for having tough administrators running a relief program. You're under tremendous pressure to come up with concrete results at the end of three years — moving so many sacks of grain or planting so many trees. This is fine, but what's lacking is any research or planning to figure out what kind of programs would be most helpful. Turkana doesn't need food-for-work. It needs food-for-thought."

Swift has always maintained that the best thing to do with pastoral nomads is to keep them pastoral and nomadic. At his urging, Oxfam and other aid agencies have begun supporting the idea of restocking nomads who have lost their animals to drought. Hoping to see a local example of this strategy at work, we make another foray deep into Turkana, this time traveling east and then south out of Lodwar toward the volcanic steam vents and bubbling mud flats of the Suguta Valley. Here Oxfam has restocked a group of

Turkana widows, giving each of them sixty female and ten male goats, a donkey, a few bags of *posho*, and some cooking gear. Their flocks should double in a year, and if the women are lucky, they will never again see the inside of another food-for-work camp.

A Turkana herder normally has sixty stock associates to whom he has lent animals that can be reclaimed at a later date. But everywhere throughout the pastoral world these self-help mechanisms are breaking down as nomads become ranchers. In the language of economics, the traditional mechanisms are undercapitalized, which means that pastoralists lack sufficient cash and animals to see them through hard times. Nomads used to be able to raise capital on their own through loans, gifts, and raiding. But with these options becoming less viable, someone has to put up the money to buy animals from neighboring areas or rich herders and give them to nomads who would otherwise be driven out of the pastoral economy.

The worsening state of this economy is often not apparent to experts on quick visits to Africa. "The landscape looks the same," says Jeremy, "but more and more pastoralists are doing nothing more than herding other people's cattle. Milk is the only payment they get as cowboys for traders and government officials. So they overmilk and overgraze, and there's high calf mortality. It's an inefficient system, like sharecropping."

As on our previous trips into the insurrection zone, Jeremy and I begin with a stop at the Agip gas pump in Lodwar. In front of us is a 240 GD four-wheel-drive diesel Mercedes with two bumper stickers saying "Christ Is the Answer" and "God Is Greater than Any Problem I Have." Waiting to gas up alongside the Mercedes are vehicles from the Salvation Army, the Inland Mission, the Diocese of Lodwar, and the Catholic Relief Services. Our congregation is suddenly enveloped in a cloud of dust as an Amoco helicopter lands from above. Out swaggers a crew of bearded geologists wearing Buck knives and shorts. After filling their gas cans, the geologists tell us they are mapping magnetic fields in Turkana as a prelude to prospecting for oil.

We drive east out of Lodwar to a large food-for-work camp at Nakurio and then head south along the sandy banks of the Kerio River. Rimming the horizon in front of us is the blue hump of

Telekis Volcano and the imposing mass of Mount Kulal, which is forested in cedar. By nightfall we reach the grass huts of four women who have been restocked with Oxfam goats. We camp outside the walls of their small *adakar* and build a fire on the sand. Nightjars, sounding like police cars equipped with whoopie sirens, whiz around us plucking insects out of the air. But the evening soon quiets into the usual animal noises, more domestic than wild.

In the morning we repair to the shade of an acacia tree to talk to the widow Nakamasune Amui and her two younger colleagues, Namanakwee Etengan and Apolou Nakero, who is suckling a baby at her breast. Counting parents and other dependents, each woman supports a family of seven. They have shaved heads, except for an ocher-colored topknot. Nakamasune and Namanakwee are adorned with the usual masses of Turkana beads and earrings, but they wear cloth rather than leather skirts, and Apolou wears no earrings or bracelets at all.

Children scurry around us, skipping stones and sneaking glances at the *wazungu* interviewing their mothers. "Do you have enough animals to live on?" Jeremy asks.

"Seventy animals should be enough to survive the first year," says Nakamasune. "But six goats were stolen and two died, and we are afraid of another drought that could wipe us out and send us back to the camps." Unlike the men we have interviewed in Turkana, there is no hand waving among the women, and all of them speak up in turn.

Jeremy sets to work collecting drought chronologies. "All the droughts we can remember were bad," say the women, "but the last one was the worst."

"What did you do?"

"We moved to the lake and fished with baskets. We foraged for fruits and berries and gave our beads to the Marile for sorghum. We sold our jewelry to white people at Ferguson's Gulf and started eating dead animals. Then the government began feeding us."

"What should be done to prepare for the next drought?"

"The government should build a big store for keeping grain. They should also raise the price of goats so we don't have to give them away for twenty shillings, no bargaining. This is obvious, isn't it? We live on food."

"Thank you," says Jeremy. "You have been the most helpful of all the people we've talked to in Turkana." The women end the interview with a round of applause.

What came of Jeremy's efforts to design a famine early-warning system for Turkana? He chose sixty-five indices for monitoring the local economy, including everything from cattle prices to the sale of spears and jewelry. Most of this information was simple enough to be collected by anyone with a notebook and a rain gauge. He wrote a one-hundred-and-fifty-page report that was well received at the highest levels, even in the office of the president. A drought contingency officer was installed in Lodwar. Oxfam continued restocking nomads, and the TRP, in a nod to "the essentially pastoral nature of Turkana," began designing earthworks for growing animal forage, rather than food.

"All that famine early-warning systems do is foster the movement of surplus grain into Africa by setting up parallel markets and making the distribution of food aid more efficient," says one critic of these systems. "I partially agree," says Jeremy. "But famine contingency planning also saves lives and reduces the economic and political chaos of famines."

Between return visits to Turkana, Jeremy carries on his work in "drought-proofing pastoral economies through the creation of herders' cooperatives, the design of appropriate credit programs, and the training of primary health care workers for people and animals." After trips to Mongolia, Ethiopia, and Sudan, he is "running out of nomads to visit," and the nomads themselves seem to be running out of time. There is a sense of urgency to his work, a willingness to propose less-than-perfect solutions, if that's what it takes to keep this way of life from disappearing forever.

While covering a lot of ground in too little time, Swift never loses sight of the fact that people's indigenous knowledge is in many ways superior to his own. This is why he spends so much time sitting on cow skins talking to herders. "I know I've already told you this," he said as we drove back from Lodwar to Nairobi. "But you should remember that the people who really know about famines are the nomads. They've lived with them for hundreds of years. They are the real experts at devising early-warning systems and life-saving responses."

As I think about why these traditional measures are no longer working, I realize that nomadism itself is in danger of vanishing. Africa's pastoralists have been buffeted by droughts and famines and, most recently, by floods. Nomads know better than anyone how to deal with an unpredictable climate. But now they must deal with a different kind of chaos, produced by the vagaries of politics and civil war, against which they have no lifesaving response.

What does it mean that another bit of the world's diversity is on the verge of blinking out of existence? Diversity is the key to adaptation, and species without it tend to go extinct. But I keep thinking about the personal consequences of this loss and what it involves for the people suffering it. The words of Apolou Nakero come to mind. "Is there anything you would rather do than keep a family herd?" Jeremy asked. "No," she replied, "because if you don't have animals, you don't know what you are."

Missing Links

You tell me that it's evolution,
Well you know,
We all want to change the world.

John Lennon

AFTER A WEEK in Goma everyone is looking glum. Noel makes his daily trip out to the airport to radiophone Kinshasa. Our truck is coming tomorrow. Our truck is coming the day after tomorrow. Our truck is not coming at all, because it is too big to fit on the airplane!

"But before I bought it, you told me the truck would slide onto a pallet with the wheels taken off!"

"No, it won't fit." So if this truck is ever going to reach Goma, someone will have to drive it upriver a thousand miles through the tropical rain forests of Zaire.

Noel retreats into his room at the Masques Hôtel. Down the street at the Hôtel des Grands Lacs, Alison and Jack are hopping mad. Noel was supposed to buy a pickup truck. Even a Ford 350 would have been big for our purposes. But an eight-ton Leyland Land Master with six wheels was *really* big. Fourteen people were now stuck in Goma with two ancient Land Rovers, no truck, and a huge hole in the budget.

Some of us had arrived from the east and some from the west to rendezvous dead center in the middle of Africa. We were supposed to drive from Goma to Ishango, a dot on the map two hundred and fifty miles north on the shores of Lake Idi Amin Dada, the former Lake Edward. Even under the best of circumstances, Goma is not a pleasant place to visit. Much of the city is built on a slag heap, and a nearby volcano occasionally dusts the trees and buildings with black ash. Parading down the main street is an unusually large collection of limbless beggars. Belgian pilots roar overhead in Mirage jets, for the street also serves as the airport's flight path.

In Kinshasa, apart from buying a truck, Noel was supposed to go shopping. But when Alison spreads out the expedition's gear in her hotel bedroom, she finds many items missing. "Here are six thousand plastic bags, but nothing to seal them with!" she exclaims. "I can't work without masking tape." Also missing is anything to eat, and the budget now holds only four hundred dollars for two months' supplies.

Total cost for the expedition is close to a quarter of a million dollars, most of it from the National Science Foundation, with smaller sums from the L.S.B. Leakey Foundation, the National Geographic Society, and the Holt Family Charitable Trust. Other support has come from the University of Wisconsin and George Washington University, which are Jack Harris's and Alison Brooks's home institutions. Noel Boaz's Virginia Museum of Natural History has provided the Land Rovers and other gear. Anthropological field seasons are expensive, and this one is about to be canceled for want of a truck.

The three principal investigators, or PIs, as the NSF contract refers to them, are no strangers to logistical mayhem. "It was the most depressing time of my life," says Jack of the six weeks he spent trapped in the Addis Ababa Hilton in 1982. Embroiled in purges and counterpurges, Ethiopia was closing its borders to anthropologists, and sixteen researchers were barred from reaching the field that summer, including Alison and her husband, John Yellen. They had stopped to visit Jack on their way to Zimbabwe for a dig of their own. It, too, would be canceled after six tourists were killed in the eastern part of the country.

"I didn't come this far not to get to Ishango," says Diana Holt, on hearing the latest news about the truck. Thinking it silly to haggle over a missing vehicle, she reaches into her handbag and pulls out a wad of traveler's checks. "We'll just have to rent a truck. And I suppose I'll also have to buy the food to put in it."

If anthropological expeditions invariably come to resemble families, one could say that I have spent the past week watching Mother Alison and Father Jack get peeved at Uncle Noel. Noel is the artist of the family, boyish and irrepressible, whose enthusiasm sometimes lands him in trouble. Alison is the brains of the operation, which does not prevent her from doing most of the housework and shopping. Jack is the rock-steady provider; during all his years of going into the field, only once did he fail to come home with the bones and stones.

Attached to the familial triad are a lot of consulting cousins and rambunctious children in the form of graduate students. Because none of the younger members of the expedition can afford to spend a week in Goma waiting for Noel's mythical truck to arrive, Aunt Diana has taken to feeding them in her room. This Palm Beach socialite and heiress to the Budweiser beer fortune describes herself as "a paleontological parasite. I started doing this at a young age. When my father took me on his fishing trips into the Pyrenees, I would go off to look at the cave paintings. I can walk by the window at Cartier's without a second thought. But when I see an Acheulian hand axe, that's when I have lust in my heart."

Paleoanthropology—the study of early *Homo sapiens* and our more primitive ancestors—is unusual in being a science popular enough to attract private patronage. Louis Leakey mastered the pitch. His wife, Mary, and son, Richard, followed him onto the lecture circuit, and by now a lot of anthropologists have learned to talk up their work at California cocktail parties. A burly New Zealander, ingenuous to a fault, Jack Harris seems an unlikely candidate for Diana's magic wand. "Jack is Donald Johanson's archaeologist. Jack is Richard Leakey's archaeologist. And Jack is Noel Boaz's archaeologist. There is no finer talent in the world," says his patron. "I tell my husband that instead of a diamond bracelet, I'd much rather go on a dig with Jack."

Buoyed by the sight of Diana's traveler's checks, we charge into the shops lining Goma's main street. From the goods piled in heaps on the floor, we buy up sixty kilos of rice, six crates of Simba vegetable oil, three hundred rolls of toilet paper, and four hundred cans of sardines, Jack's favorite food. A triumphant Alison arrives back at the hotel with eighteen rolls of masking tape and an undisclosed number of chocolate bars.

The next day at dawn, as a rented truck from Tout en Est pulls up to the verandah, Diana appears at the front door of the Grands Lacs wearing a rattan pith helmet over her nest of blond hair. "Has anyone heard the stock market report?" she asks. "I want to know if we can eat tonight." Blue tennis shoes, an oversized blouse, and a pair of well-thumbed spectacles complete her safari costume. "There must be an easier way to find cocktail conversation for Palm Beach," she says.

Piled around her on the verandah are boxes filled with shovels, nails, string, aluminum foil, trowels, hammers, rock chisels, line levels, and pans like those used by gold miners. "You can run a perfectly respectable dig with these few simple items," says Alison. "But without them, you're lost."

On top of the basics lie three Polaroid cameras, a triple beam balance, a dozen dustpans, a copy of *Where There Is No Doctor: A Village Health Care Handbook*, four ampoules of snake bite serum, seven solar-powered calculators, a fishing pole, fifteen mattresses, five plumb bobs, a surveyor's transit and tripod, twelve rolls of flagging tape, sixty kilograms of plaster, a grease gun, a bottle of hydrochloric acid, fifty feet of galvanized hardware cloth, and two dozen machetes. "This should get us started," says Jack.

Loaded down to the leaf springs, our "Everything in the East" truck and two Land Rovers finally begin the long climb north into the Virunga National Park. We are headed up the Rift Valley into the foothills of the Ruwenzori Mountains, to where the Semliki River falls out of Lake Amin. Here sits the grassy bluff known as Ishango. The site has been famous among anthropologists since the 1950s, when Jean de Heinzelin de Braucourt uncovered here the remains of a twenty-thousand-year-old "aquatic civilization" that invented bone harpoons, mathematics, and possibly even writing. Ishango was in the news again in 1985 after Jack and Alison discovered nearby some of the world's oldest stone tools. The magnet drawing us up the Rift Valley a year later is the possibility of finding the hand that made those tools.

Out of Goma, we traverse the ashen flanks of Mount Nyiragongo. Above us floats a lava lake, while down below lie valleys filled with cinders and the new shoots of banana trees. As the road opens onto Rift Valley savanna and great herds of Cape buffalo and kob, a sign announces that we are entering the Virunga National Park, the former Prince Albert National Park, the oldest in Africa. Then we pass a memorial to the thirty guards who have died defending it. At Ishango the previous summer Jack had apprehended a band of poachers and put them to work digging his archaeological trench. If he had followed park rules, he would have shot them.

The park stretches two hundred miles up the Western Rift Valley, where it encompasses some of the most incredible geography in Africa. It was created in 1925 as a sanctuary for mountain gorillas, which survive in the bamboo forests that straddle the volcanoes near Goma. North of the volcanoes lies the high savanna surrounding Lake Amin and the Semliki River. As de Heinzelin wrote of the upper Semliki after a decade spent exploring the area, "Still living on the plains is a large fauna of elephants, ungulates, and wild animals similar to those that populated Europe in the Pliocene. On every day's walk I shivered on encountering the last true remnants of the prehistoric world."

Farther north the Semliki descends into tropical rain forests and hanging valleys whose rock faces resemble the great cathedrals of Europe. As the river falls, the surrounding land rises in a frantic pitch that climbs in sixteen miles through every habitat found in Africa, with the exception of desert sands and maritime coastline. Mounting through great vistas of white heath and alpine tundra, the park ends in permanent glaciers atop the ten Ruwenzori peaks that are over sixteen thousand feet high.

Calling them the Mountains of the Moon, and correctly describing them as the watershed of the Nile, the Egyptian geographer Ptolemy featured the Ruwenzoris in his famous map of Africa drawn almost two thousand years ago. Ptolemy's latter-day counterparts at the Royal Geographical Society, doubting that snow could exist on the equator and thinking that it must really be salt, commissioned Henry Stanley to take a look. Stanley undertook this added assignment while on his mission to "rescue" Emin Pasha — born Eduard Schnitzer — in 1889.

By the time he reached the lower Semliki after a year-long march across the Congo, Stanley had already outlived all the Europeans and most of the Africans in his entourage. When he asked his guides for the name of the river and a description of its headwaters, it is understandable why they replied, "Semuliki," which in Kinande means "there is nothing there." Stanley named the river's source Lake Edward, after Britain's Prince of Wales. But it was the reluctant Pasha who was the first European to set foot on the lakeshore. After being rescued by Stanley and carried to Zanzibar, Pasha headed straight back to Central Africa for a walk around the lake.

The only mishap on our first day in the field comes when Noel's heater catches on fire and fills his Land Rover with smoke. The problem is solved by pulling out the offensive item. We stop for the night at Rwindi, a cluster of huts built for game watching in the middle of the park. That evening we are the only visitors drinking the warm beer at the bar.

Lake Amin, which is also known as Lake Rutanzige or Ex Amin or Ex Edward or simply Lake Ex, fills the Rift Valley above Rwindi, so the only road north runs along the top of the escarpment. We start off at five in the morning to make the three-thousand-foot ascent up the Rift wall before the midday heat can play havoc with our radiators. The early start also gives us time to stop and walk the *falaise* above the Rwindi River. De Heinzelin described the site as Oldowan because he thought it held stone tools similar to those discovered by Mary Leakey at Olduvai Gorge, which is dated at slightly less than two million years old.

As we stroll through a prehistoric landscape of euphorbia and thorn trees, above a green river filled with hippos, I observe the differing styles of our three principal investigators at work. Noel is way ahead, moving fast over the eroded hills, stooping now and then to pick up fossils, which he wraps in toilet paper and stuffs in his knapsack. Alison lingers behind, poking at rocks with the toe of her hiking boot. "This is something I'd put a number on," she says, fingering a stone tool that eventually gets tossed back on the ground. Jack has disappeared into a ravine, where we find him scratching in the soil with his knife. "This is worth returning to later," he says, and everyone agrees.

Back on the road, we scatter a herd of antelope while driving toward the blue wall of the Western Rift. This is not to be confused with the Eastern Rift, the younger offshoot that runs through the Kenyan game parks before petering out south of Olduvai Gorge. The major fault knifing through the continent from the upper Nile to Mozambique, the Western Rift is the joint out of which the Great Lakes of Africa have been carved. We will spend the day climbing the escarpment on a dirt track that switches back and forth in an apparently endless succession of blind curves.

On top of the wall, we plunge into the tumult of Kanyabayonga, a market town that straddles the Rift for miles. The front yards of the houses look east over Prince Albert's refuge, while their back yards give onto a series of steeply cut mountain valleys, every inch of which is cultivated in nearly vertical fields of cassava and bananas. Far below, the fields merge into the sea-green mat of Africa's largest tropical rain forest.

We drive over a series of ridges newly torched for slash-and-burn agriculture before reaching another surprising sight. The little farms of maize and bananas give way to pastures grazed by dairy cows. The great Belgian estates have tumbled into ruin— one house has a tree growing out of its roof—but suddenly, alongside a road lined with eucalyptus trees, appear wooden stands selling cheese and butter and baskets full of strawberries. When we stop for a continental picnic, our maps tell us we are sitting on the equator.

Late the following afternoon we drop off the escarpment and wind our way down to the northern shore of Lake Amin. It has taken us three days to traverse a body of water sixty-five miles long. Leaving behind the last village and the Boulangerie de la dernière chance, we descend into the valley and cross the Semliki on an iron bridge spanned with railway ties. On the other side of the river, the road opens onto a vast plain rolling off to the foothills of the Ruwenzoris and the Ugandan border. Winking at us on the horizon are the blue waters of Amin.

This is the loveliest savanna I have seen in Africa. It rolls like the Great Plains north of Yellowstone, but the thorn trees and antelopes and pastel light make it uniquely African. We turn onto a narrow track, which is nothing more than a mat of grass laid over the black cotton soil, and drive for an hour until the road dead-ends at Ishango.

We stop the car and walk to the edge of the bluff. Below us lies the Semliki where it rises out of the lake. The water is so clear that thousands of *Barbus* and other fish can be seen swimming with their noses pointed upstream. What look like boulders on the river bottom are actually hippos. One of them breaches like a whale and sinks back into the current. Hundreds of water birds line the sandy banks, while behind them, on the far shore, a procession of bushbucks and warthogs is coming down for an evening drink. "*Un des plus grandioses sites de la planète,*" the sign at the Ishango gate to the park had announced. This was no exaggeration.

The only buildings at Ishango are three white cottages that once served as summer houses for the Belgian royal family. The cottages are now inhabited by bats and fleas, and one of them has lost its red tile roof. Also standing on the site is the queen's *paillote*, a thatch-roofed gazebo overlooking the river. In the hour before sunset, we hurry to pitch our tents and run down for a swim. A fish eagle plops midstream. Herons watch us undress on the beach, and behind them a backstop of hippos grunts in surprise as we enter the water. I keep an eye cocked for behemoths emerging from below as I take one of the most pleasurable, if wary, baths of my life.

The sun goes down, a red fist over the Rift wall. We light an oil lamp in the *paillote* and dine on fresh *Barbus* in tomato sauce. A breeze comes up to blow away the mosquitoes. Below us floats a pod of young hippos, gathered by their mothers into a circular nursery. Jack opens a liter of wine to toast our arrival. "Shall we wish for hominid?" he asks, raising his cup. "To hominid!" everyone shouts.

Working out of Queen Faviola's gazebo, the three principal investigators busy themselves at dawn the following morning creating a little village of our own. Word has gone out for one hundred and fifty workers. A runway has to be cleared for the airplane hired to carry away Diana, and the guano has to be shoveled out of the cottages, which are being commandeered for an archaeological "museum" and a carpentry workshop whose first assignment is the manufacture of chairs for us to sit on.

In the middle of unloading the Tout en Est truck, I ask everyone to pause for a photograph. The picture will come out fuzzy, and some important faces are missing, but this is the closest I get to a family photo of the Semliki Research Expedition. The attire is already bush: hiking boots, crusher hats, work shirts. Faces are unshaved, hair wild. With knives on their belts and boxes of toilet paper in their hands, expedition members look halfway between mean and green.

Present in the photo are Noel Boaz, hominid hunter; Alison
Brooks, Stone Age expert; Jack Harris, archaeologist; Diana Holt,
heiress with a lust for Acheulian hand axes; Jacques Verniers,
Belgian geologist; Jean Sept, plant food connoisseur; Kanimba
Misago, Zairean Iron Age specialist with a Ph.D. from the University of Hamburg; Leo Mastromatteo, Promethean mechanic
charged with keeping all our moving parts moving; Mugangu
Trinto-Enama, zoologist; and Pote Nghanza, plant ecologist. The
last two are carrying Winchester carbines. Completing the line-up
are six graduate students, three of them women, who are responsible for supervising daily work on the digs.

Missing from the photograph, but scheduled to arrive later in
the season, are John Yellen, archaeologist famous for collecting
Bushman rubbish; Raymonde Bonnefille, who studies fossil pol-
len to find out what was growing in Africa two million years
ago; Peter Williamson, Harvard snail man; Kathy Stewart, fish
bone enthusiast; David Helgren, geological haberdasher adept at
clothing the ancient landscape; and Frank Spencer, fossil feces
maven.

Providing off-site support for the expedition is another group
of people. Basil Cooke will calibrate the pig clock. This is the name
given to evolutionary changes in pigs' teeth, which have proved
quite helpful in dating archaeological sites. Frank Brown will handle paleomagnetism, and Jean de Heinzelin will do the geology.
Laboratories in France, Belgium, England, Canada, and the
United States will look at more specialized problems.

"Everyone here is trying to reconstruct the ancient environment
as it existed two million years ago," says Jack. Reconstructing ancient environments is obviously a complex business. Ever since
Raymond Dart plucked the fossilized skull of the Taung Child
from a South African lime kiln in 1924, Africa has come to be
viewed as our ancestral birthplace. Very few people initially believed that Dart's "child" had anything to do with human evolution.
They thought it was an ape at best. But over the years, as more
fossils were recovered from Africa's caves and weathered valleys,
most of us have come to assume that hominids — the evolutionary
line on which we come last — originated in Africa.

If hominids are defined as erect-walking primates, their African fossils can be divided into two basic types. The australopithecines, dating back over five million years, are the older, more primitive of the two. Younger by three million years are the larger-brained *Homo* species from which we are descended. Dart named his fossil *Australopithecus africanus*, which means "the southern ape of Africa." Its name aside, *A. africanus* is not an ape but a hominid. It forms a branch on our family tree, either as cousin or direct ancestor of *Homo sapiens*, and it appears there *after* our evolutionary split from the apes.

If australopithecines are not apes, are they human? On this question hinges the current debate between Richard Leakey and Donald Johanson. Leakey says no. The australopithecines are a side branch, a dead end separate from the *Homo* line. Johanson says yes and places *Australopithecus afarensis*—Lucy being the most famous member of that species—at the base of our family tree, where she gives rise to both the australopithecine and *Homo* lines.

While the phylogeny of early hominids is hotly debated, so too are the scenarios created to describe their behavior. When it comes to early (Wo)Man—why s/he adopted upright posture, whether s/he lived by hunting, foraging, or scavenging, and how s/he managed to juggle sex and family life—no version of the story remains uncontested. What all these scenarios have in common, though, is their political context. In the 1960s Man the Naked Ape, an accomplished hunter and cannibal, was thought to have cut a wide swath through his fellow creatures. By the 1970s Early Woman had converted to pacifism, become a vegetarian grazer on salads and nuts, and moved into the world's first matriarchal commune. In the 1980s a new being appeared: Man the Scavenger, a crafty opportunist living off other animals' labor.

"Oh, it's crazy," Mary Leakey told me in Nairobi, where we met while I was waiting for the Ishango team to assemble. "Opinion swings to one side and then goes *whoosh* right to the other side again. After Robert Ardrey argued that man was a bloody, violent character, he then became meek and mild, peace-loving, eating nuts and berries. And now he's not even supposed to have hunted."

The search for our prehistoric ancestors has been limited mainly to the eastern, drier side of Africa. But if human beings evolved from tree-climbing creatures, then why not look for basal hominids, otherwise known as Missing Links, on the western, wetter side of the continent? After all, this is where our cousins the great apes still reside. The only problem with this approach lies in the difficulty of pursuing it. Bones rot rather than fossilize in jungles, and the specimens that do exist are impossible to see for all the trees.

Lying on the edge of Zaire's central forest refuge, but endowed with eroded gullies and rock outcroppings not unlike those found in East Africa, the Semliki River valley struck Noel as the perfect solution to the problem. If an expedition into this little-explored part of Africa could discover bones and stones as old as those at Olduvai Gorge, or perhaps as old as the three-million-year-old Lucy, this would be a coup worthy of the great names in the profession. In the mid-1970s, as the idea took fire in his brain, Noel Boaz had no choice but to go west.

When *Science News* reported the Semliki Research Expedition's first major findings near Ishango in 1985—three hundred quartz tools and various animal bones and teeth dated at two to two and a half million years before the present—the magazine described them as having "been discovered in a rain forest in Zaire." They were actually discovered in the lovely savanna on which my tent is pitched a year later. But the rain forest lies a day's walk to the west, and who knows what the weather was like two million years ago?

The article goes on to describe how these tools are several hundred thousand years older than those found at Olduvai Gorge. Their age is rivaled only at two other sites in Africa, Omo and Hadar, both in Ethiopia. "They are definitely from the hand of man, with repetitive technological features characteristic of tools," said Jack at a Washington news conference announcing the discovery. "In studying them, we are sampling the behavior of the earliest humans." What Jack did not say was that one of his fellow investigators was disappointed by these findings. It was all well and good to sample their behavior, but what Noel Boaz really wanted was the earliest humans themselves.

We are trotting over the Lusso beds, the oldest ironstone and clay deposits on the shores of Lake Amin, when Jacques Verniers and

I are surprised to see Noel fall off a cliff. We look over the edge to find him hanging onto a tree halfway down to the lake below. He too is surprised and a bit shaken, although he manages a joke. "That's a nice sequence," he says, looking up at the path he carved during his rapid descent.

For ten hours we have been sprinting along the lakeshore, with Noel jumping into gullies and stooping to pick up anything that looks to his trained eye like fossilized bone or wood. Jacques, the team geologist, has been sent out as a kind of professional watchdog to shadow his colleague. The worst thing an expedition can have is fossils marked "provenance unknown." Stripped from their geological context, they are useless as anything other than souvenirs. So every time Noel picks up a bone, Jacques has been instructed to run over and remind him to map its coordinates and snap a Polaroid picture of the location.

While Noel takes notes, Jacques charges up and down the cliffs describing the six cycles of inundation that formed the lakeshore. He yells out the names of the layers. "Lusso beds! Semliki formation! *Basse terrasse*! Fossiliferous *zone brune*!" Listening to Jacques, I get the idea that the ground under my feet is not as solid as I thought. "Twenty million years ago the African continent flopped up, while part of the crust, along the lines of weakness, collapsed." This is his explanation of how the Rift Valley was formed.

Jacques reads the land as if it were a drama played by giants in the earth. Oceans invade. Volcanoes explode. Land masses collide to push up mountains. Each event leaves its trace on the earth's crust, which is nothing more than a layer cake of deposits marking different moments in history. Gray for volcanic eruptions. Sandy brown for lakes that evaporated. The work of distinguishing these deposits is known as stratigraphy. It is an old-fashioned science, requiring a lot of crawling around in the dirt, but no single task is more important to an anthropological expedition. If you get the wrong date on the fossiliferous *zone brune*, then all the bones coming out of it will also be misidentified.

A lanky young man with silver spectacles and a crest of brown hair rising from his head like a rooster comb, Jacques is a hard scientist. He counts everything. Water temperature, pebble size, soil color, the number of steps he takes. In 1985 he spent five months at Ishango, four of them alone, mapping the site. His car was broken. Since the Uganda border was closed, there was no fuel anyway. It was the rainy season, overcast and cold. The clay exposures along the river were treacherous. But Jacques went out every morning to climb the cliffs with his rock hammer and munsell chart for identifying twenty different shades of gray clay. After he had covered most of it on his hands and knees, the terrain was as familiar to him as his own body.

"I was going to do some more geology on this trip," Jacques says wistfully. "But everyone wants me to go with Noel and find out where the fossils come from. I guess I'll play the guide this year."

Rather than digging them up, which is a time-consuming process, paleoanthropologists generally pick their bones off the ground. "You don't go around digging holes looking for hominids," says Jack. "If that were your strategy, you'd be out of business pretty quick."

Finding exposed bones involves an element of chance, so anthropologists tend to be superstitious. Hence the talk of "Leakey's luck" and Donald Johanson's writing "feel good" in his notebook the morning he found Lucy. The geologists who chaperone them in the field are often surprised by their fellow researchers. Someone had to inform Johanson about the context of what he was looking at as he scurried around picking up anthropological detritus. In that case it was Maurice Taieb, a French geologist who had already spent four years exploring Ethiopia before he invited Johanson to join him at Hadar.

Taieb was initially appalled by the "unlimited ambition" of his American colleague. On their first day together in the field, "Donald began picking up bones with the firm idea that there had to be a hominid among them. He began thinking from that moment of the glory that would befall him on his return home. He also thought of the big budgets that numerous American foundations would give him without delay." Unfortunately, Johanson's first find, a hominid tibia, is now marked "provenance unknown" because it was collected before Taieb hove into sight.

Noel's hurry to pick up bones at Ishango is partly owing to the same ambition that drives his colleague, but it also stems from his peculiar experience in the Libyan Desert. Noel spent four years exploring the area around the old Byzantine fort at Sahabi, in a part of the desert "hot enough to fry you into a little grease spot. We had to quit by ten in the morning and lie in the shade." With a fossil record stretching back over five million years, the area is of great anthropological interest. But its secrets lie buried under a moving carpet of sand, and all one can do is wait for little windows into the past to open with the shifting winds.

At times it was infuriatingly like a peep show. A window would open to reveal a broken urn dropped by a Roman gypsum miner or a Paleolithic stone tool or a Second World War jerry can. And then the window would blow shut again. One morning while out surveying, Noel discovered the skeleton of an extinct animal halfway between an elephant and a horse. Thinking the location perfectly evident, he neglected to mark it, but when he returned a few hours later, the fossil was gone, buried back in the past and never to be recovered.

"I don't buy the theory that East Africa is the site of human origins," he says. "That just happens to be the only place we've looked. If you speculate that hominids emerged from the African forests, then along with the eastern edge as an area of emergence, you should also have one on the north, south, and west." But in spite of Noel's claims to the contrary, no one has found any significant remains of early humans anywhere but in eastern and southern Africa.

During one of the trips Boaz and de Heinzelin made together into the desert, de Heinzelin picked up a long bone at Sahabi that went unidentified until Noel carried it back to New York and convinced himself it was a hominoid clavicle — the shoulder bone from a member of the superfamily that includes both apes and humans. Noel believed he had discovered Lucy's grandmother, a really hoary fossil that could have ranked as one of the major finds of the century.

The Berkeley anthropologist Tim White, who may have been getting revenge for having his own mistakes corrected in print, accused Noel of mistaking a dolphin rib for a hominoid clavicle. What came to be known as the *Flipperpithecus* affair was one of the reasons why Noel was denied tenure at New York University, where he had taught for several years before leaving to found a natural history museum in his home town of Martinsville, Virginia. "I still think it looks more hominoid than dolphin," he says. "But my little scraps of bone from Sahabi aren't really anything to write home about. That's just the breaks. Hominoids were small animals who got chewed up a lot by carnivores."

Noel first got the idea of exploring Libya and Zaire in 1973 when he met de Heinzelin on the Omo dig in southern Ethiopia. Noel at the time was a lowly graduate student at Berkeley and de Heinzelin a senior geologist at the University of Ghent, but they shared a predilection for rising early and eating a bowl of corn flakes before heading into the field for the day. Omo and the other East African digs were getting all the publicity and money in the 1970s, but de Heinzelin assured his young colleague there were other rich claims to be staked in Africa, and he described the sites that he himself had worked twenty years earlier. The only problem was logistics. Both the Libyan Desert and the Western Rift Valley were hellishly difficult places to negotiate.

The 1970s were a time of tremendous excitement in African anthropology. Donald Johanson stumbled on Lucy and the First Family; Richard Leakey opened up the rich vein at Koobi Fora; and Mary Leakey uncovered "perhaps the most remarkable find I have made in my whole career," the 3.6-million-year-old hominid footprints at Laetoli. But the Golden Age was over by the end of the decade, when Ethiopia closed its borders to paleoanthropologists, Richard Leakey underwent a kidney transplant, and Mary Leakey retired from the field.

Ready to lead the charge out of East Africa into other, relatively unknown parts of the continent, Noel thought a move into Libya looked like a brilliant tactical maneuver. "In Libya we were hitting not only a new area, but also a new time horizon. We expected to find new things and we did," including a long list of vertebrate species never seen before in North Africa, or anywhere.

In the process of becoming a leader of anthropological expeditions, Noel developed what he calls his "Woolworth philosophy." "You want to run as many expeditions as possible to amortize the cost of your overhead. As long as no one else is working in the field, I might as well be out there doing it." He built up a stock of Land Rovers and other gear. He started flying rotating shifts of Earthwatch volunteers into Ishango, and he dreamed of buying an oceangoing boat large enough to sail from Virginia to Africa. "It would cut out air fare, freight charges, and theft, and you could hold two-week seminars on the passage over."

After exploring Libya and the upper Semliki River, Noel dreamed of leading an expedition into the *lower* Semliki. Racing through a canyon below the Ruwenzoris, this stretch of river is markedly different from its placid headwaters at Ishango. The lower Semliki, a gray stream filled with crocodiles, flows through a kind of tropical badlands. Waterfalls cascade off the edge of the Rift into the scorching, tsetse fly–infested valley. Cathedral spires and outcrops dating from the Miocene hold five- to fifteen-million-year-old fossils that should rightly be collected by helicopter.

The biologist Xavier Misonne, who descended into the lower Semliki in the 1950s, had come back out with a Miocene monkey tooth that he said was discovered below a hill called Ongoliba. If someone could get back to Ongoliba and find the skull that held that tooth, the world would have another chapter to read in the evolutionary history of apes and humans. "No one has ever found a Plio-Pleistocene ape tooth at any of the hominid sites in East Africa," says Noel, "because apes didn't live in East Africa. They lived here. The chance to find apes and hominids inhabiting the same area, and the ancestral figure to both of them, is unique to the lower Semliki."

Noel and his wife, Dorothy, who is also an anthropologist, and two graduate students set out to rediscover Ongoliba in 1982. They hiked along the Rift wall through gold mining country, where all the valleys have been gouged out by placer mines. Their passage was recorded by unseen drummers beating out the news. "There are no secrets in Zaire," someone told them. It was assumed that Boaz's group, like everyone else, was looking for gold. De Heinzelin had been trying to get to Ongoliba in 1960 when he was kidnaped during the Zairean civil war. He managed to escape and flee from the country, but no white person had been seen in the valley since then.

They dropped into canyons that were deathly still except for the buzzing of tsetse flies and the rustling of crocodiles disturbed in their midday naps. With so many flies and crocodiles it was impossible to camp along the Semliki. So they explored the area in forced marches that took them twenty miles up and down the Rift wall each day. Except for Noel, everyone's knees gave out. He wore the skin off his feet by wading downstream in boots filled with sand, but he pressed on to find the Ongoliba hill where Misonne reported finding his monkey tooth. They located Miocene mineral deposits in the area, but no fossils of any kind.

When Noel told de Heinzelin about his expedition, the geologist went to have a chat with his Belgian colleague. "No, it wasn't really at Ongoliba that I found the tooth," said Misonne. "It was in a nearby river valley whose name I can't remember. After all, it was thirty years ago."

Noel talked de Heinzelin into returning to Zaire with him in 1983, but they failed to reach the lower Semliki. Twice since then, Noel and one or two hardy companions have succeeded in dropping into the valley, and on the last of these visits they discovered Miocene deposits loaded with fossils. Though it may be worthy of Noel's hero Henry Stanley, hit-and-run fossil collecting is not the kind of research that gets financed by the National Science Foundation, who prefer a more corporate, cerebral approach to scientific problems. His friends urged Noel to retreat upstream to Ishango. The deposits were younger, but if an expedition succeeded there, he could eventually work his way back downstream to the old fossils that interest him most as a participant in what he calls "the hominid game."

Noel bought the argument. He allied himself with academically prestigious colleagues and became a team player on a new expedition to the younger, southern end of the valley. The National Science Foundation awarded him twenty percent of their spring 1986 budget in anthropology, and made him co-principal investigator on the decade's largest paleoanthropological expedition to Africa. But unless I am mistaken, I sometimes saw Noel casting wistful glances downstream a hundred miles into the valley where the old, the really old fossils lay.

Waking one morning to the buzz of the expedition's motorboat, I crawl out of my sleeping bag and look toward the river. A shoeless Boaz and a stern-looking Verniers are nosing downstream through a pod of hippos. I listen to the motor misfiring in one cylinder until the boat disappears around a bend in the river.

There has been a divorce in the family. Father Jack and half the children have moved ten miles downstream to a new camp at the Senga rapids, where he is excavating the site at which he found his stone tools the previous summer. Alison has stayed at Ishango, where she is reexamining de Heinzelin's cliff and an older, Middle Stone Age horizon nearby. It is not really a divorce, as the split was foreseen, but the esprit de corps of getting to Ishango has given way to the sober reality of exhuming bones and stones on the shores of Lake Idi Amin Dada.

A few days later I, too, follow Jack downstream to Senga, where I pitch my tent under a thorn tree and walk out to find him in his hole directing three graduate students and ten Zairean laborers in the fine art of archaeological excavation. A red-bearded New Zealander wearing shorts and wool socks, Jack looks like an early hominid in hiking boots. His hands are bloodied around the knuckles from overzealous digging, and his chest is bronzing in the sun. At first glance, one might think this was a construction crew preparing the subsoil for a two-car garage. But then why is everyone down on his hands and knees crawling around with dental picks and toothbrushes? Every bone and stone chipped out of the purple, iron-rich soil gets dusted, numbered, measured, and mapped in three dimensions.

Jack runs a tight ship. He rises at dawn and jumps in the river at quarter of six for a bath. He breakfasts at six and then works without a break until midday, when he sits down to the first of his two sardine meals; this one is plain sardines. For dinner he might dress them up with a plate of spaghetti.

The only two things Jack does in excess are smoke and work. Otherwise, he is rock-steady and fair to friend and foe alike—or would be, except that he has no foes, which is exceedingly rare in his profession. Two thirds of the stone tools over two million years old found in Africa have been excavated by Jack, and he has dug at all three of the sites from which they came—Omo, Hadar, and Senga. When someone wants an archaeologist with a good eye for vintage stone and the meticulous brawn capable of retrieving it, they phone Jack.

John William Kendal Harris got interested in anthropology when he was a New Zealand schoolteacher assigned to handle "discipline problems" in the lower grades. This meant students from Maori and Pacific Island cultures. Unable to get an advanced degree in New Zealand, he left to study anthropology at the University of California at Berkeley. In the late 1960s Berkeley was in the grip of Africa fever, and Jack soon found himself following Professor Clark Howell out to Ethiopia to work on his dig at Omo. Howell, who recruited experts from every branch of the anthropological sciences as they were then practiced, can be credited with inventing the team approach to paleoanthropology. The Omo expedition was also responsible for training many of the scientists still working in Africa today.

From Omo, Jack carried his rock hammer across East Africa to work with Richard Leakey at Koobi Fora, with Mary Leakey at Laetoli, and with Johanson and Taieb at Hadar. In all the photos of remarkable fossil finds from those years, Jack is in the background chipping away. After digging up the two-and-a-half-million-year-old stone tools at Hadar that are currently the oldest in the world, he was scheduled to excavate another Ethiopian site in 1982, and lead his own expedition south of Hadar, when he got trapped in the Addis Ababa Hilton and never reached the field. The following summer Jack stayed home in Milwaukee and painted the trim on his house. That was the first time in fifteen years he had missed a field season in Africa. Then Noel phoned looking for someone to dig holes in Zaire . . .

Like Noel, Jack is intrigued by origins. "If you're asking questions about the ape-human split, you have to be working in rocks older than three to five million years old. In Ethiopia the rocks go back seven million years. In the lower Semliki they go back six. There are very few places in the world with rocks this old, which means there are very few places where you can look for the possible ancestors to apes and humans, what we call missing links."

But the younger rocks at Ishango hold secrets of their own. "The next crucial time period comes between two and three million years ago. That's when you see the emergence of bigger-brained hominids of the genus *Homo* and the making of artifacts. There's a dramatic change in climate to drier conditions and more marked seasonality, which brings about a change in diet. I look on the advent of stone tools in the archaeological record as a symptom of dietary change."

"This was a real shot in the dark for me," Jack says of his decision to follow Noel to Ishango. "No one had ever excavated a paleontological site in the Western Rift Valley. Everyone thought our survey last year would turn out negative, but finding the tools really extended the province of early hominids. The artifacts are a clear sign of penetration into the area."

The way Jack talks about them, stone tools become "markers on the landscape," clues for reconstructing the behavior of our ancestors. "Gone are the days when you can get money to go out, dig up artifacts, and put dates on them," he says. "The field is now problem oriented. We're 'using' tools for what they can tell us about diet and movement over the landscape and the environmental changes that led the hominid line in the direction it took. This is all part of the story about the unique sets of behavior that we recognize as human."

"It's obvious no one comes to visit you for your food," says Peter Williamson, staring at a plate of sardines.

"No," says Jack. "They come for the bones off my table."

A mustachioed Englishman whose ruddy face has gone blotchy from an overdose of tropical sun, Williamson has flown out to Africa to look at the Semliki fossil snails and clams. He goes about his job with great gusto, spending the day collecting specimens that later get displayed on the dinner table. "Look at this beautiful *Pseudobovaria murayana!*" he exclaims, pointing to a clamshell with a toothy edge. Holding up a smaller variety, he suggests that Jack try cooking some of its still-living relatives in spaghetti sauce.

Williamson uses fossil mollusks to tell him what the weather was like two million years ago. He also uses them to distinguish what are known as speciation events—those moments when the geological clock ticks out the birth or death of species. From Williamson's perspective, the Semliki River valley is a snail graveyard. Their shells outnumber all the other fossils put together by a hundred to one, or more. Everywhere he looks in the exposed sediments he sees white snail shells packed into layers. These are die-offs, the remains of species that failed to adapt in a world that was getting drier, wetter, more acidic, or more basic. But whatever twist the environment has thrown at them, snails have always managed to evolve new species that could step in and survive where their predecessors failed.

Snails are thought to be slow-moving creatures. But what impresses Williamson about them is their evolutionary speediness. If the geological record snoozes through long periods of stasis, it also witnesses moments that by comparison look like Baryshnikov leaping across the stage of the Paris Opera. "Evolutionary explosions happen when the conditions are right. As a result of these punctuated events, the geometry of the snails changes. You get all sorts of weird patterns and shapes. In two places in the Lake Turkana basin, I think I've documented a rapid change like this taking place in as short a period of time as five to fifty thousand years."

While working with Richard Leakey at Koobi Fora, Williamson found evidence of a "rain forest pulse" in an area that today is desert. "Just when hominids are sorting out their evolutionary options, West African rain forest snails start appearing in the East African geological record. It looks to me like the climate changed and the rain forest zipped over to Turkana, before it retreated again."

Williamson gets excited when he finds evidence for a similar "punctuated event" in Jack's Lusso beds. "The invertebrates take on all sorts of strange geometric shapes and then die off. The same thing happens at roughly the same time in the Lake Turkana basin, and if the evidence falls together, you might be able to verify some sort of pan-African desiccation that took place two and a half million years ago."

Williamson's findings offer the best proof yet for Niles Eldredge and Stephen Gould's theory of punctuated equilibrium, but not everyone buys the argument. "There are about forty papers on my work in Turkana," says Williamson, "most of them attacking me." By allowing for revolutionary change in nature, the theory has a leftist tinge, and most scientists still prefer to leave the *r* out of evolution. Noel is one of them, which leads to some rousing debates at the dinner table. The first sticking point between the scrappy Englishman and the equally emphatic Virginian concerns the nature of the evidence itself.

"The hominid fossil record is one of the *worst* places to look if you want to say anything significant about evolutionary process," says Williamson. "There are more anthropologists than specimens. How many skulls do you have? Five, or ten at most? That's not a serious sample, is it?"

Noel admits that "all the hominid specimens put together would just about cover this table, but there are still enough to generalize from."

Williamson chuckles. "We have eight parameters, all mathematically controlled and modeled, for looking at mollusk evolution, with millions of samples stretched over eons. There's no such agreed-on system for measuring human change, a skull being far harder to map than a mollusk. So the discussion, by definition, becomes qualitative and judgmental. That's why you chaps are always attacking each other."

Noel counters by restating an argument against punctuated equilibrium that he published in the British journal *Nature*, which is also where Williamson publishes his snail data. According to Noel, the most parsimonious way to interpret the evidence is by the old Darwinian model, which sees evolutionary change as slowly accreting over long periods of time.

While Jack slips off to bed, the continuing argument reminds me of a visit I paid to Tim White in his Berkeley office. Decorating the wall was a full-color, six-page foldout from the *National Geographic*, entitled "Faces from the Past . . . Lining Up the Fossil Evidence." Pictures of skulls culled from the bone rooms of the world marched across the page. Looking closely at the layout, I noticed a lot of plaster and acrylic filling in for the missing parts. There was a crucial gap, for example, between the face and the cranium of *Australopithecus afarensis*, Donald Johanson's famous find.

Of the thousands of hominid fossils retrieved since the first skulls were accidentally found in Germany's Neanderthal Valley in 1856, most are isolated teeth. On top of this great mound of molars sit a few long bones and mandibles, and a skull or two. "When you look for decent whole crania," said White, "there aren't many all the way across the board. We chose the best ones for the *Geographic* layout, but if you're looking for typical specimens, you'd be hard pressed to find any second-stringers."

The *Geographic* photo shows nine species in two genera evolving through time in an orderly fashion, from the small-brained, large-faced australopithecines to the small-faced, noble-brained *Homo sapiens*. It looked to me like a tidy display until White enumerated the scant evidence used to distinguish these genera and species. "For *Australopithecus africanus* we have two fairly complete adults, some broken specimens, and one child. For *A. afarensis* there's one cranial reconstruction and other parts. For *A. boisei*, there are two whole crania, three or four halves, and five other facial fragments. For the classical form of *Homo erectus* there are only one or two crania from Java with faces."

White picked up my notebook and sketched a family tree, while giving a running commentary on evolutionary theory as we know it today. "You've got a form called *habilis* which presumably, somehow, question mark—whether it's stepwise or straight—gives rise to *erectus* and so forth into *sapiens*. To be perfectly honest, you can't identify a point in there where we don't need more fossils, and we're not going to get them in my lifetime."

White's tree begins at the bottom of the page with *A. afarensis* as the trunk. A variety of alternative evolutionary trajectories shoot up from there to the top branches of human life. The drawing is peppered with so many question marks, diversions, switchbacks, and alternative routes that the middle of it has turned into a gray swirl, out of which grins a little fossil skull, species unknown.

Mornings at Senga are misty and cool before the clouds burn off and the day heats up into the nineties. The air is thick with the noise of birds singing in the trees and geese honking on the river. From downstream comes the muted roar of the Senga rapids. It is the dry season, but every third night a storm blows over. The rain falls in sheets before moving off to hit the Rift wall, then bounces back for a second pass over camp an hour later.

Toward the end of the season, when Jack starts exploring other potential excavations, he leaves his graduate students and Zairean workers in charge of the Senga dig. Schoolteachers moonlighting on their summer vacation, the Zaireans are paid a dollar a day and all the cassava they can eat. For many of them, this is their second season digging for Jack. They have become quite expert by now at field archaeology, although they have their own idea of what the work is about. First of all, since no one in his right mind would camp in savanna filled with lions, they spend much of the night singing and banging on pans before falling asleep huddled around a fire.

Excavating bones—even those that have lain in the ground for two million years—is a serious and potentially risky business. "You can't just go out and dig up the bones of your ancestors," says Bunduki Paluku, the head excavator. "You have to have special authorization from the chief, although in this case, we've indirectly consulted him by getting authorization from the state.

"We won't find anything if they don't want us to, so we invoke the spirit of our ancestors to aid us in the work. They give us the vigor to go out in the morning and dig. They allow us to remove the bones intact. We have a prayer, a secret incantation, that we use to talk to them."

When I ask him about the prayer, Bunduki says, "I can't tell you what it is, or it will evaporate. All I can say is that the ancestors give their answers in dreams or in signs. For example, fog in the morning is a good sign."

Dressed in shorts and T-shirts emblazoned with slogans like "Salisbury Mobil" and "Siemens Ltd.," the Zaireans, as they wield their rock hammers, keep up a nonstop running commentary in Swahili, Kinande, French, and their newly acquired English. When they run out of things to talk about, they break into responsive song, filling in the women's parts in falsetto.

One day they engage me in a long discussion about the injustice of their salaries, which are sixty zaires a day. A bottle of local banana wine costs eighty zaires. A goat costs twenty-two hundred zaires. A fish, on the other hand, goes for as little as seven zaires. These are official prices in the cash economy, but everyday life in Zaire is actually conducted in a gray market based on barter, truck farms, foraging, gifts, bribes, poaching, and other petty tergiversations. The men had gone on strike at the beginning of the season and had succeeded in boosting their salaries from forty to sixty zaires. As this was sixty zaires more than anyone else in the valley was paying, when Jack told them it was his final offer, they went back to work.

The work itself is meticulous, with every object of any conceivable interest getting measured and mapped in place with an alidade, stadia rod, and compass. Objects standing on edge reveal evidence of trampling. A group of objects oriented in one direction indicates deposition by water. Water also has a tendency to size sort, leaving big things behind while carrying the small ones away. If one can prove they are "behaviorally associated," bones lying next to stone tools are the best news of all.

Digging alongside the Zaireans are Jack's three graduate students. One is a former model trying to get her life together. Another comes to work in a string bikini that provokes a strong reaction from the men. *"Crocodeel! Crocodeel!"* they squeal in high-pitched voices, before falling to the ground with laughter. They are imitating the student's first sighting of a crocodile in the Semliki River, or perhaps alluding to certain subliminal urges of their own. In either case, the men are fond of their bikinied assistant, and one of them pays her the compliment of saying she looks like his sister.

Dug in three-centimeter layers called spits, the excavation is beginning to produce a nice collection of horns, femurs, small bones, tools, fossilized feces, and quartz flakes. The site itself is littered with string, nails, plastic bags, tags, dustpans, and chisels. "As you can see," says Jack, "you have to be patient in this line of work."

Left standing in the middle of the hole is an unexcavated square of earth called a baulk, which is being preserved as a reference point. "Once you dig a site, it's gone forever," he says. "So you want to leave some of it in place. But for all we know there could be hominid under there."

When not working on his dig, Jack's students are all engaged in something called actualistic studies. This is the experimental wing of archaeology. Trying to find modern analogues for the behavior of early hominids, researchers begin with a sympathetic act of imagination. If I went out on the savanna and tried to live like a naked ape, what foods could I forage, kill, or scavenge? Where would I drop my tools and bones, and what would they look like when someone dug them up in two million years?

These experiments have done a good job of tightening the rules of evidence in anthropology. As Mary Leakey told me in Nairobi, "It always seemed to me that if you get a concentration of broken-up bones and stone tools in a restricted area, it's reasonable to assume they're associated. But other people don't believe that. They think it's fortuitous." Leakey called these concentrations of bones and stones "living floors," and the behavior they recorded was that of a "home base" where hominids congregated to share food. Her successors at Olduvai Gorge are now attacking her ideas as "wildly inaccurate."

Tim White, Mary's former assistant at Laetoli, tells me, "Living floors will never again be seen as Boy Scout camps where all the little hominids shared their food around the fire. They didn't even have fires in those days, so who knows what they sat around! Forget it. These land surfaces are going to be seen as places where hominids and carnivores and geological processes combined in making a signature, and it's difficult for archaeologists to know what the hominid contribution to that signature was. I think for a lot of these sites, we're up against a wall."

"We're asking simple questions," says Jack, "but there are real problems with the inferences and sorts of jumps we make, which can be highly speculative. The whole field is going through a revolution. Ten years ago, based on nothing but circumstantial evidence, we would have said immediately that Senga was an important site for indicating the hominid diet. Now we're a lot more careful about making these assumptions, and we put the evidence through a whole series of interpretive screens."

One of Jack's students, Martha Tappen, specializes in taphonomy, the study of bones and how they get deposited and preserved. She maps lion kills on the savanna and watches where the refuse collects. The bones scatter so fast that in a year only one in ten can be recovered. This has led one researcher in the field to posit what she calls the "killer tree" hypothesis. Anthropological sites in Africa owe their existence not to the butchering of animals, but to the fact that carnivores like to sit under shade trees while gnawing on scavenged bones.

Randy Bellomo, another of Jack's students, spends a lot of time burning holes in the savanna to simulate archaic hearths. Unlike

Tim White, Jack believes that early hominids did have fires to sit around at night. He thinks the human control of fire goes a long way back in the archaeological record, and his hearth experiments are designed to help people identify the evidence.

"Hominids were relatively defenseless, which means they must have spent a lot of time up in the trees. I argue that it wasn't until they had fire that they could come down and secure places on the ground. You find the first traces of fire a million and a half years ago with *Homo erectus*. A million years ago *erectus* radiated out of Africa to colonize the cooler, temperate parts of the world. One of the burning questions in anthropology is what made this species so successful. I think it was fire.

"Fire changed the biological clock of humans. Before that we were blundering around in the dark. It extended daylight and altered the human psyche. When hominids could sit around the fire and exchange ideas on the day's happenings, that's when you see the development of language. Unfortunately, vocal cords don't preserve, so the evidence is necessarily fragmentary."

The interest of Jack and his students in fires and foraging and the movement of bones over the landscape will culminate in the Great Goat Roast. An animal will be butchered with stone tools, cooked over a fire, gnawed to the bone, and flung from camp in a carefully controlled experiment meant to simulate archaic practices. This will also be our first good meal in weeks.

It is not unusual for scientists to eat their subjects. A taste of ant or monkey gives that extra perspective on the data. I am not suggesting that anthropologists studying archaic humans will sneak a taste of flesh, but one day they will probably feel the urge to *act* like archaic humans. It was Louis Leakey, after mastering the art of making stone tools and using them to butcher animals, who first popularized this kind of anthropological dressing up.

Alison and the rest of the Ishango camp drive over to Senga for the day. They have scoured the valley for delectable things to eat, finding a lot of fish and some fresh vegetables. Leo provides a goodly quantity of *kindingi*, or cassava liquor, and *kasiks*, fermented banana wine. Jack knaps some quartz cobbles into stone tools. A fire is lit for cooking the *brochettes de chèvre*, and the sacrificial animal is led to his tree.

Two Zairean excavators have volunteered to experiment with Jack's stone tools. After the goat is strung up and slaughtered in the modern fashion—with a knife—the men begin butchering it with large quartzite blades. For the tight spots around the tail and head, they switch to the smaller flakes. Jack times their progress. It takes twenty minutes to cut the meat off the ribs with a stone tool. Ten minutes with a knife. When the job is finished a couple of hours later, the stone tools still have an edge to them.

"Have you done the deed?" asks Peter Williamson, poking his head out of his tent.

"We did it in the name of science," says Jack.

"Bloody butchery, if you ask me," says Williamson. "But do you mind saving me the liver?"

We spend most of the day feasting on roasted goat and *kindingi*. Later in the afternoon the bones are carried down to a sandy stretch along the river. Here Jack and his students have dug three hearths that are wired with digital thermometers to record their burning temperatures. The hearths are piled with acacia branches and various antelope and buffalo ribs scavenged off the savanna. We top the display with our stone tools and goat roast remnants to recreate a Plio-Pleistocene butchery site on its way to becoming a "living floor."

The riverbank is littered with carcasses and tools. As the sun goes down over the Rift wall, Jack asks if everyone is ready and lights the first match. In the evening chill, with the dew beginning to settle and fresh bones on the fires, it will take more than one match to get this prehistoric scene properly lit. A bare-chested Jack picks up a burning branch and starts jumping among the fires. Stoking them furiously and looking for all the world like a latter-day *erectus* drunk on burnt flesh and *kindingi*, he yells to me over the flames, "This should put some meat on your story!"

While Noel researches the bones and Jack the old stone tools, the rest of the work at Ishango is left to Alison Brooks. She intends to excavate the major sites and sort out the archaeological record for the last two million years, from the Early Stone Age to the development of agriculture. A Harvard magna cum laude, Alison began studying archaeology at a time when the subject, at least in the United States, was reserved for men interested in hacking their way through South American jungles. "In 1965 there were no women anthropologists on the faculty at Harvard, and none of the men who worked in the New World would accept a woman in the field. A mix of exploration, adventure, and treasure hunting, it was a terribly macho thing."

The daughter of a Harvard classics professor who later became undersecretary of the Smithsonian Institution, Alison started college thinking she would be a classicist like her father. Then she jumped from Far Eastern studies to medieval history and literature before settling on astrophysics. "Astrophysics has a lot of parallels to digging up the past. You're digging up past light structures in the sky, and it's probably equally useless.

"Then I went through a sophomore crisis, and being in calculus and astrophysics wasn't recommended for someone who was having trouble getting out of bed in the morning. So I thought I'd try a course in anthropology. It looked as if it could encompass all my interests in languages, the Near East, classics, medieval history, and literature. Even the astrophysics would come in handy."

At the age of nineteen she told her parents she was going to Syria for the summer to join a team of archaeologists excavating Paleolithic rock shelters. "As you can imagine, they were appalled." She went off to discover that "suddenly I had my own rock shelter to excavate and a crew of seven Arabs, all of whom had strange ideas about a nineteen-year-old girl telling them what to do. But we worked out an arrangement."

Alison traveled to other digs in the Near East, where she met the two great women archaeologists then working in the field, Diana Kirkbride, who was famous for doing her surveys by camel, and Kathleen Kenyon, who was excavating Jerusalem. "I was absolutely enchanted," she says of the day she spent with Kenyon in Jerusalem. "I saw for the first time how exciting it could be to work as a scientist in the field making new discoveries." These encounters made Alison think there might be room for her in the profession after all.

She was headed back to the Near East in 1967 when the Six-Day War broke out, marking the first of many expeditions she has had to cancel for political reasons. Alison traveled instead to

France's Dordogne Valley, which holds the world's greatest concentration of Paleolithic remains. There she helped excavate one of the two hundred Ice Age rock shelters that have been discovered around the town of Les Eyzies. This one had escaped the attention of previous archaeologists because it lay under a medieval barn filled with four centuries of manure.

Her Harvard adviser assigned her Aurignacian tools as a Ph.D. topic. Thirty thousand years old, these are the first tools in the European Stone Age to reveal the stylistic details of a particular culture. Alison devised systems for quantifying these details and began working her way through thirty thousand stone tools housed in the Les Eyzies museum. "There was an enormous amount to do, and I didn't have a wife," she says, referring to advice she received early in her graduate student career. The spouse of an illustrious professor, who herself had been trained as an anthropologist, had told her, "My dear, it takes two people to make one archaeologist."

Her adviser was convinced that marriage and archaeology were incompatible for a woman. At the end of her first year in the field, when Alison told him she was marrying John Yellen, "the man just about died. In fact, he had a stroke shortly thereafter, and I've always thought I had something to do with it. He threatened to remove me from the site. He refused to speak to me. He said if I was getting married, I should go teach kindergarten."

John Yellen was involved in the Harvard Kalahari project, a team effort to study the Bushmen before their way of life disappeared forever. If someone wants to know how humans have lived throughout most of their time on earth, it makes sense to look at present-day hunters and gatherers. What the Harvard people found when they got to the Kalahari "set the anthropological world back on its collective ear," says Yellen. "We had it all wrong. To be a hunter and gatherer wasn't that bad after all. They didn't work that hard, even in this land of thorns. For an adult it came to less time than a nine-to-five office worker puts in on the job. They lived a long time, too."

Alison made her first trip to Africa with Yellen in 1968. "It was an extraordinary experience. Here were hunters and gatherers living a kind of life we hadn't been able to imagine before. It seemed very important to study if one was going to understand the Stone Age."

She returned to France for three and a half years and left with her dissertation half finished to teach at George Washington University. It took her another ten years to write the other half. But in the meantime, Africa had got a hold on her imagination. In 1975 Alison returned to the Kalahari for what would be the first of ten field seasons.

Every aspect of !Kung Bushman life, from story telling to trance, was put under the Harvard microscope. Yellen and Brooks studied their patterns of settlement. Yellen had the good fortune to meet a !Kung tracker with total recall of the desert landscape. The man led him on a walk backward through time, taking him to the site of every hunting camp he had occupied since the 1940s. This "neat, almost laboratory situation" allowed Yellen to recover artifacts that had weathered in the Kalahari for five, ten, fifteen, thirty years. By observing "how things fall apart," he could graph a model of site formation that arced "back into the true archaeological past."

That was where Alison began. As she excavated a dozen sites up to a hundred thousand years old, the Kalahari offered her direct continuity between past and present, with the Stone Age ending here only about a hundred years ago. "It was a perfect laboratory for testing various models about what an archaeological site represents. The Bushmen aren't the ancient hominids of Africa, but you can study their behavior for adaptations to the African landscape, and extrapolate backward to reconstruct what hominid behavior might have been like."

Alison also developed a theory about the placement of archaeological sites. "I'm interested in locational strategies, in trying to figure out in advance where the sites should be, and then going out to see if I can find them. Bushmen living in a home base for two months will leave no permanent trace on the landscape. Even their six-month camps leave no more than a smear. Only their hunting venues, occupied repeatedly over the last ten thousand years or more, persist in the archaeological record."

These observations led her to conclude that archaeological sites "are not going to be located in good places to live, but in good places to extract things from. People come back to rock shelters, lookout posts, the tops of ridges, and narrow gullies useful for trapping animals. These are the sites that exist as magnets on the landscape."

During her time in the Kalahari, Alison had to juggle her personal and professional lives. She went to the desert one year with her fourteen-month-old daughter, and another year she took her eighteen-month-old son. Her children grew up speaking sentences made out of !Kung verbs and English nouns. "My daughter was carried off during the day, tied to the back of a !Kung woman gathering edible plants. I would leave things for her to eat at home and return to find that nothing had been touched. I complained that my daughter wasn't being fed, and the woman protested vehemently, 'Of course she's being fed!' That's when I discovered she was being breast fed along with all the other children."

On a typical morning I find Alison sitting under the queen's *paillote* organizing everyone's schedule before getting on to her own work. A soft-spoken woman with a curly thatch of blond-brown hair, she makes !Kung clicks to herself while reviewing the expedition's accounts. A fisherman arrives with a big *Barbus* for sale. A delegation of workers comes to complain about a shortfall in their cassava ration. A sick graduate student needs doctoring for a stomach ailment. A researcher sorting berries wants to know if the same varieties can be found in the Kalahari. Jack drives into camp looking for extra tins of sardines and coffee. "Jack," she says, "your rates of consumption are alarming. Are you sure you're not feeding everyone in the park?"

Later in the morning we walk along the bluff to de Heinzelin's original Ishango site, which is being reexcavated. Alison discusses a problem with Catherine and Leith Smith, the students leading the dig. How are they going to keep three-ton hippos from falling in the hole? A thorn-tree barrier seems the easiest solution, but the hippos have been coming up at night and scent-marking it with excrement. "We'll just have to do some extra digging every morning," Alison concludes.

When de Heinzelin excavated Ishango in the 1950s, he found a wealth of fossils and tools that he dated at roughly nine thousand years before the present. Among these artifacts was a bone handle with a quartz blade inserted in the tip. De Heinzelin speculated that this might have been used for engraving or tattooing or even writing. Some of the many harpoons he discovered were marked with a base-ten number system that showed knowledge of multiplication and prime numbers. Because these objects predated by several thousand years the mathematics developed in dynastic Egypt, de Heinzelin argued that the true source of Western civilization lay at the headwaters of the Nile.

"Because the Egyptian number system was a basis and a prerequisite for the scientific achievements of classical Greece, and thus for many of the developments in science that followed, it is even possible that the modern world owes one of its greatest debts to the people who lived at Ishango," he wrote in an article published in *Scientific American*. De Heinzelin produced a carbon-14 date for the Ishango tools of twenty-one thousand years before the present. This was way ahead of similar stages of development in Europe, and no one at the time was willing to credit black Africans with being more advanced than their northern counterparts. So de Heinzelin cut the figure by two thirds. At the risk of offending him, Alison was going to use new techniques to redate Ishango, which she thought as old as his original numbers.

Alison sets to work surveying the dig with a transit, but first the equipment has to be calibrated. It is a new Leitz model, modified for work in the southern hemisphere. The needle of a normal compass, when carried below the equator, will drag on the bottom of the case. This can be corrected by weighting the southern end of the needle. "I don't know who put this weight on," says Alison, unscrewing the case, "but they must have thought I was going to the South Pole."

While she fixes her compass, I sit down with a collection of stone tools borrowed from the Ishango "museum" in one of the old royal cottages. For more than two million years humans made all their tools out of stone. In fact, the Stone Age represents all but one one-thousandth of the time we have lived on earth, so I was surprised to learn that stone tools were not recognized as such until the 1800s. Prior to that these strange objects were thought to have been forged by thunderbolts or dropped ready-made from the heavens.

I spread a tool kit around me, a nice sequence of cultural styles ranging from Acheulian hand axes to Levallois flakes. Like most of the names in Stone Age archaeology, these come from France. Hand axes were first found at Saint Acheul, and the flakes were discovered while digging the Levallois metro stop in Paris.

"It's impossible to lay out an irrefutable sequence showing how one style develops from another," Alison warns me. "The Oldowan and Acheulian overlap. Middle Stone Age people made Late Stone Age tools. Fast learners were a hundred thousand years ahead of their time, and in general the African scale is two to three times more advanced than the European." Still, it looks to my untrained eye as if people got a lot better at making their tools as time went on.

I pick up an Oldowan chopper, a heavy mass of rock that fits securely into the palm of the hand. My thumb rests in a groove on the ventral face, while my fingers find a nice grip on the front. This is definitely a tool, well used, well made, with a ready heft and pleasing practicality. This stuff is old, and it is human.

I finger my way through a succession of spheroids, hand axes, and choppers until I come to some large flakes. The flakes reveal further proof that these objects are tools. Their upper surfaces are flared into bulbs of percussion, with radiating lines of force that reveal the direction from which they were struck. These discrete bulges under the point of contact make me realize that stone is soft enough to be worked by human hands.

The flakes give way to smaller tools such as triangular points and backed blades, designed with platforms on which my fingers can rest away from the cutting edge. This was a nice idea for someone to have come up with a hundred thousand years ago. By the time I get down to the microliths, geometrics, and crescents, the technology has miniaturized itself—like the computer-age jump from vacuum tubes to transistors.

I pick up a microlith to get the feel of it. If there was any doubt lingering in my mind as to whether these pieces of stone are actually tools, the matter is settled when I cut myself. Thousands of years after someone made it, the blade on this quartz knife is sharp enough to draw blood.

A few days later, Alison, her excavators, and I drive downstream to her Middle Stone Age dig at Katanda. We walk the last few hundred feet to an imposing cliff high above the Semliki. At the bottom of the slope lies the purplish red rock of the Lusso beds. Above this rise layers of gravel, sandstone, calcite, and ironstone. To someone trained in decoding them, these exposures can be read like the lifeline of an ancient hand. Here we see sweet rains and a pleasant lakeshore life. Here volcanoes exploded and people close to you died. Up near the top of the series, Alison has found a goodly stash of Middle Stone Age tools and fossil bones.

"Sites of this age with tools and fossils together are as rare as hen's teeth," she says. "A lot of people collect things off the ground and call them Middle Stone Age, but I'm interested in isolating a living floor and looking at the spatial relationships *between* objects. This site should tell me something about how it was occupied over a long period of time."

From our cliffside perch, we look west across the river to the Rift wall. Behind us, over the savanna, rise the Bukuku Mountains and the Katwe volcanoes, which merge into the snow-capped Ruwenzoris. Also remarkable are the bones and stones dating from one hundred and fifty thousand to fifty thousand years ago that are lying all around us on the ground. "This is a crucial period in history, as it marks the origins of *Homo sapiens sapiens*," says Alison. "The Acheulian stands on the far side of the divide, the Middle Stone Age on this side. The important question is, how did we get from one side to the other? I think the answer is going to come from Africa."

The workers shoulder their tools onto a ledge hanging over the river and divide up into teams of diggers and sifters. "What I wouldn't give for a bulldozer to take off the top of this hill," says Alison, who has to settle for fourteen men with shovels. *Giwe mingi mifupa kidoga* — a lot of stones, not too many bones — is their name for the site. Today's excitement comes from the discovery of "human features" — two circles of dark earth that might be a pair of archaic hearths. "This could be headline news," says Alison, who calms herself by thinking of alternative hypotheses. Maybe the circles were made by hippo footprints or elephant dung?

If Alison's site is recommended for its view, it loses points for the windless heat that rises off it in the afternoon, when the thermometer reads a hundred degrees. A blue haze hangs in the valley like a shower curtain. To keep from having to stand in the sun holding a plumb bob, I sit under an acacia tree and pretend to write. I slept badly last night. Big waves like ocean surf were crashing on the lakeshore. This was added to the usual night sounds: yapping hyenas, panting leopards, coughing lions, and hippos grazing so close to my tent that I could hear their lips squeaking up the grass from the savanna.

I was also kept awake by a question that still worries me as I sit under my acacia tree. How am I going to get out of here? The pilot who was supposed to swoop down onto our runway and carry off Diana Holt never came. He is scheduled to touch down next week with a fresh load of anthropologists, but what if he misses us again? Diana was eventually driven out of the valley in a Land Rover, but no one is going to spare a vehicle to carry a writer out of the field. Now that I am sitting on top of their bones, the ancestors who had been so coy about my coming seem to be equally stubborn about letting me go.

With no airplane in sight, I eventually hitch a ride up the Rift wall on a fish truck and then travel north to an airstrip large enough for a weekly flight to Goma. After landing back under the gray volcano, I scurry across the Rwandan border and make my way by bush taxi down to Kigali, where I catch another once-a-week flight to Nairobi. Retracing my steps out of Africa, I keep thinking, "It's true. Ishango really was *un des plus grandioses sites de la planète.*"

The ancestors by the end of the summer had begun smiling on everyone. Jack found a pig jaw sitting in the middle of his excavation and other archaic bones with what appeared to be tool cut marks. Noel added a healthy number of fossils, including some new species, to the expedition's thirty thousand samples of Semliki fauna. The redug Ishango site revealed a human jaw, three skull fragments, and other good evidence that it really is three times as old as de Heinzelin reported. Alison uncovered an Early Stone Age horizon under her Middle Stone trench at Katanda, and it too disclosed a nice collection of bones and stone tools.

No one went back to Ishango the following year, but in the summer of 1988 the Semliki Research Expedition returned in force to the shores of Lake Idi Amin Dada. Over fifty researchers trav-

eled to Zaire, including Earthwatch volunteers brought in as laborers. Heavy rains washed out the roads in the valley. A student
was trampled by a hippo and had to be evacuated by helicopter.
Diana Holt, still lusting after Acheulian hand axes, came for a visit,
while the principal investigators and their Zairean excavators continued searching for archaic bones and stones.

It was a mixed season for the PIs. Some of them made unbelievably lucky finds, while others got confused by contradictory
data. No fewer than five geologists joined Jack Harris at Senga.
But it took only one word from one of them to send him into a
funk. Having flown in to examine the dig, de Heinzelin pro-
nounced it "derived." There is no nastier word a geologist can
utter about an archaeologist's site. It means that the artifacts so
laboriously chipped out of the ironstone might be a lot younger
than the original estimate of two million years. De Heinzelin
guessed they may have washed in as recently as ten thousand years
ago, and Jack got so depressed by the news that he moved away
to camp in a mud hole.

The season was happier for Alison and her excavators, who
unearthed a remarkable series of levels at Katanda. Digging from
the top of the cliff down toward the Semliki, they discovered platforms littered with quartzite tools, animal bones, and other archaeological features, including a stone floor laid down at least
forty thousand years ago. This sequence of Stone Age levels shows
how the Semliki River valley emerged and was settled over the
past million years. Whenever a surface evolved, people came to
live on it. "There's something wonderfully attractive about Katanda," says Alison. "It's a real magnet on the landscape."

Digging near his wife at a site called Katanda 9, John Yellen
uncovered the oval carpet of stones that was the major archaeological find of the season. As a bonus, Yellen found an array of
bone and stone tools lying on the floor. Exquisite examples of their
kind, the tools include the world's oldest carved bone points and
harpoons. They provide surprisingly early evidence of fishing, and
they offer one of the earliest proofs of long-distance trade in Africa. Some of the stone tools are made of brown flint, which is not
local to Ishango, and de Heinzelin speculated that they may have
come from as far away as Lake Turkana. "If the site is what we

think it is," says Alison, "it could clinch the argument that modern humans evolved in Africa."

Alison is hoping to return to Ishango in the near future, but Jack will probably head over to East Africa. Don Johanson has asked him to do some work at Olduvai Gorge, and there is always the chance that Ethiopia could open up again. Noel still has his heart set on an expedition into the lower Semliki, and the eight-ton Land Master truck he bought for carrying supplies into the field has finally reached Ishango.

It took Leo the mechanic more than two months to extract the truck from the customs office in Kinshasa and another month to float it upriver and then drive it overland into the Rift. As he was carrying most of the supplies for the 1988 season—including four cases of minced garlic, six pounds of pepper, and all the Earth-watchers' tents and bedding—Leo's arrival in the "White Elephant" took on the mythic proportions of a cargo cult. "When Leo gets here we'll have beds to sleep on. When Leo gets here we'll have something to eat. When Leo gets here . . ." With the season half over and the truck still not in sight, the suspense was so great that whenever the Zairean excavators heard a vehicle in the distance, or even an airplane overhead, they would put down their shovels and start chanting, *"Léo! Léo! Léo!"*

Virus Hunting on the Niger

Only a masochist with an exuberant taste for
self-violence will pick Nigeria for a holiday.

Chinua Achebe

WHEN OYEWALE TOMORI went to lunch in New Haven, the counter man noticed something strange about his customer. He spoke a lilting English, possibly Caribbean in origin, and he consumed his submarine sandwich with tremendous gusto.

"Where are you from?" asked the man.

"The Yale Arbovirus Research Unit," said Tomori.

"I mean, where are you *from*?"

"I'm from Nigeria."

"You're from Africa!"

"Yes, I told you, I'm from Nigeria."

"I've watched a lot of films about Africa. Do you know Tarzan?"

"Sure I know Tarzan," said Tomori. "We're good friends."

There was a pause before the next question. "Is it true they hunt heads and eat people in Africa?"

"Yes, it's true. But heads are very difficult to come by now. So we're sending people out to search for heads in other parts of the world. In fact, I'm here in New Haven hunting for heads."

The terrified look on the man's face gave way to a smile when Tomori assured him he was joking. For the next few weeks, whenever the African headhunter came to lunch, he was served second helpings on the house.

"Basically I think I'm a very shy person, but it doesn't show," says Tomori. "Over the years I've become the man who is master of ceremonies. The Yoruba are a flamboyant people, and I'm often the life of the party."

Tomori, who directs the virus laboratory at the University of Ibadan, is telling me stories about his early experiences in America as we drive along the Niger. We have been sticking close to the river, bleeding people in settlements and schools, before swinging west into the less populated inland areas. Here we will try to collect blood from field rats and other mammals. We are crossing into what virologists call the zone of emergence—the boundary area through which viruses escape from their wild animal hosts to infect a human population. The back of the station wagon is filled with the red ampoules of a successful mission, but it will be several weeks before we know if any of this blood contains a new virus.

As at other major decisions in his life, when the twenty-nine-year-old Tomori told his family he was getting on an airplane for the first time and flying to America, they were horrified. They had been frightened before, when the twelve-year-old boy left his ancestral home in Yorubaland to go to boarding school in the tropical rain forest of southern Nigeria. And they were frightened again when he went to study veterinary medicine at Ahmadu Bello University in the Hausa north. But neither of these adventures was as reckless as leaving western Nigeria for the United States.

"From the stories we know, America is gangster country," says Tomori. "Everybody carries a gun, and they shoot you at the drop of a hat."

Soon after his arrival in Atlanta, where he would spend two months researching viruses at the Center for Disease Control before moving up to Yale, Tomori stopped a passer-by to ask for directions to Five Points on Peachtree Street. "The man gave me a dirty look and said, 'Hey, brother, you jiving me?'

"It went through my mind as he turned around and started walking back to me that I was a dead person. But he must have realized I wasn't a native American, because instead of shooting me, he said, 'Brother, you *on* Faa Pon on Peach.'

"It took me a while to get used to people's accents—the speech of black Americans was particularly hard for me to understand—but after I got the knack I felt right at home. I enjoy American food, hamburgers and hot dogs, and the weather in Atlanta was fine, almost like Nigeria."

But what Tomori enjoyed most was the chance to spend long days in the CDC "hot lab." This is a special maximum-containment laboratory built for handling the world's most dangerous viruses. Dressed in a space suit and breathing through a regulator, Tomori could work in Atlanta on African viruses that no one in Nigeria is allowed to touch.

"I sing when I'm working," he says. "It takes off the drudgery and loneliness of being away from family. There was an intercom in the hot lab, and I never thought much about it, until one day somebody yelled down to me, 'Wally, that was a good song! Give us more!'" Tomori became such a familiar figure at the hot lab that two years later, when he returned for a visit, the guards at the gate waved him through without a pass.

After finishing his work in Atlanta on Lassa fever, Tomori went to New Haven to look at another African disease, Orungo virus, which he was researching for his Ph.D. in virology from the University of Ibadan. He was excited at the prospect of meeting so many great scientists at Yale, people whose names he had seen for years in the published literature on African viruses. There was Max Theiler, who had won a Nobel Prize for developing the yellow fever vaccine; Jordi Casals, who had isolated the Lassa virus that almost killed him; and Robert Shope, who had discovered a whole new series of rabies viruses, some of them carried by mosquitoes.

Orungo and yellow fever are arboviruses, or *ar*thropod-*bo*rne viruses, which are transmitted through the blood-sucking bites of mosquitoes, ticks, flies, and other joint-footed creatures. Some arboviruses are fatal to humans, while others cause little more than a few aches and pains. Built originally by the Rockefeller Foundation and the United States Public Health Service, the Yale Arbovirus Research Unit is the world reference center for arboviruses. Five hundred varieties are listed in the *International Catalogue of Arboviruses*, and an equal number are waiting for people like Tomori to characterize them in the laboratory or discover them in the field.

Besides being a flamboyant people, the Yoruba have a highly developed sense of hierarchy. Kings and chiefs are traditionally greeted by subjects prostrating themselves in the dust. "Our leaders are used to being served," says Tomori. "But the problem with this is that once you become a leader, you stop doing any work."

One of the things that surprised him about America was that people in positions of authority often worked harder than those below them.

At the end of his stay in New Haven, Tomori mentioned to Robert Shope that he wanted to prepare some chemical reagents to carry back to Africa. Shope offered to help, and they agreed to meet early the next morning. "When I got to the building at half past six, he was already there mixing up reagents. This was the director of the laboratory! It would never happen here in Nigeria. I said to him when I left, 'If I ever become director of the Ibadan virus laboratory, I want to be a director like you. Rather than sitting in my office, I'll put in my hand and do the basic work.'

"When I went back to Yale for a week in 1985, Shope asked me, 'Are you the kind of director you said you'd be?' " Tomori gives me a sly grin. I already know the answer is *yes*.

"If you be ready to leave for New Bussa, we pick you tomorrow at 7:00 A.M.," said the note. The next day, around ten in the morning, I am ushered into a battered Peugeot 504 by Sheidu Opeloyeru, our driver, and introduced to three of Tomori's graduate students, with whom I will spend a week virus hunting in northern Nigeria. "Prof" Tomori, who is already out in the field, will be driving from the new Nigerian capital at Abuja to meet us at the Kainji dam, which spans the Niger below the former rapids at Bussa.

As part of their training in virology at the University of Ibadan, Tomori's students are required to learn how to search for viruses in the bush. The Kainji trip is meant to elucidate a cardinal rule in field epidemiology. Because many viruses survive by maintaining a natural cycle of infection in wild animals, human beings can get in trouble when they come in contact with these animals or the arthropod vectors that carry their viruses. One example of this phenomenon may be a monkey virus that is thought to have switched hosts and mutated on its way to becoming AIDS.

Viruses capable of jumping from animals to humans thrive in disturbed environments, and both the Kainji lakeshore and the new Nigerian capital at Abuja offer fertile ground for disaster. In 1968, the year it was finished, the Kainji dam created a five-hundred-square-mile lake. It also pushed sixty thousand people off the banks of the Niger; they retreated into scrub savanna filled with animals and endemic diseases. This breach in the established boundary between nature and civilization opened the area to epidemics of yellow fever and other African viruses.

As director of Nigeria's only virus laboratory, Tomori wanted to search out these potential epidemics before they struck. He knew he would have to deal with them sooner or later, and he preferred to do it sooner. This required actively hunting for live viruses in the field by drawing blood from animals and humans. Finding a virus in a person or animal who is sick with it is relatively easy. But isolating viruses in blood samples from random populations is far more difficult; the odds slip to two in a hundred. If one does find a potentially dangerous virus living in monkeys or other wild animal hosts, the infected animals can be killed and the surrounding population vaccinated as a barrier against the disease spreading. The discovery may also tell you something about the distribution of viruses in nature, a subject that is still largely unknown.

My student companions on the drive to Kainji include the Nigerians Ayo Bamgboye and Atanda Olabode and the Ghanaian Ben Sam. Wearing a long dress in a bold yellow pattern, with a matching jacket flared at the waist, Ayo has left her husband and four-year-old son in Ibadan to make her first trip into the field. Atanda, a sturdy, good-humored fellow who will be my roommate at Kainji, tries to scare her with stories about the large number of lions roaming around the lake.

Ben Sam fixes me with the stern gaze of an African leftist and embarks on one of the many lectures I will hear on the subject of AIDS. According to Sam, AIDS is an American disease, a first-world syndrome developed in the cities of a decaying empire. After exporting it to the third world, American scientists are now doing everything possible to blame the disease on its hapless victims. "Why is it that people only hear the bad news out of Africa?" he asks.

At half past ten we are still trying to get out of Ibadan's sprawling mass of bungalows, which stretch for miles over the low hills of Yorubaland. Instead of freeways, this African Los Angeles is laced with a grid of mud streets. Traffic policemen wearing white gloves are perched on islands at the major intersections, but the flow of vehicles around them is so chaotic that the police look like ship-wrecked survivors waving for help.

Located at the edge of the forest a hundred kilometers inland from the Gulf of Guinea, Ibadan has none of the skyscrapers and smart restaurants found in Africa's other large cities. Most of the buildings that attempted to rise over two stories are unfinished shells, relics of the Nigerian oil boom that came and went. What Ibadan has instead is a teeming central market that sells everything from monkey skulls to smoked bush rats on sticks.

Defended by its endemic diseases, Yorubaland under British colonial rule was left mainly to the Yoruba. Even today I can walk the main streets of Ibadan for hours on end without seeing another white face. Most of the city's inhabitants live without running water, and electricity is sporadic. But before the recent growth of West Africa's coastal capitals, Ibadan reigned for centuries as the largest city in black Africa.

Although the city's population is estimated at two million, no one knows how many people actually live in Ibadan—or in Nigeria, for that matter. Demographers guess that a sixth of Africa's six hundred million people live in this densely settled country. But there has been no census in Nigeria since 1963, and every attempt since then to count the population has ended in charges of fraud. Nigeria's three major regions—the Yoruba west, the Ibo east, and the Hausa and Fulani north—are all afraid to find out how numerous their neighbors are. From the standpoint of public health, this is more than inconvenient. Imagine the difficulty of ordering measles and polio vaccines for an unknown number of children.

Apart from the hawkers selling soap powder, toilet paper, and coils of white grass used as sponges, the most prominent roadside feature on our trip to the north is a harvest of wrecked automobiles. Some of them are freshly smashed, while others have begun to disintegrate and spread over the countryside like industrial mulch. With the cheapest gasoline in the world and no traffic laws or speed limits, the Nigerian highways are a mayhem of cars over-taking each other to the left and right. As confirmed by UN statistics on traffic fatalities, Nigerians are the worst drivers in the world.

After stopping to get buzzed on kola nuts, Sheidu dashes around his own share of automobiles as we pick up speed through the forested hills of the Yoruba Plateau. We cross the Niger at Jebba, and immediately the houses change from square to round. Built within grass-walled compounds, they are flanked by granaries made of red mud. We have entered the dry savanna of the north, the land of the Hausa and the tall Fulani, whom we see walking along the road switching the rumps of their zebu cattle. The scene is as foreign to the other Nigerians in the car as it is to me.

At day's end we drive over the dam and skirt the town of New Bussa to arrive at the Kainji Lake Research Institute, where we will be staying during our visit. I appreciate the fact that I am looking at the site where Mungo Park met his demise, although its history is now under water. Park, a Scottish surgeon, was dispatched in 1795 by the African Association to chart the course of the Niger from its headwaters to the Atlantic. He confirmed Herodotus's claim that the river flowed to the east, wrote his bestselling *Travels in the Interior Districts of Africa*, and then returned ten years later to trace the river to its mouth. Rather than dicker over requests for safe passage, Park developed the habit of shooting every African he saw. This policy got him twenty-five hundred miles downstream, but he was still six hundred miles from the coast when he was attacked and killed in the narrow rapids at Bussa.

The rapids are now buried under a sluggish lake, and New Bussa is nothing more than a construction site with a borrowed name. As I stand on the shore, watching pirogues filled with fishermen paddling home for the night, I wonder about this strange body of water. Is it a manifestation of Park's avenging spirit? How else can one explain why the Bussa rapids were wired into the Lagos power grid, while the local inhabitants were left in the dark?

Later that evening another Peugeot, a station wagon, arrives in a swirl of dust. Out hops Tomori to greet everyone warmly and lend a hand unloading syringes and rat traps from the back of the car. He is a slender man with a boyish face. In spite of the white curls flecking his nap of black hair, he looks younger than his forty-odd years. He wears a loose blue shirt, chinos, and aviator-frame spectacles. There is something American about his casualness, and within minutes I am tagging along behind him on his first errand in New Bussa.

The houses and laboratories at the Kainji Lake Research Institute are surrounded by maize gardens, and the place looks more like a village than a fisheries research center, at least to my Western eyes. Ushered in to pay a courtesy call on the director, we find him sprawled on his living room floor watching a movie on his VCR. He wears the pants and undershirt of what, when fully assembled, must be a very fine *boubou*. Delighted to see each other, he and Tomori try to carry on a conversation over the voices of Faye Dunaway and Jack Nicholson in *Chinatown*. Nicholson, playing the private detective, is about to learn some nasty facts about the Los Angeles water wars.

"My husband is seeing another woman."

"So you're back in town looking for viruses?"

"Do you love your husband, Mrs. Mulray?"

"We found some interesting things in the national park."

"Why, yes."

"Human or animal?"

"Then you should go home and forget about it."

"Maybe both."

Blood is the place to look for viruses. So for the next week we will roam the shores of Kainji Lake collecting blood and other bodily fluids from rats, lizards, hedgehogs, ticks, birds, mosquitoes, and humans. No one is a willing donor. Everyone has to be cajoled. For the animals we have box traps, rat traps, light traps. For the humans we have nothing more effective than reason. This Dracular phase of Tomori's field work will produce a station wagon full of blood samples. Back in Ibadan, three or four of these samples may reveal a live virus. Others will reveal the antibodies that viruses leave as their calling cards after a visit. And if he finds a new virus for which no one has antibodies, then Tomori will get on the phone to the World Health Organization and sound a global alert.

Six of us are lodged for the night in three rooms in a motel-like bungalow. Our two drivers sleep on couches in the living room. We wake at dawn and grab a quick cup of Nescafé before heading out for a day of bloodletting in the Kainji Lake National Park. To reach the park headquarters, we follow a track through thirty kilometers of forested savanna. The grass has been burned off for animal viewing, but we are the only viewers in sight. A roan antelope, a kob, a great bustard, and a couple of wart hogs flee on our approach. Even the baboons show us their rear ends.

On reaching headquarters, Tomori unloads eight Can't Miss rat traps, some box traps, a bottle of palm oil, and a loaf of bread. He gathers a half dozen park wardens under a mango tree and gives them a lesson in baiting rat traps: attach a piece of bread soaked in palm oil, cock the spring, and watch out for your fingers.

Because he has already found viruses in the wardens' blood, Tomori has returned to ask them to trap the animals that might have infected them. Game parks protect both animals and the diseases they carry, and park employees, tree cutters, and poachers are most at risk from these diseases. People wandering into a natural cycle of infection stand a good chance of spreading it into the zone of emergence, and from there it can jump into the population at large.

We walk through the tall grass along the Oli River, a tributary of the Niger, to set some traps at a water hole. We bait other traps near the wardens' houses and then turn to a row of abandoned workers' quarters that Tomori calls "the condominiums." Ayo steps forward to load her first rat trap, and everyone laughs as Tomori tells her, "Don't worry about your fingers; there's a very good hospital in New Bussa."

Looking for more blood, we drive around to various primary schools, a teachers college, and the federal school of wildlife management. Tomori visited these places in the winter, when the dry fields were being burned off, which is when rats move indoors. He has found viruses, not yet identified, in rodents trapped near people's houses, and now he wants human blood for further testing.

Entering the grounds of the wildlife school, we pass a girl in a green blouse, with braids spiking the top of her head. As his male students crane their necks to stare at her, Tomori says, "I see there will be no problem finding volunteers to come back in the morning and check our rat traps." Then he breaks into pidgin English. "If blind man miss snail wey he match, which eye he go use see another." Roughly translated, this means, *An opportunity once lost cannot be regained*. Everyone laughs.

The director of the school has gathered fifty prospective wardens in a classroom, and Tomori begins talking to them. "The only way to be sure that the rodent viruses we found here have anything to do with humans is to collect blood and see if it has antibodies to the viruses involved. If you have antibodies, then you are already protected. But people new to the area are seldom protected, and there's always a chance of finding a virus for which no one has antibodies."

From outside comes the high-pitched drone of cicadas. The ceiling fan whirs overhead, but the room is hot and close. Students begin raising their hands to ask questions. "Is it dangerous to give blood?"

"Humans have half a bucket of blood, and all we want is five milliliters. By the end of the day your body will have made it up."

"What viruses exist in Nigeria?"

"We have forty viruses that infect people."

In response to another question, Tomori steps to the blackboard and begins a lecture on the human immune system. He distinguishes between primary infections, when viruses multiply in target organs, and secondary infections, when they begin coursing through the blood. He describes how the memory cells known as antibodies never forget a virus once they have seen it. He mentions cross-immunization and the fact that exposure to one virus can sometimes spare you from infection by another.

He assures his audience that most viruses produce little more than mild fevers and joint pains. But he mentions the names of some local killers. "In 1969 Lassa fever was found in this country. Then there was Ebola fever in the Sudan, and now everyone is shouting about AIDS."

Seeing that people are stalling for time, the director of the school steps forward and rolls up his sleeve. "It's important for you to seize this opportunity," he says. "This is your chance to confirm you don't have any viruses." While Tomori and Ben Sam prepare their syringes, half the students escape around the back of the building.

Afterward, while driving to another school, we swap stories

about the reticence of blood donors in Africa. "When it comes to the Fulani," says Atanda, "you can't even bleed their cattle. Maybe they'll let you vaccinate, and after doing a hundred cows, you might be allowed to draw blood from one of them."

Tomori tells about the police chief in Abuja who was very keen to own a Can't Miss rat trap. "After I gave him one, he called up the entire staff of two hundred to give blood. It was a good investment."

Following a dinner of okra soup served in the Kainji guest house, we report to the dissecting laboratory to process the day's catch of rodents and arthropods. Using himself as human bait, Adekunle Adeniji has trapped a handful of mosquitoes that are now being mashed into a virological stew. Something similar is happening to our collection of *Rattus rattus*. Hearts, lungs, livers, and kidneys are removed, ground up in a blender, and diluted to a ten percent solution, which will later be injected into the brains of suckling mice. Each virus has its own rhythm of replication and destruction, so if the mice drop dead on the seventh day after injection, one might start looking for yellow fever.

The human blood samples have begun to settle in their stoppered tubes, with red blood cells on the bottom and the yellowish serum on top. Spinning the samples in a centrifuge would squeeze out more serum, which is the most interesting part of the blood for virologists, but the centrifuge is broken. Liberally coated with dust, the shelves and cupboards in the room are bare except for a few bottles of nitric acid and ammonia. The only light comes from a couple of neon tubes in the ceiling, and the overhead fan is wobbling so erratically that I fear we might soon be adding our own blood to the experiment.

Pointing to the lizards scampering up the walls, I ask Tomori about the viruses they carry. He names three—Marco, Timbo, and Chaco—which exist in a viral category of their own. Inspired by my question perhaps, he grabs a lizard off the wall and turns it over to Ayo for dissection. "If this produces a virus," he says, "I'll send out the army with instructions to catch every lizard they can find."

Tomori slips into his Indian accent and starts regaling us with stories of his work on Lassa fever. In the CDC hot lab he had met an Indian scientist who was puzzled that an African would come to America to work on such a deadly disease. "Your goorrment sent you here to die? Vy, my friend, vy do you want to die in America?"

We finish by eleven and head to the bar for Fantas and a game of Monopoly. The night's conversation turns to AIDS. As a viral epidemic, Acquired Immune Deficiency Syndrome lies within Tomori's area of expertise. But it is the politics of AIDS that interests him tonight. He wants to argue against the so-called Africa connection, which claims that the virus originated in Africa and spread from there to infect the rest of the world.

AIDS emerged as a recognized viral epidemic in the early 1980s, first in the United States, where the syndrome was identified among homosexual men in Los Angeles, and then in France, where the virus was isolated by Luc Montagnier at the Institut Pasteur. AIDS is currently the leading cause of death among males in New York City between the ages of twenty-five and forty-five. The CDC estimates that one and a half million Americans are infected with the AIDS virus, and a third of them will die in the next five years. One finds roughly the same scenario in Brazzaville and Kinshasa, but not in Lagos and Ibadan, where the virus has only recently arrived to infect a handful of people.

The AIDS virus appears to have emerged simultaneously in North America and Africa. So why is the latter claimed to be its source? "The search for the origin of AIDS in Africa is motivated by a desire to move it out of home base," says Wilbur Downs, the former director of the Yale Arbovirus Research Unit. "We tried to stick it on the Haitians, and when that failed, we pushed on to Africa."

Luc Montagnier, the discoverer of the virus, has also voiced some doubts about the African origins of the disease. "It appears that the virus came to Europe from the United States, and it might have reached Africa via the same route," he told me over lunch in Paris. Among alternative explanations, Montagnier entertains what he calls "the American hypothesis." "The epidemic might have been caused by the traffic in blood. An isolated population of South American Indians could have been the focus for a natural infection that was amplified by the sale of blood products to the United States."

"If you spend enough time and money trying to look for the origin of AIDS in Africa," says Tomori, "you'll find it. We cannot divorce science from politics. They always go together. It may very well be that AIDS developed in Africa, but the epidemiologists are treading on very slippery ground."

Because it suffers from a related, simian form of the disease, some people suspect that the African green monkey is the source of AIDS. But there are several problems with this theory. Only one of the two major strains of the AIDS virus resembles the green monkey virus. And the pygmies of Zaire, who eat a lot of green monkeys, are free of AIDS. "Green monkeys are innocent of giving AIDS to humans," says Montagnier, "and this might be true of all monkeys."

Another shaky piece of evidence for the Africa connection comes from retrospective serology — the study of stored blood. Antibodies to the AIDS virus have been found in African blood dating back to the 1960s, but this is not conclusive. "I've seen a lot of false positive AIDS tests," says Tomori. "People with kuru, a virus found in New Guinea, will test positive for AIDS. It's quite common for antibodies to cross-react with each other, which is what could be happening in Rwanda and Burundi. Anyone can speculate, but they shouldn't use speculation as fact."

Another theory about the African origin of AIDS sees it as an endemic disease, localized for hundreds or thousands of years in an isolated population before it escaped to infect the world at large. A high percentage of people on the shores of Lake Kivu possess antibodies to AIDS, and this percentage has remained unchanged for the past fifteen years. "But for all we know," says Montagnier, "we could collect the same data from a tribe of Indians in the rain forests of Brazil."

"You Americans have the moon," says Tomori. "Why can't you also take credit for AIDS?"

When Tomori first told the Nigerian government that he wanted to search for viruses at Kainji Lake and Abuja, they told him there was no money for this sort of thing. He appealed, but his letters went unanswered. He finally hit on the idea of sending a hand-written note, marked "personal," to the military governor at Abuja. This letter slipped past the general's secretary, and Tomori was summoned to present his case.

Conceived during the Nigerian oil boom of the 1970s, Abuja was meant to be the Brasilia of West Africa. A new capital rising on virgin land would symbolically unify a country that recently concluded a deadly civil war. The site chosen for the city was an existing community of Hausa and Gwari farmers and hunters in central Nigeria. This town of a few hundred people is projected to welcome another million and a half inhabitants by the year 2000.

The plan to build a federal capital at Abuja almost foundered once before on medical grounds. When word got out that onchocerciasis, commonly known as river blindness, was prevalent in the area, officials in Lagos refused to move there. The district was saturated with DDT to kill the female fly that carries the onchocerciasis parasite, but no one knew what other endemic diseases were likely to emerge once Abuja's ecology was disturbed. Tomori suggested to the military governor that somebody should get into the field and look for potential epidemics before they actually arrived. The general nodded his approval, and "in one hour we did everything I had been struggling to do for seven years."

Abuja lies three hundred and fifty miles northeast of Ibadan. One has to zigzag northwest another two hundred and fifty miles to get to New Bussa. To search for viruses in both areas at once, four times a year, Tomori has to be away from home for weeks on end. But once in the field, he finds it easier to stay in the field. He sends his students back to Ibadan with relays of fresh blood, while he himself sticks to collecting it.

Soon after I last saw him, and within a year of beginning his virus survey in Abuja, Tomori was rushing back to the area to respond to an epidemic of yellow fever. Deaths in the thousands have been reported, and twenty-five million people are still at risk today. Tomori tells me in a recent letter that he has isolated two new viruses from the rodents and mosquitoes in Abuja, but he has been too busy to identify them.

*

Warm climates are bad for your health, and the worst of these climates, in terms of human disease, is tropical Africa. Its diseases have shaped the history of the continent, dictated its patterns of human settlement, shaved years off the average lifespan, and altered the very nature of human relations. Public health officials talk about the burden of disease, and nowhere in the world is this mass of parasites, fungi, bacteria, and viruses heavier than in Africa.

Africa is unique among continents in that the equator bisects it into northern and southern halves. This distribution of land mass around the equator, with most of the continent lying between the tropics of Cancer and Capricorn, makes Africa hot and wet, a perfect climate for disease. It also allows for a flourishing, year-round community of arthropods and other disease-spreading organisms.

The potency of its diseases helped to keep Africa relatively isolated until the colonial era of the nineteenth and twentieth centuries. The environment also encouraged the rapid spread of diseases that were introduced onto the continent, including smallpox, cholera, and syphilis from Europe and the Near East. In exchange, Africa exported to the rest of the world yellow fever, hookworm, river blindness, and several strains of malaria and dysentery. But diseases lethal to foreigners are often tolerated by their original hosts, and before the arrival of Europeans, Africa actually suffered few major epidemics. These would come with colonialism.

A parasite that kills its host endangers its own survival. As a result, selective pressure over time tends to produce more moderate pathogens. Antibodies and cultural responses also help to keep us out of harm's way. But it takes many years of association before a group of people and its diseases reach a state of balanced pathogenicity, and the isolation necessary to obtain this balance is becoming increasingly rare. As the world becomes a "global village," we are waking up to the fact that diseases spread as fast as information. Luc Montagnier is only half joking when he tells me that "the Boeing 747 is the vector of the AIDS virus."

The social historian William McNeill describes the world as organized around gradients of infection that "make it perilous for human beings to migrate into warmer and wetter lands. . . . The most striking modern example of this phenomenon was illustrated by the fate of Europeans in tropical Africa who, early in the nineteenth century, survived on the average less than a year from the time of their arrival."

It is safer to migrate *down* a disease gradient into cooler and drier lands, but anyone changing environments courts the risk of being done in by unfamiliar infections. Even temporary changes, like pilgrimages, can be dangerous. Engaged in what McNeill calls "institutional forms of behavior that prepared people for death," religious pilgrims rivaled armies in spreading cholera through Europe. West African Moslems flying on hadj trips to Mecca perform the same function today.

Patterns of infection defined by climate have given way to other disease gradients stemming from the invention of cities. Cities concentrate populations that become vulnerable to the spread of viruses like smallpox, measles, polio, and influenza—viruses that have no animal host other than humans. The fact of the matter is that cities are bad for your health. They increase the frequency of encounters among strangers and multiply the number of potential hosts. In the absence of medical intervention, measles requires half a million people to sustain itself. Only where the virus finds a sufficient number of babies without antibodies—approximately seven thousand—can it survive indefinitely as a human infection. Cholera in its classic form can exist only in cities, and AIDS, according to Luc Montagnier, is another urban disease that "thrives on the promiscuity and weakened immune systems of city dwellers."

If one looks back to the invention of cities, it appears that the Neolithic revolution itself was bad for human health. Francis Black, an epidemiologist at Yale, speculates that hunter-gatherers in the preagricultural world had a very limited spectrum of infectious diseases. "In large measure," says Black, "modern advances can do no more than return us to the state of health that mankind enjoyed ten thousand years ago." Another consequence of the Neolithic revolution, the domestication of animals, has also taken its toll on human health. The list of viruses originating in animals includes influenza from birds, respiratory viruses from cattle, measles from dogs, pneumonia and the common cold from pigs, mumps from poultry, and intestinal viruses from cats and horses.

For William McNeill, the mark of a successful civilization is its ability to master its disease. A victorious race is distinguished by the strength of its antibodies. Modern history is filled with examples of disease being the secret weapon that allowed invaders to wipe out a previously unexposed population. The Spanish conquest of Mexico and Peru owed more to smallpox than any other single factor. Within one hundred and thirty years of Cortez's arrival in Mexico, the native population of pre-Columbian America had shrunk by ninety-five percent. Several North American Indian tribes met a similar fate when they were given blankets intentionally infected with smallpox.

Another telling example of what happens when two formerly distinct disease environments are joined comes from colonial Africa. Medical historians generally agree that the unhealthiest period in Africa's history occurred at the height of colonial contact with whites, between 1890 and 1930. Introduced by trade caravans from the East Coast, cholera reduced the lifespan of the average Tanzanian male to twenty-five years. Cholera and smallpox eliminated the Masai as a major tribe, and East Africa was generally depopulated during the first three decades of this century. Invading the continent in the 1890s, the rinderpest virus wiped out livestock from the Nile to South Africa. Deprived of food, many Nilotic herders followed their cattle into extinction, which explains why the White Highlands of Kenya—East Africa's choicest real estate—were fortuitously empty when the European settlers arrived to occupy them.

Precolonial Africa suffered other epidemics during the Bantu migrations from the north, the Zulu *mfecane* from the south, and the days of Arab slaving off the coasts, but nothing equaled the disruption of colonialism. A dispersed population of hunter-gatherers and agriculturalists, who had worked out a modus vivendi with their pathogens, was suddenly confronted with new diseases and means for spreading them. Viruses were the advance guard of colonialism, and the continent's present disease environment is one of its legacies.

As European explorers and their African bearers crisscrossed the continent, they introduced respiratory and intestinal diseases. They spread sleeping sickness up the river routes from the west, and rinderpest and pleuropneumonia down from the north. Other colonial policies did a good job of disseminating disease. Forced labor, head taxes that required seasonal migrations, the building of plantations and mines, and the concentration of people into towns and cities all added to Africa's disease burden. Various epidemiological blunders, like the evacuation of sleeping sickness victims into previously unaffected areas, also made the situation worse. As a sign of how quickly it had become integrated into the global disease economy, Africa contributed two million victims to the influenza pandemic that followed the First World War.

Shocked by the diseases spreading around them, and afraid for their own survival, the colonial powers invented tropical medicine. This was a subspecialty of the scientific enterprise that in the nineteenth century mastered the diseases rampant in Europe's cities. Using public health measures like evacuation and containment, colonial governments set out to control the epidemics they were helping to create, although in the ideology of colonialism, it was the victim who was blamed for his suffering. Buttressed by the myth of the Dark Continent, which imagined Africa as a place of disease and superstition, colonialism was conceived as a saving venture, an act of charity that took no credit for engendering the mayhem around it.

The first aim of tropical medicine was to protect the lives of white immigrants. Only then, with what resources were left over, did it turn to protecting the labor force required for colonial enterprises. This explains why even today there is no correlation between the number of people killed by a disease in Africa and the amount of money spent controlling it. Ignored were the diseases of children and other major killers like diarrhea and respiratory infections, while a lot of money went into researching cures for yellow fever, smallpox, and sleeping sickness. Today the African disease of greatest interest to Europeans is AIDS.

Tropical medicine came into vogue at the turn of the century, when Robert Koch, discoverer of the tuberculosis bacterium, and other European scientists led expeditions to Africa. While their predecessors had been looking for new territory, the scientists were searching for new diseases. Expeditions retraced the steps of Stanley and Livingstone to discover the causes of sleeping sickness, malaria, and yellow fever. These early forays became the prototype for European science in Africa. Outsiders would march into an obscure part of the continent, collect the blood and tissue needed for Western science, and then retreat to their laboratories, where one man's parasite becomes another man's puzzle.

It was not until 1945, after the invention of sulfa drugs and antibiotics, that Africa's high birth rates began to balance its equally high death rates. Aided by preventive and curative medicine, the continent since then has entered a period of rapid population growth. To outsiders in non-Catholic countries, this growth rate seems precipitously high. But Africans generally view their fecundity as a positive phenomenon. They also see it as a necessary corrective to the underpopulation resulting from centuries of slaving and disease. However one interprets it, Africa's rise in population is another major legacy from the latter stages of the colonial enterprise.

The means by which one can die young in Africa are still remarkably numerous. Mortality on the continent today is higher than it was in Europe in the middle of the eighteenth century, prior to the Industrial Revolution. Infant mortality rates of two hundred per thousand live births are common. Mortality of children between the ages of one and four is fifty times higher than in the industrial world. Malaria causes eight hundred thousand deaths a year in Africa, seventy-five percent of them in children under the age of five. As one observer put it, "The white man's grave remains the African child's grave."

It is generally not the exotic parasites associated with tropical medicine that kill people in Africa, but the common bacterial and viral infections that were once endemic in the cities of Europe. Diarrheal diseases and respiratory infections cause two thirds of the deaths in the third world. Rotaviruses are one cause of diarrhea, while influenza and adenoviruses are implicated in respiratory infections. Malaria comes next on the list, as the primary or contributing cause for a third of the deaths in sub-Saharan Africa, which is the epicenter of the disease. But as public health officials know, the underlying cause of death in most of these cases is not a virus or a parasite. It is an acquired immune deficiency syndrome known as malnutrition.

At the international conferences he attends on tropical medicine, Tomori often comes away with the feeling that people are using the same names to talk about different diseases. Ninety-five percent of the world's research is conducted by first world scientists on first world problems. As a legacy from colonial days, some of these problems include tropical medicine, but Tomori often finds himself at odds with the European approach to African diseases.

"I go to these conferences in Abidjan and Kuwait, and among three hundred and fifty Western experts on the tropics, I find twenty Africans. The Westerners are all excited about bioengineering and genetic techniques for making new vaccines. At all the meetings I stand up and say, 'This is very good. But in Africa we haven't succeeded in controlling viruses with the vaccines we already have. Vaccines that have worked in Europe and America are not working in Africa. *This* is the problem we have to look at.'

"In the 1970s when I was saying these things they thought I was a rabble-rouser. Now that I'm in charge of a laboratory, I'm still saying these things, and people have started listening. At a meeting in Rabat I went up to the head of the Organization of African Unity and said, 'It's time we had a conference of *African* scientists talking about Africa's viral diseases,' and he finally agreed." At this first meeting, held in Nairobi in 1986, Tomori spoke on Lassa fever and related viruses.

Why do vaccines that work in Europe fail in Africa? The answer involves both politics and medicine. "A lot of vaccines close to expiring get dumped in Africa," says Tomori. "Graft is often involved, with a bribe going to the purchaser. The pharmaceutical companies send us a million doses three months before expiration, knowing full well that we don't have the capacity to distribute them.

"Nigeria hasn't had a census for twenty-five years, and without knowledge of your birth rate, you don't know how many doses to deliver. Live vaccines have to be kept as cold as possible. In the midday heat they can die in an hour, and exposure to sunlight will wipe out a vaccine in thirty minutes. In the end, you don't even know what you're putting into the children."

Vaccination programs in Africa have also encountered problems dealing with maternal antibodies. Passed from mothers to their offspring, these antibodies protect babies against disease during the first six months of life, and then they wane. If children are vaccinated too early, their antibodies are used up fighting the vaccine, and they actually become *more* susceptible to disease.

"Doctors in Europe, to be sure that children have lost their maternal antibodies, wait fifteen months before vaccinating against measles. But in Africa, where measles is endemic and children get it as early as six or seven months, we can't afford to wait that long. We vaccinate at nine months. But many children who have been vaccinated *still* get measles and polio. Every day we walk a thin line between vaccinating too early and too late."

A similar problem arises when adults are vaccinated against a disease for which they already have immunity. "Some people have antibodies to yellow fever that have come from being infected by related viruses, like dengue. This preimmunity to yellow fever may disappear when they are vaccinated. All the vaccine does is mop up the antibody and leave you defenseless."

Vaccination campaigns are based on the concept of herd immunity. If eighty percent of a population are protected by antibodies against infection, this suffices to protect the twenty percent who are still unexposed. But to guarantee this kind of coverage, a campaign has to be mounted every year. Otherwise one creates a susceptible population with no antibodies at all.

"This happens all the time," says Tomori. "Some government gives you money for a year. They get their names in the paper as generous donors, and then the next year the money disappears. A program like this is useless."

Another problem is that different people react differently to vaccines. To see if people are actually developing antibodies, a campaign should be accompanied by blood tests. "Before vaccinating you draw blood to establish a baseline, and then six weeks after vaccinating you draw blood again to observe the change. But it's not done this way in Nigeria, because no one has the time or money. We wait for a disease to strike and then see if vaccinated people come down with it."

When I follow the high-tension wires back from the lights of Ibadan to the villages surrounding Kainji Lake, I find that all but two of them lack electricity. I also find, as is true elsewhere in Africa, that development can be bad for your health. As a general rule, the bigger the technology the worse the consequences.

After being paid five pounds sterling per acre of productive farmland, forty-four thousand people were resettled into new villages around the lake. Three kinds of houses were built to approximate their traditional structures. Domes with slit windows were erected for the Kamberi, a tribe of pastoralists who file their teeth to sharpened points. Square houses were built for the Bussawa and Maguzawa. Round houses clustered into compounds were put up for the Hausa, a Moslem tribe that keeps its women in purdah. While their original dwellings had mud walls and thatch roofs — good building materials for the tropics — the new houses were built of concrete blocks and roofed with asbestos. By midday the houses turn into furnaces hot enough to bake bread.

Parts of New Bussa were supplied with water and electricity. Two more villages got water piped straight from the lake. But the other one hundred and thirty-six villages received neither electricity nor water, which they had to raise from wells. "There was no attention given to the human health aspects of the lake," says Margaret Tayo, who is staying with us at the Kainji Lake Research Institute. "The emir managed to get an air force base and a research center in New Bussa. But ten miles away there is no electricity, and people are being taken off by the most debilitating tropical diseases."

Tayo is another African scientist working at Kainji on a shoestring budget. While Tomori handles viruses, Tayo researches just about everything else, and between the two of them, one gets a good idea of how dangerous dams can be to tropical health.

Tayo is a strikingly handsome woman, with stylish, loosely curled hair, gold-frame spectacles, lacquered nails, and lipstick highlighting shiny white teeth. She likes to rise late in the morning and linger over a cup of coffee. One reason she is a late riser is that she often stays out in the field bleeding people until midnight.

To take care of their medical problems, the Kainji tribes are regularly dusted with DDT to kill the black flies that carry river blindness. Otherwise they are left to fend for themselves. On three occasions, World Health Organization medical surveys of the region have been abandoned for lack of passable roads. It took a woman equipped with an ancient Land Rover and a lot of courage to succeed where her predecessors had failed. Arriving seventeen years after the dam was built, Tayo was the first medical officer, and probably the only person other than the tax collector, to visit all the villages remaining on the shores of the lake.

Tayo heads the Division of Public Health at Nigeria's National Institute of Medical Research, which occupies the old Rockefeller Foundation yellow fever laboratory at Yaba, on the Lagos lagoon. With a master's degree from the London School of Hygiene and Tropical Medicine, and a Ph.D. from Ahmadu Bello University, Tayo runs an eight-man team in the field. In the course of a year, the team makes one complete sweep around the lake. As there are too many of them to fit into her Land Rover, they travel in shifts. They work twelve-hour days, and sometimes longer, due to the odd fact that some of Tayo's blood samples have to be collected at midnight. Her budget for this landmark study of dams and tropical health is twenty thousand naira a year. Her salary is eight thousand naira a year. At the current rate of exchange, four naira equal a dollar.

Along with demographic and social data, Tayo methodically gathers the physical evidence of disease at Kainji Lake. She counts the eggs of schistosome flukes in urine. She examines blood for parasites and malaria. She snips a piece of skin from people's buttocks to look for the worms that cause river blindness. "It requires a fair degree of trust to arrive in a village and ask for these things. Sometimes people say they'll help you, and then when you come back, the village is deserted."

It is standard practice to omit women from studies like this, but Tayo wants them included. As the only female on her team, she has to work alone when visiting the Hausa women in purdah, and she says that "their health is generally very bad."

To be done properly, an epidemiological survey like Tayo's should range over different seasons and times of day, requiring multiple visits. The parasitic flatworm *Wuchereria bancrofti*, for example, which causes elephantiasis, hides in people's internal organs during the daylight hours, where it is undetectable. But around midnight, in tune with the night-flying mosquitoes that suck it up in their blood meal and transmit it from host to host, the worm surges into the peripheral blood. "This is when you have to look for bancroftian worms," says Tayo, "but people don't smile on your collecting blood at midnight."

From my evening conversations with Tayo and Tomori, I get the idea that public health is a house with three rooms, and you report to one room or another depending on whether you are suffering from a virus, a bacterium, or a parasite. The afflicting agents are sorted by size. Viruses are the smallest, parasites the biggest. The viruses infecting people at Kainji include measles, polio, yellow fever, and rabies. The bacteria cause typhoid, cholera, meningitis, and syphilis. The parasites produce malaria, river blindness, and schistosomiasis. There is also a dazzling array of parasitic worms, including Guinea, round, flat, tape, thread, and hook. Parasites are Tayo's specialty.

"Everyone suffers from malaria, which is no big news, except that it kills a lot of children," she says. "This is the holoendemic zone; we're in the middle of the problem." Transmitted in the saliva of infected female *Anopheles* mosquitoes, the malaria parasite burrows into the liver of its human host, where it replicates for ten days before bursting forth to invade the body's red blood cells. Here it multiplies furiously in the stage of the disease that manifests the classic symptoms of chills and fever.

"You can find all the different types of malaria here, including the cerebral type that kills you, and we're identifying more virulent strains. The usual drugs are no longer taking care of malaria in Nigeria. Resistance is developing." Every infectious agent has chemical features, known as antigens, that the body recognizes as foreign and protects itself against by producing antibodies. But parasites, with their multistage life cycles, are quite adept at eluding the body's natural immune system. This also complicates the search for an effective vaccine.

One of the nastiest of the disease-carrying organisms that flourish along the Niger is the female black fly *Simulium damnosum*, which carries the worms that produce river blindness, one of the great scourges of West Africa. Growing up to thirty inches long, these worms have a preference for breeding in the tissue of the human eye. River blindness afflicts millions of people and depopulates the river valleys that would otherwise be the area's most productive land. "I find entire villages filled with blind people," says Tayo, who estimates that over ten percent of the Kainji population is infected.

Because of the host snail's preference for still water, all the dams built in tropical Africa have burdened the people around them with schistosomiasis, and Kainji is no exception. The snails that harbor the disease proliferate along the shore, and anyone touching the water is liable to have his internal organs invaded by schistosome worms. Guinea worms, whose intermediate host is the *Cyclops* crab, are another waterborne plague in the Kainji villages. These milky white worms destroy the muscle tissue in which they live. "I have seen people who have lost their arms and legs to Guinea worms," says Tayo, who has found villages where two thirds of the households are infected. There is no drug that kills Guinea worms.

An adult resident of Lagos whose death is reported to the authorities is likely to have died between the ages of forty and fifty. Infant mortality is twenty-five percent. Shave five to ten years off the former figure and double the latter for a sense of how much harder life can be around the dam that supplies Lagos with its electricity.

"There's an atrocious problem with the water in the area," says Tayo. "But no one thought about this when they built the dam. There is nothing for people to do now, other than move away." Tayo is the first outsider to observe villages around the lake being abandoned to the flies and mosquitoes. No one knows where the people are going, but a good guess is that many of them are working their way down the high-tension wires to the slums of Lagos.

While she works in the laboratory, Tayo suggests I visit the lakeshore village of Monai with Alhaji Aliyu Usman, her assistant and translator. Dressed in a sky-blue *boubou* and purple fez, Usman is a small man of regal bearing. The regalness, I soon learn, is owing to the fact that he is related to Alhaji Musa Muhammadu Kigera III, emir of Borgu, the feudal chief whose suzerainty includes New

Bussa and the entire western side of the lake. Chiefs still wield great influence in Nigeria, and to have one of their family members on your team is a great boon to a researcher.

As we drive through New Bussa, a village bustling with motor scooters and bush taxis zigzagging around the potholes, I count five churches of various do-it-yourself Christian denominations and a new mosque under construction. In the courtyard of his palace, we see the emir himself sitting in the front seat of his Mercedes Benz. "He must be getting ready to travel," says Usman. "Would you like me to introduce you?" I decline the invitation, fearing that the meeting could be prolonged. We continue around the palace and down a dirt track to Monai, a town of five hundred people barely a mile from where the emir is sitting.

Monai has no electricity, and until recently the only source of water was a well. Now there is also a pipe that runs directly from the lake. The town is built of round houses clustered into compounds that are filled with goats, cooking fires, and little granaries resembling pots with straw hats. With the elaborate courtesy of the Moslem north, Usman is greeted by men prostrating themselves on the ground.

We walk through town listening to the thud of wooden mortars pounding cassava into flour. Bleating goats exhort the herd boys to hurry up and bring them forage. A herd of zebu shuffles by on its way into the neighboring fields of *bourgou*. Down at the lake, fishermen load their pirogues with nylon nets and paddle offshore for the day. From overhead comes the crack of a Nigerian air force MiG-21 breaking the sound barrier, and we crane our necks to stare up at a plume of jet exhaust unfurling in an otherwise perfectly blue sky.

"None of them has been vaccinated against measles or polio or the other common childhood diseases," says Usman, pointing to the children following us through town. "We have no refrigerators for vaccinating in the field, so half the children you see here are likely to die before the age of five."

On leaving the women drawing water at the well, Usman assures them that he and Dr. Tayo will be returning soon. I adjust the rearview mirror in our Land Rover to look at the town receding behind us. When the concrete houses are obscured by dust and the heat haze of a midday sun, Monai looks like any one of thousands of villages in West Africa. It is.

I ask him if he comes from a large family, and Tomori, doing a mental calculation, gets lost somewhere around the number twenty. This is the number of his father's wives. "My father had thirteen, fifteen, or twenty wives," he says. "It's difficult to tell, since we had no census then.

"If your father died, the younger wives were inherited by the children. They were shared out to the men in the house and became wives to the sons. It was the vogue then to have many wives and many children, especially male, but there were also economic reasons. Given the high rate of infant mortality, you hoped at the end of the day to have enough people to work on the farm." His father was a cacao farmer, and Tomori himself spent Fridays and Saturdays in the fields harvesting his mother's allotment of yams.

Oyewale Tomori was born in 1946 in Ilesha, one of the ancient Yoruba towns east of Ibadan. His grandfather was a chief, third in rank to the king. "In those days chiefs were important, and the king was king. He owned the land. He owned everything. The food was his and people must give him food from their land. Nowadays nobody gives the king what he wants, so he has to find other ways of surviving. You pay him money to be made a chief. I could resume the family title, but nobody wants to bother now with so many problems around.

"My mother was wife number ten, I think," says Tomori, before pausing to think about it. "Ten, eleven, or thereabouts. Apart from those he inherited, she was one of the last wives my father married. Some of my father's children are older than my mother."

Because she was one of his youngest wives, Tomori's mother lived in his father's house, a two-story structure built in the middle of the family compound. Two rooms on the ground floor were reserved for new wives, who later moved to houses in the courtyard.

"A young child stays with his mother until the age of six, when he moves into the big yard, where all the children stay, the boys in one place, the girls in another."

"How many brothers and sisters do you have?"

"I wish I knew! The last time I looked there were about fifty.

We're talking about those who are alive. I was in the last set, quite low in rank, maybe ninth or tenth from the end." In his immediate family, Tomori is the third of five brothers.

"When your mother wasn't around, there was always someone to care for you. You could walk into anyone's house and take your food. Your mother was my mother. This was the beauty of the extended family."

Life in the compound was meticulously organized by Tomori's father. "Everything worked like clockwork. He came home from the fields at four-thirty each day, and by five his food was ready on the table. The wives knew their work, no arguments. One woman in charge of cooking the soup. One in charge of pounding the yam. My father insisted we eat together as a family. Everybody would come into the house to eat a piece of pounded yam, which we call 'father's food.' My father couldn't read, but he was very smart in the way he handled his family, his business, the way he trained us. It takes a lot of intelligence for a man to control fifteen wives and sixty children and yet maintain peace in the house."

Most of his wives were traders and market women dealing in wholesale produce and long-distance shipping. One of them ran a *bukateria*, a restaurant attached to the front wall of the house. Tomori's mother sold kola nuts, a seasonal fruit she hulled and preserved for sale throughout the year. "She must have been a good businesswoman to pay for sending her children to school," says Tomori. The only book she herself knew how to read was the Bible, in Yoruba.

According to the British system of education imposed on colonial Nigeria, a child was old enough to go to school when he could bend his hand over his head and touch his ear. "They didn't take account of midgets and people with short arms. Some children were fifteen before they went to school, and some never went at all."

Tomori himself started at the age of five, when he followed his older brother to school one day and was allowed to stay. After the Church Missionary Society primary school in Ilesha, he would have followed his brother to the Government College secondary school at Ibadan, but he was assigned instead to the Government College in Ughelli. This caused great consternation in his family. Ughelli lies in the tropical rain forests of a coastal region filled with Ibo immigrants. His mother considered a trip to Ughelli more dangerous than going to London or New York. But for Tomori this journey into a "foreign" part of Nigeria was the formative experience in his life.

"It made me what I am. If I had gone to Ibadan my attitude toward life probably wouldn't be as broad-minded as it is now. It exposed me to different types of people, different cultures. Nigeria wasn't like it is today. People were quite suspicious of each other, particularly if you couldn't speak their language."

Nigeria's government colleges were modeled on the great public schools of Britain. "Most of the teachers were white, and the students were taught how to play cricket and become gentlemen." Tomori was strong in mathematics and science, but he also toyed with the idea of becoming a journalist. One of his articles in the school paper set the tone for his later provocations. He attacked the idea of having an American Peace Corps volunteer teach English at Ughelli. "Much as I like the freedom of expression in American English, it was of no use to us. You needed British English to exist in this country. Americans could teach physics and chemistry, but not English. So I wrote an article, 'How Can an American Come and Teach English in Nigeria?' which got me in a lot of trouble. The principal made me apologize, but I didn't change my mind."

In 1963, the year before taking his final exams, Tomori caught the first whiff of the political chaos that would soon push Nigeria into civil war. The government redrew the country's political boundaries, and the Yoruba, who had lost some territory, retaliated by pulling their teachers out of Ughelli. Tomori and his classmates spent their final year studying on their own. He passed his exams, but with marks too low to get into medical school. He went off to Lagos to sell duplicating machines and become a young man about town, until he was accepted into medical school on the second try. But by then Tomori had said, "To hell with medicine. I'll become a veterinarian."

"I went to the library to read about vet medicine. I watched a few films about cowboys and cattle rides. I thought I'd like a life like that. I'll get a large piece of land covered with a lot of cattle. I'll wake up in the morning, check my cattle, drive about, sleep, wake up, and look at them again. And of course make money, although making money wasn't my main concern."

The only veterinary school in Nigeria at the time was at Ahmadu Bello University in Zaria. Tomori left for ABU in 1966, the year before the outbreak of civil war. "I ignored all the entreaties from my family, who considered going to the north a dangerous adventure. Ten days after I got to Zaria the big troubles broke out. All the Ibo were killed or chased out by the Hausa. I had been to school in an Ibo part of the country, and without the Yoruba face marks, I look every inch an Ibo. Even the way I speak English is with an Ibo accent.

"I was putting my neck in the lion's mouth. But by the grace of God I survived, and it was a good experience for me, because I got to know the Hausa better. I could not accept what they were doing, but I understood why they did it. I'm a better Nigerian because of this up-down-south-north kind of education. I fit into any part of this country today—Ibo, Hausa, Yoruba—because of this experience."

When Tomori later visited Iboland in 1972 in response to an outbreak of yellow fever, he found the war had taken a high toll among his former classmates. "I couldn't believe my eyes at the amount of destruction that took place during the war. At one point I started crying. Whenever I asked about my friends from Ughelli, I was always told they had died on one war front or another. You saw the maimed, the gunshot wounds, the paralyzed walking on crutches. For a long time I never got over it."

At ABU Tomori had a second, more fruitful encounter with American teachers. The veterinary school had been financed by the United States Agency for International Development. Many of the teachers were American, as was the system of instruction. The school term began on a Friday, and Tomori's anatomy professor told his class to report to the Zaria racetrack the following morning.

"It was exciting for us and a lot of fun. Luckily, or unluckily, one of the horses broke its leg. The man took us around and said, 'This is the bone. This is the muscle.' Nobody was listening. We were saying, 'Poor horse,' and that kind of thing. On Monday he gave us a test, and we all got zeros.

"The American system was alien to us, this coursework business, tests and exams every week. In the British system they ask you five questions at the end, and if you're lucky enough to guess them in advance, you don't have to read the whole book." After getting the hang of it, Tomori rose to the top of his class.

Another important moment in his brief career as a veterinarian came when Graham Kemp and Vernon Lee, researchers at the Rockefeller Foundation virus laboratory in Ibadan, arrived on campus. They had been traveling in northern Nigeria, responding to the first epidemic of Lassa fever, before stopping at the university to give a lecture on viruses. Kemp had been trained as a veterinarian, and he thought ABU a good spot to look for his replacement in Ibadan when the Rockefeller Foundation pulled out of Africa.

"They told us how Lassa fever was wiping out people, how it was a devastating disease, with mortality rates of sixty to seventy percent. They frightened the hell out of us. At the end of their lecture, Kemp asked if anyone in the room was interested in working with Lassa virus. In my usual way, thinking life is not all that difficult, I said, 'Yes, I want to work with viruses.' He told me to finish my course, and if I was still interested, to get in touch with him later."

When a government job was slow to arrive, the newly graduated Tomori knocked on the door of the Ibadan virus laboratory, and in 1971, with a month's instruction from an expatriate scientist on her way out of town, he took over as head of the serology department. "They were trying to replace Rockefeller people with Nigerian counterparts, and I just walked in at the right time."

"The early years were quite hectic for me. Reading about x-y tests is different from doing them in the laboratory. The little tricks you learn along the line are not in the textbooks. At the end of the day I would stay behind and repeat all the experiments, before going home at ten o'clock. This established the pattern I've followed ever since.

"I enjoy puttering around the laboratory, mixing things, looking for results, inoculating animals, going to see if they're falling sick, collecting them, and running tests. Challenges are something I like. When people think things are too risky, I always say, 'Let's take a look and see what we can get out of it.'

"The good thing about veterinary training is that it taught me how to adapt. If you have to treat a cow, you can't ask it, 'What's wrong with you?' If you did, it would probably kick you. This gives you the ability to make diagnoses when you're dealing with people who can't talk back to you. It was training that proved quite helpful for working on viruses, where you're exploring the unknown."

Several Rockefeller scientists prolonged their stay in Ibadan until 1974, which gave Tomori the chance to learn his field virology from the best practitioners in the business. His first trip was a viral survey of the Nupeko forest—a great bloodletting of monkeys, mosquitoes, and humans in a search for the reservoir of yellow fever in Nigeria. "It was exciting for me to go out in the field and sleep in a tent. All the way home I kept wondering, 'Am I going to get a virus?' "

Lying at the junction of the Niger and Kaduna rivers, Nupeko is a gallery forest filled with a tangle of climbers and creepers. The river valleys flood from June to September, when the inhabitants paddle between their isolated villages by canoe. Because the area is moist and thick with mosquitoes and monkeys, it is perfect terrain for yellow fever. It is also less than a hundred miles from the new Nigerian capital at Abuja.

After two weeks in the Nupeko forest, Tomori's team went home with their cars full of blood. Back at the laboratory they found no live viruses, but they did find antibodies to yellow fever—the signature of its having come and gone—in seventy percent of the monkeys and almost all of the humans over the age of forty. These are the survivors of epidemics, the hardy ones who will produce a new crop of infants for the virus to infect.

In the early 1960s one of the largest arbovirus epidemics on record infected two million East Africans with a disease called O'nyong Nyong. No one knows where the virus came from or where it went after the epidemic, and it has yet to reappear. A recurrent theme in the annals of public health is that many viral epidemics go unrecognized. They are often misdiagnosed as malaria, and they generally kill more people than the mortality figures would indicate. Nigeria reported two hundred and eight cases of yellow fever in 1969, but an epidemiological survey revealed that in that year alone there were actually a hundred thousand cases.

"The virus is constantly wandering," wrote one of Tomori's colleagues in an article about yellow fever and the Nupeko survey. From its original source in East Africa, yellow fever was carried to the New World with the slave trade. Thirty-seven epidemics were registered in North America in the nineteenth century alone, with mortality rates of up to fifty percent. Yellow fever killed twenty-five thousand of Napoleon's soldiers after they landed in Santo Domingo, and the virus stopped Ferdinand de Lesseps from building the Panama Canal. It was only twenty years later, after Walter Reed and his colleagues discovered that mosquitoes were the vector of yellow fever, that work on the canal could begin again.

Virologists once nursed the hope that yellow fever could be eradicated by wiping out the *Aedes aegypti* mosquito that carries the disease among humans. By 1930 the mosquito had been eliminated from the cities of Brazil, but researchers faced the unsettling fact that yellow fever itself had not been eliminated. Historically, the disease had been associated with urban populations. But after observing cases of yellow fever in rural areas, scientists began to wonder if there might be a second cycle of transmission among monkeys and forest mosquitoes. Their optimism about controlling the disease received a rude shock when it was discovered in 1932 that yellow fever does in fact have a jungle cycle of transmission, and that jungle yellow fever is exactly the same virus as the urban strain.

The vectors for spreading jungle yellow fever are sun-loving mosquitoes that live in the forest canopy, where they feed on monkeys and other arboreal mammals. But a woodcutter chopping down a tree may provoke the virus into switching levels. It will move down to humans and homophilic mosquitoes, then make its way out to the zone of emergence. Should the virus jump from there into a population with insufficient antibodies, it will rage into an epidemic.

Sixty years after its discovery, many details about the jungle yellow fever cycle remain unknown. How can the virus survive among monkeys that either die of the disease or develop a high level of resistance? To answer these questions the Rockefeller scientists launched a program of active surveillance. Rather than relying on notoriously unreliable reports from hospitals and public health officials, they tried to locate the source of yellow fever epidemics-in-the-making.

They studied hospital records, paying special attention to diagnoses of fever and jaundice. They bled hospitalized patients. They conducted retrospective surveys of blood serum. They made seasonal insect counts. They monitored human populations from year to year. And they trapped and bled a lot of animals. Tomori would later extend these techniques into areas being ecologically disturbed by dams and new cities.

On January 9, 1986, speaking to a crowd of a thousand people, Oyewale Tomori gave his inaugural lecture as a professor at the University of Ibadan. He began with a Biblical quotation that he said was pertinent to both the current hiring freeze in Nigerian universities and his own rise in status. "For promotion cometh neither from the east, nor from the west, nor from the south. But God is the judge; He putteth down one, and setteth up another."

"Viruses have never been associated with anything good," said Tomori, warming to his subject. The word *virus* was synonymous with *poison* or *venom* until the end of the nineteenth century, when the porcelain filter was invented. This allowed scientists to trap bacteria, and by a process of deduction they then figured out that viruses were neither parasites nor bacteria, although exactly what they were remained unknown well into the twentieth century.

When Wendell Stanley crystallized the tobacco mosaic virus in the 1930s, viruses were recognized for the first time as discrete particles. Stanley's work, for which he won the Nobel Prize, provoked a debate still raging today. How can a biological organism become a crystal? Are viruses living or dead or somewhere in between? It was not until after the invention of the electron microscope in 1952 that anyone actually saw a virus. Stanley's crystals revealed themselves to be composed of individual virus particles, or virions, that can be arranged symmetrically into cubes, like the herpes virus, or helixes, like the tobacco mosaic virus, or more complex shapes, like the smallpox virus.

"A virus is a piece of bad news wrapped in protein," Sir Peter Medawar has said. Viruses are parasites that can survive only by splicing their genes into functioning cells. Afterward, whenever the cells replicate, they make copies of the viruses infecting their chromosomes. Consisting of a single nucleic acid surrounded by a protein coat, a virus is the simplest form of life. It is also the only other organism on earth, besides ourselves, capable of threatening human survival.

Some viruses are fast and others slow to multiply, and speed of replication provides the first clue in identifying a virus. AIDS is a *lentivirus*, which is derived from the Latin word for *sluggish*. It can lie dormant for fifteen years before springing into action. Chikungunya, a common African virus that produces symptoms like arthritis, will kill a baby mouse in a day, while rabies requires anywhere from fourteen to twenty-one days to kill its victims.

Taking up the subject of "virus research in Nigeria, past, present, and future," Tomori described how the Rockefeller Foundation in 1925 established the West African Yellow Fever Commission in Yaba, Nigeria. The Yaba laboratory tested Max Theiler's yellow fever vaccine and isolated another long list of African viruses. In the field of virus research, the Rockefeller Foundation was a fairy godmother waving her magic wand over scientists around the world. After a brief absence from Nigeria, the foundation returned in 1963 to establish the arbovirus research laboratory at the University of Ibadan. This was one of a chain of laboratories that Rockefeller built from India to Brazil.

Rockefeller scientists Ottis Causey, the first director of the Ibadan laboratory, and his wife, Calista, who was also a virologist, were curious to see if the methods they had invented for finding viruses in the rain forests of the Amazon would work in tropical Africa. When not busy vaccinating people and dealing with epidemics, the Causeys traveled around Nigeria collecting blood samples from virgin communities, that is, communities with no previous exposure to a virus. These are the areas most likely to succumb to an epidemic, and the Causeys hoped that their virus surveys would act as an early warning system. A community with an insufficient level of antibodies and a nearby source of infection could be inoculated against disease.

The Causeys also launched a series of studies for isolating the viruses found in African arthropods and mammals. They had developed the practice in Brazil of using sentinel animals to trap viruses. Newborn mice, monkeys, and chickens are exposed to free-flying insects at carefully controlled sites and times of day to see if they succumb to a virus. The mist netting of birds and bats, the trapping of rats, and the use of human beings as mosquito collectors are other methods that Tomori inherited from the Causeys and would later apply to his virus surveys in Kainji and Abuja.

After spending seven hundred thousand dollars over a decade of virus research in Nigeria, the Rockefeller Foundation turned its laboratory over to the University of Ibadan in 1974. For the next decade, with budgets as low as a thousand dollars a year, the laboratory hovered near extinction. "In 1984, when the first nail of the coffin was being knocked in, I took over as head of the department," Tomori told his audience.

He and his colleagues had survived until then "because of the surplus material and reagents left by the Rockefeller Foundation. If we needed a rat trap or a syringe, we went to the storeroom to get it. Even our Purina chows were left over from the Rockefeller days. But by the time I became head of the laboratory, the storeroom was empty."

Tomori began beating the bushes for money. "Over a hundred letters later, and after numerous journeys in hot pursuit of would-be donors, fortune began to smile on us." Government agencies, banks, trading companies, and private individuals donated the funds needed to keep the laboratory running.

"They restored confidence in Nigeria to those of us who, like Andrew, were on the verge of checking out of 'di God'dem country.'" His audience laughed uproariously at Tomori's reference to Andrew. Andrew is a legendary Nigerian, a talented, ambitious young man who feels compelled to migrate to the northern hemisphere in order to get ahead in the world. As part of its War for National Survival and Economic Recovery, the Nigerian government ran television commercials showing Andrew packing his bags to leave the country, then changing his mind and deciding to stay in Nigeria.

In summarizing its accomplishments, Tomori said the Ibadan laboratory had isolated 2,531 viruses from 109,873 blood samples, an isolation rate of 2.3 percent. This is par for the course, and it indicates the difficulty of tracking down a live virus before it rages into an epidemic. The laboratory has been involved in the discovery of twelve new viruses, which bear the Nigerian place names of Mokola, Kotonkan, Dugbe, Sabo, Shamonda, Jos, Ife, Igbo-Ora, Potiskum, Abadina, Sango, and Lassa. Most of these viruses cause aching joints and fever. But two of them, Mokola and Lassa, are deadly.

The relationship between Mokola virus and rabies was one of the laboratory's important discoveries. Popular lore in Yoruba-land said that shrew bites cause madness and death, like rabies. Taking these reports seriously, the laboratory trapped shrews in the Mokola district of Ibadan and found in them a virus that was indeed related to rabies, which until then had been considered a unique disease. Now Nigeria, which is the historic home of rabies, has disclosed Mokola and another rabies variety called Lagos bat virus.

The laboratory's most celebrated research has been on Lassa fever, a "new" virus discovered in the Nigerian village of Lassa in 1969. "In order for a virus to become famous, it has to kill important people," Tomori told me, and within a year of its discovery, Lassa had become famous enough to figure as the hero of a book and two front-page articles in the *New York Times*. In many ways the sudden emergence of the virus and the terror surrounding its appearance prefigured events a decade later when another "African" virus sparked the AIDS epidemic. But Lassa differs from AIDS in being transmissible through the respiratory tract, which means that one can catch it as easily as the common cold. Lassa is every virologist's nightmare of a disease waiting to break out of its endemic area of infection to attack the world.

It first came to the attention of the Ibadan laboratory when a radio call from Jos reported a strange ailment that had just killed two missionary nurses. The doctor making the call would also die of what later came to be known as Lassa fever. This is now recognized as its common pattern: a sick patient admitted to a hospital ignites an infection that sweeps through the wards on its way up to the nurses and doctors. Lassa fever has become so feared in Nigerian hospitals that people suspected of having it are no longer admitted. In one notorious case a German doctor and two nurses were thrown out of their own hospital. The doctor was later evacuated from the country in an empty airplane flown by a pilot wearing a space suit.

Lassa fever became really famous when it started attacking medical researchers in the United States. Blood samples from a mission nurse evacuated from Nigeria had been sent to the Yale Arbovirus Research Unit, where Jordi Casals headed a team responsible for isolating and describing the new virus. They worked under the tightest security, but Casals and a technician still came down with Lassa fever, and the technician died of it. "New Fever Virus So Deadly That Research Halts," ran the four-column headline in the *New York Times*. The article went on to explain that Yale was closing down its research on Lassa fever, which would henceforth be restricted to the CDC hot lab in Atlanta.

As no one knew where Lassa fever had come from, scientists in Ibadan set out to discover if the disease had an animal reservoir. They tracked down a woman who had survived an infection and began working up her life history. They studied her village and her patterns of activity—anything that would give them a clue to the origins of the disease. Then they started trapping animals inside and outside her house, eventually finding the culprit in virus-laden rats.

Tomori was part of the team that investigated the last reported outbreak of Lassa fever in Nigeria. "Since 1974 it would appear that Lassa fever had disappeared from the Nigerian scene. This is not quite correct," he told his audience in 1986. "Because of subtle pressure from the government, it's understood you don't report cases of Lassa fever. Nigeria has no cases of Lassa fever because no one is looking for them."

Turning to talk about the future of virus research in Nigeria, Tomori said that "research for national development" had become his "watchword and guiding principle." His laboratory was trying to do something about the three and a half million cases of measles reported annually in Nigeria, which cause over a hundred thousand infant deaths. As secretary of Rotary District 911, he was monitoring a three-million-dollar polio vaccination program financed by the Rotary Foundation. The World Health Organization had asked his department to look at viral diarrheas, and the United States National Academy of Sciences was paying for a study of childhood respiratory infections.

Tomori directed his final remarks to the Young Turks in the audience. "This is the most important aspect of my lecture," he said, before describing how he often despaired of accomplishing anything in Nigeria, a country known for "the squandermania of its talent and resources." He called for setting up "good research centers" built "around a core of young scientists who are highly motivated and well trained. At the present level of our development, with no sound research foundation, I suggest we lay emphasis on basic research."

Tomori ended his lecture—already well into its second hour— with encomiums of praise for his wife, Omowumi, and their four children. But his fullest praise was reserved for someone else in the audience. "Present here today is a woman who has listened intently, but without understanding a word I have said. Yet she was the one who taught me how to read the first Yoruba words." Introducing his mother, he switched into Yoruba to sing her *oriki*, the praise song that summarizes a person's character and accompanies them from birth to death. Tomori, who goes out of his way to learn these songs and sing them on public occasions, knows thousands of Yoruba verses. His own *oriki*, which begins with his traditional name, goes like this:

"Okokomọki," a ji mu taba ogun
Omo a tẹ ni wijọ
A be le jo koju
Mo jejo mo jejo, ogbé ori oka sẹnu

"Okokomoki," who smokes the medicine tobacco early in the
     morning,
The son of the man who sits on the mat to talk,

The man who is not afraid to confront anybody,
Told not to eat a snake, he bites off the head of a cobra.

Tomori takes the phone off the hook and locks the door. He cuts off the air conditioner, and we begin to sweat. This is the only way we can hope to carry on a conversation in his Ibadan office. The walls are painted recovery-room green. Two curtained windows overhead plunge us into sepulchral gloom. The air conditioner, which had been bathing our heads in a prop wash of cold air, sounds like a DC 9 ready for takeoff. People with urgent questions have been opening the door every few minutes. The telephone has been ringing with a lot of dubious connections, the kind that invariably lead to yelling and gesticulation. "I sometimes wonder if it wouldn't be easier to go outside and shout across town," says Tomori.

He gives me a thumbnail sketch of his tenure as director of the Ibadan virus laboratory. "In 1984 I ran around the country looking for money. In 1985 the money arrived, and in 1986 we started work." Tomori's immediate predecessor had been a one-time graduate student and political rabble-rouser at Yale, where his former professors remember him as a "worthless sort." After running the Ibadan laboratory into the ground, he went on to become oil minister of Nigeria.

The laboratory inhabits a rambling building on the grounds of the University of Ibadan hospital. A statue at the entrance used to depict a Yoruba soldier shooting a lion with a musket, but the lion has collapsed and been carried off to rest under the eaves. A virus laboratory consists of three basic departments: tissue culture, inoculation, and serology. Around these you put your animal rooms and library, and if you care about treating people, you add a fourth department in epidemiology.

The tissue culture room, which is reserved for the preparation of cell lines, is equipped with three Leitz microscopes that are out of service for want of missing objectives and eyepieces. The inoculation chamber is outfitted with a new Forma Scientific contamination hood and bench unit provided by the United States National Research Council, but the hood is unusable because the room lacks a working air conditioner.

The corridors are lined with a broken autoclave and five Revco freezers in similar condition. When they last worked, the freezers stored blood and tissue at −70 degrees Centigrade. "This is our high-tech museum," Tomori joked one day, as he ran his fingers through a layer of dust. Badly dented on its arrival in Lagos, a new Revco sits on a screened porch, where the night air keeps it from overheating.

In the serology laboratory, Tomori's old domain, Atanda, Ayo, Adekunle, and Ben Sam are busy analyzing the blood samples collected at Kainji Lake. Serology is the end point in diagnosing a viral infection. Here you test blood serum for the presence of viruses and antibodies. Every reaction is tracked through an increasingly narrow range of suspect viruses. To isolate yellow fever, for example, requires eliminating everything with similar reactions, including Dengue, Zika, Dakar bat, Potiskum, West Nile, and Orungo, a virus that Tomori found in Nigeria in 1972. It is one of the half dozen viruses that his surveys have discovered for the first time in West Africa.

Adjoining the serology laboratory is an animal house filled with plastic boxes holding four thousand Swiss albino mice. A good laboratory needs several systems for isolating viruses. Tissue cultures made of ground-up monkey kidneys are good for finding polio, but baby mice are particularly susceptible to arboviruses. Some of the mice in the room show signs of infection. They are dazed and lethargic. Soon they will go into convulsions and die. How does one know if it was a virus that killed them? Because antibiotics, which work against bacteria but not against viruses, have no effect on the patient.

"Everything looked much better in the Rockefeller days," Tomori tells me during our tour. "Now because of austerity it's hard to keep the place up." The library, for example, has a stopped clock on the wall next to a Michelin map of Africa that has lost its southern regions to mildew. Other than a dictionary and some scientific journals, the most recent of which dates from 1974, the library holdings consist mainly of spiral-bound, color-coded reports from the old Rockefeller virus laboratories. Orange for Belém, Brazil. Blue for Poona, India. Red for Port of Spain, Trinidad. Yellow for Cali, Colombia. Black for the Rockefeller laboratory in

New York. And green for Ibadan. The most recent of the green editions is the ninth, from December 1974.

Tomori's laboratory can identify about two hundred viruses. What he cannot identify has to be sent either to Dakar or to Fort Collins, Colorado. What *they* cannot identify has to go to the Yale Arbovirus Research Unit. But Yale itself is prevented from working on the so-called savage viruses—Rift Valley, Ebola, Lassa, and Marburg—which can be analyzed only at the CDC hot lab in Atlanta. "When you think about the shortage of facilities available in Africa," Robert Shope told me during a visit to Yale, "it's like combining the United States and Canada, and instead of having virus laboratories in every state and territory, you'd have only three, in New York, St. Louis, and San Francisco."

During the years when his laboratory was being run into the ground, Tomori kept himself busy on the international research circuit, working in New Haven, Atlanta, Antwerp, and Tokyo. "Every time I went out, I came back to a vacuum. On any one of these trips I might have become a statistic added to the third world brain drain, but something kept drawing me back to Nigeria. I'm a politically minded sort, and there really is a lot of work to be done here."

On being appointed director of the Ibadan laboratory in 1984, Tomori approached all the usual sources in the United States and Europe for money, but to no avail. " 'What are you doing asking us for money?' they said. 'You come from the richest country in black Africa and your colleague, the oil minister, is grossing twenty-five billion dollars a year! If Nigeria cares about virus research, you can pay for it yourselves.' "

Tomori then launched himself on what he calls his search for the Nigerian Rockefeller. "I started knocking on the doors of rich men with factories and banks. I was trying to entice them into doing what Rockefeller did, putting their money into research or a foundation that would immortalize their name. But we don't have this tradition in Nigeria; everybody wants to make his money and get out."

Nigeria has an unusual system of financing its public facilities. The state governments hold fund-raising drives. Many of the same names appear as donors in different campaigns, and the sums involved often run into the millions of dollars. "When a man donates two million naira to your state fund, if he wants anything in the state, you're going to give it to him. With one big contract at inflated prices he makes back his money and has enough left over to donate again next year."

Putting aside his scruples, Tomori sent off two hundred letters to the country's top donors. "A few wrote back reminding us, as if we didn't already know, that the economy was so bad that it was difficult to get the stamps to post their reply. I threw their letters in my Nigerian Rockefeller file and forgot all about it.

"This is when I began thinking of checking out of 'di God'dem country.' We were ready to troop out like Andrew to the land of milk and honey, where no man is poor. Address books were dusted off, to contact the guys over there in God's Own Country, when out of the blue came a letter by courier. Not from London. Not from New York. It came from Lagos!"

Tomori was being summoned to meet Chief W. I. Folawiyo, chairman of Yinka Folawiyo and Sons. The virology department was down to one working vehicle with no shock absorbers and doors that opened only from the outside. Tomori prayed the rainy season would be delayed until after his return from Lagos, as the car had no windshield wipers.

The reception room at Folawiyo's Unity House was crowded. Tomori calmed his nerves with a trip to the toilet. Then he was ushered in to greet the deputy chairman of Yinka Folawiyo and Sons, who apologized for bringing "a whole professor" all the way from Ibadan, and introduced to Mr. Folawiyo himself. The chief said he had only one question to ask, but Tomori, who had prepared a little speech for the occasion, went ahead and gave it anyway. He described how his department investigates viral epidemics across the country, monitors immunization programs, diagnoses cases of yellow fever and other diseases, and searches for new viruses in West Africa.

Chief Folawiyo asked his question. "How much money do you need?" Tomori jotted down a shopping list of equipment and material, and Folawiyo's deputy wrote him a check for eighty-two thousand naira. At the time, one naira was worth a dollar.

Reviving his once-promising career as a journalist, Tomori wrote two articles for Nigeria's *Guardian* newspaper about his meeting with Mr. Folawiyo and the special problems of doing science in Africa. He described how, out of necessity, he had had to do much of his own research *outside* of Africa, at places like the National Institute of Health in Tokyo, where he went to work on hemorrhagic fevers in 1983. "Suddenly it dawned on me," wrote Tomori of his visit to Japan, "that there is hardly any aspect of our life that Japan does not hold us by the jugular vein. So close to our daily life is the stamp of Japan, that even our pounded yam machine was made in Tokyo. The only Nigerian who is not making use of a Japanese product is a dead Nigerian, although this may not be strictly correct, as our coffins and tombstones are now custom made in Japan."

Japan attained this global dominance by investing in scientific research, said Tomori. He noted that the Japanese Council for Science and Technology is chaired by the prime minister, while the equivalent agency in Nigeria is lost in the bowels of the education department. As well as being out of touch with their government, Nigerian scientists are also isolated from each other. "We become aware of other Nigerians working in Nigeria in the same field only through reading foreign journals." As for the supposed beneficence of foreign aid and its willingness to transfer technology to the third world, Tomori reminded his readers that most aid money goes to pay foreign salaries and suppliers. "At the end of it all a department may have a German centrifuge, a Japanese rotor, a British switch to turn it on, and a Korean expert as the project coordinator.

"The greatest problem we have in what one of my colleagues calls 'the deteriorating world' is that we do not know our own environment. For example, in Nigeria we have no clear-cut national policy on vaccination against certain diseases. At what age should children be vaccinated? What types of vaccines do we use? What diseases should we vaccinate against? These are all questions that only basic indigenous research can solve."

Tomori realized after his visit to Mr. Folawiyo that he had to be more forceful in arguing the economic benefits of scientific research. He advised Nigeria to follow the Japanese model, where science is the base on which the economy is built. Now that he had begun thinking of himself as "doing science for development" and "research to solve our national problems," he was convinced that what he and his fellow Nigerians "need and what we lack is self aid."

Soon after his visit to Unity House, Tomori began finding other Nigerian Rockefellers. A bank came up with some money. Then a trading company. Then Chief Bode Akindele wrote out a check for fifty thousand naira and put Tomori on the board of directors of a new medical center. No longer thinking of checking out of "di God'dem country," Tomori put away his address book and got down to work.

SELECTED BIBLIOGRAPHY

ACKNOWLEDGMENTS

INDEX

Selected Bibliography

Achebe, Chinua. *The Trouble with Nigeria.* Enugu, Nigeria: Fourth Dimension, 1983.

Axelrod, Herbert R., and Warren E. Burgess. *African Cichlids of Lakes Malawi and Tanganyika.* Neptune City, N.J.: T.F.H. Publications, 1973.

Bâ, A. Hampaté. *L'Empire peul du Macina au xviiie siècle.* Paris: Mouton, 1962.

Barker, Jonathan, ed. *The Politics of Agriculture in Tropical Africa.* London: Sage Publications, 1984.

Bayliss-Smith, Tim P., and Sudhir Wanmali, eds. *Understanding Green Revolutions: Agrarian Change and Development Planning in South Asia.* Cambridge: Cambridge University Press, 1984.

Bovill, E. W. *The Golden Trade of the Moors.* 2nd ed. Oxford: Oxford University Press, 1968.

Brokensha, David W., D. M. Warren, and Oswald Werner, eds. *Indigenous Systems of Knowledge and Development.* Lanham, Md.: University Press of America, 1980.

Brooks, Alison, and Catherine Smith. "Ishango Revisited: New Age Determinations and Cultural Interpretations." *African Archeological Review* 5 (1987): 65–78.

Caillié, René. *Journal d'un voyage a Temboctou et à Jenné, dans l'Afrique Centrale: précédé d'observations faites chez les Maures Braknas, les Nalous et d'autres peuples, pendant les années 1824, 1825, 1826, 1827, 1828.* 3 vols. Paris: l'Imprimerie royale, 1830.

Carr, Archie. *Ulendo: Travels of a Naturalist in and out of Africa.* New York: Knopf, 1964.

Chambers, Robert. *Rural Development: Putting the Last First.* London: Longman, 1983.

Chirimuuta, Richard C., and Rosalind J. Chirimuuta. *AIDS, Africa and Racism.* London: Free Association Books, 1989.

Clarke, Thurston. *The Last Caravan.* New York: G. P. Putnam's Sons, 1978.

Cole, Sonia. *Leakey's Luck: The Life of Louis Seymour Bazett Leakey, 1903–1972.* London: Collins, 1975.

Conrad, Joseph. "Heart of Darkness." *Blackwood's Edinburgh Magazine*, February–April, 1899.

Copans, Jean, ed. *Sécheresses et famines du Sahel.* 2 vols. Paris: François Maspero, 1975.

Curtis, Donald, Michael Hubbard, and Andrew Shepherd, eds. *Preventing Famine: Policies and Prospects for Africa.* London: Routledge, 1988.

Dalby, David, and R. J. Harrison Church, eds. *Drought in Africa: Report of the 1973 Symposium.* London: University of London, School of Oriental and African Studies, Centre for African Studies, 1973.

Darwin, Charles. *The Origin of Species by Means of Natural Selection, or the Preservation of Favoured Races in the Struggle for Life.* London: John Murray, 1859.

Delson, Eric, ed. *Ancestors, the Hard Evidence.* New York: A. R. Liss, 1985.

Deschamps, Hubert J., ed. *Histoire générale de l'Afrique noire, de Madagascar et des archipels.* 2 vols. Paris: Presses Universitaires de France, 1970–1971.

Eldredge, Niles. *Time Frames: The Rethinking of Darwinian Evolution and the Theory of Punctuated Equilibria.* New York: Simon and Schuster, 1985.

Fage, J. D., and Roland Oliver, eds. *The Cambridge History of Africa.* 8 vols. Cambridge: Cambridge University Press, 1975–1986.

Ford, John. *The Role of the Trypanosomiases in African Ecology: A Study of the Tsetse Fly Problem.* Oxford: Clarendon Press, 1971.

Forde, Cyril Daryll, ed. *Ethnographic Survey of Africa.* London: International African Institute, 1953–.

Fossey, Dian. *Gorillas in the Mist.* Boston: Houghton Mifflin, 1983.

Franke, Richard W., and Barbara H. Chasin. *Seeds of Famine: Ecological Destruction and the Development Dilemma in the West African Sahel.* Montclair, N.J.: Allanheld, Osmun, 1980.

Freund, Bill. *The Making of Contemporary Africa: The Development of African Society Since 1800.* Bloomington: Indiana University Press, 1984.

Fryer, Geoffrey, and T. D. Iles. *The Cichlid Fishes of the Great Lakes of Africa: Their Biology and Evolution.* Edinburgh: Oliver and Boyd, 1972.

Fuller, John G. *Fever: The Hunt for a New Killer Virus.* New York: Reader's Digest Press, 1974.

Gallais, Jean. *Hommes du Sahel: espaces-temp et pouvoirs, le delta intérieur du Niger, 1960–1980.* Paris: Flammarion, 1984.

Glantz, Michael H., ed. *The Politics of Natural Disaster: The Case of the Sahel Drought.* New York: F. W. Praeger, 1976.

Goldsmith, Edward E., and Nicholas Hildyard. *The Social and Environmental Effects of Large Dams.* Camelford, England: Wadebridge Ecological Centre, 1984.

Gorer, Geoffrey. *Africa Dances: A Book About West African Negroes.* London: Faber & Faber, 1935.

Graham, Alistair D. *Eyelids of Morning: The Mingled Destinies of Croco-*

diles and Men, Being a Description of the Origins, History, and Prospects of Lake Rudolf, Its Peoples, Deserts, Rivers, Mountains, and Weather. Illustrated by Peter Beard. Greenwich, Conn.: New York Graphic Society, 1973.

de Gramont, Sanche. *The Strong Brown God: The Story of the Niger River.* London: Hart-Davis MacGibbon, 1975.

Greenberg, J. H. *The Languages of Africa.* Bloomington: Indiana University Press, 1963.

Grigg, David. *The World Food Problem, 1950–1980.* Oxford: Basil Blackwell, 1985.

Grove, A. T. *Africa.* 3rd ed. Oxford: Oxford University Press, 1978.

Gulliver, Philip H. *The Family Herds: A Study of Two Pastoral Tribes in East Africa, the Jie and Turkana.* London: Routledge & Kegan Paul, 1955.

Hailey, William Malcolm. *An African Survey: A Study of Problems Arising in Africa South of the Sahara.* Rev. ed. Oxford: Oxford University Press, 1957.

Hansberry, William Leo. *Africa and Africans as Seen by Classical Writers.* Washington, D.C.: Howard University Press, 1977.

Haraway, Donna J. *Primate Visions: Gender, Race and Nature in the World of Modern Science.* New York: Routledge & Kegan Paul, 1989.

Harlan, Jack R., Jan M. J. de Wet, and Ann B. L. Stemler, eds. *Origins of African Plant Domestication.* The Hague: Mouton, 1976.

Harris, J. W. K., et al. "Late Pliocene Hominid Occupation in Central Africa: The Setting, Context, and Character of the Senga 5A Site, Zaire." *Journal of Human Evolution* 16 (1987): 701–728.

Hartwig, Gerald W., and K. David Patterson, eds. *Disease in African History: An Introductory Survey and Case Studies.* Durham, N.C.: Duke University Press, 1978.

Hay, Margaret Jean, and Sharon Stichter, eds. *African Women South of the Sahara.* New York: Longman, 1984.

de Heinzelin, Jean. *Exploration du Parc National Albert, Mission Jean de Heinzelin de Braucourt.* 6 vols. Brussels: Institut des Parcs Nationaux du Congo Belge, 1955–1961.

de Heinzelin, Jean. "Ishango." *Scientific American* (1962): 105–116.

Hiernaux, Jean. *The People of Africa.* London: Weidenfeld & Nicolson, 1974.

Hillaby, John. *Journey to the Jade Sea.* London: Constable, 1964.

Hoagland, Edward. *African Calliope: A Journey to the Sudan.* New York: Random House, 1979.

Höhnel, Ludwig R. von. *Discovery of Lakes Rudolf and Stefanie: A Narrative of Count Samuel Teleki's Exploring & Hunting Expedition in Eastern Equatorial Africa in 1887 & 1888.* Trans. Nancy Bell. 2 vols. London: Longmans, Green, 1894.

Howell, Paul, Michael Lock, and Stephen Cobb, eds. *The Jonglei Canal:*

Impact and Opportunity. Cambridge: Cambridge University Press, 1988.

Iliffe, John. *The African Poor: A History*. Cambridge: Cambridge University Press, 1987.

Independent Commission on International Humanitarian Issues. *Famine, A Man-Made Disaster?* London: Pan, 1985.

Johanson, Donald, and Maitland Edey. *Lucy: The Beginnings of Humankind*. New York: Simon and Schuster, 1981.

Jones, Roger. *The Rescue of Emin Pasha: The Story of Henry Morton Stanley and the Emin Pasha Relief Expedition, 1887–1889*. London: Allison and Busby, 1972.

Juma, Calestous. *The Gene Hunters: Biotechnology and the Scramble for Seeds*. London: Zed Books, 1989.

Leakey, Louis S. B. *White African*. London: Hodder & Stoughton, 1937.

Leakey, Mary. *Disclosing the Past: An Autobiography*. London: Weidenfeld & Nicolson, 1984.

Leakey, Richard E. *One Life: An Autobiography*. London: Michael Joseph, 1983.

Lee, Richard B., and Irven De Vore, eds. *Kalahari Hunter-Gatherers: Studies of the !Kung San and Their Neighbors*. Cambridge, Mass.: Harvard University Press, 1976.

Leighton, Alexander H., T. Adeoye Lambo, et al. *Psychiatric Disorders among the Yoruba: A Report from the Cornell-Aro Mental Health Research Project in the Western Region*. Ithaca: Cornell University Press, 1963.

Levtzion, Nehemia. *Ancient Ghana and Mali*. London: Methuen, 1973.

Lewin, Roger. *Bones of Contention: Controversies in the Search for Human Origins*. New York: Simon and Schuster, 1987.

Lewis, David L. *The Race to Fashoda: European Colonialism and African Resistance in the Scramble for Africa*. New York: Weidenfeld & Nicolson, 1987.

Lhote, Henri. *Les Touaregs du Hoggar*. 2nd ed. Paris: Payot, 1955.

Livingstone, David, and Charles Livingstone. *Narrative of an Expedition to the Zambesi and Its Tributaries and of the Discovery of the Lakes Shirwa and Nyassa, 1858–1864*. London: John Murray, 1865.

Lowe-McConnell, Rosemary H. *Fish Communities in Tropical Freshwater: Their Distribution, Ecology, and Evolution*. London: Longman, 1975.

Magasa, Amidu. *Papa-commandant a jeté un grand filet devant nous: les exploités des rives du Niger, 1902–1962*. Preface by Claude Meillassoux. Paris: François Maspero, 1978.

Maltby, Edward. *Waterlogged Wealth: Why Waste the World's Wet Places?* London: International Institute for Environment and Development, 1986.

McKelvey, John J. *Man Against Tsetse: Struggle for Africa*. Ithaca: Cornell University Press, 1973.

Miracle, Marvin. *Maize in Tropical Africa*. Madison: University of Wisconsin Press, 1966.

Monod, Theodore, ed. *Pastoralism in Tropical Africa*. London: Oxford University Press for the International African Institute, 1975.

Moorehead, Alan. *The White Nile*. Rev. ed. London: Hamish Hamilton, 1971.

Moreau, Reginald E. *The Palaearctic-African Bird Migration Systems*. London: Academic Press, 1972.

Murdock, George P. *Africa: Its Peoples and Their Culture History*. New York: McGraw-Hill, 1959.

Nichols, Lee, ed. *Science in Africa: Interviews with Thirty African Scientists*. Washington, D.C.: Voice of America, 1982.

Odhiambo, Thomas R. "East Africa: Science for Development." *Science* 158 (1967): 876–881.

Ogot, Bethwell A. *History of the Southern Luo*. Nairobi: East African Publishing House, 1967.

Omer-Cooper, John D. *The Zulu Aftermath: A Nineteenth-Century Revolution in Bantu Africa*. London: Longman, 1966.

Ouologuem, Yambo. *Le Devoir de violence*. Paris: Editions du Seuil, 1968.

Pacey, Arnold, and Philip Payne, eds. *Agricultural Development and Nutrition*. London: Hutchinson, 1985.

Pachai, Bridglal, ed. *The Early History of Malawi*. London: Longman, 1972.

Park, Mungo. *Travels in the Interior Districts of Africa: Performed under the Direction and Patronage of the African Association in the Years 1795, 1796, and 1797*. London: W. Bulmer and Co., 1799.

Pearse, Andrew. *Seeds of Plenty, Seeds of Want: Social and Economic Implications of the Green Revolution*. Oxford: Clarendon Press, 1980.

Phillipson, David W. *African Archeology*. Cambridge: Cambridge University Press, 1985.

Ransford, Oliver. *Livingstone's Lake: The Drama of Nyasa*. London: John Murray, 1966.

Richards, Paul. *Indigenous Agricultural Revolution: Ecology and Food Production in West Africa*. London: Hutchinson, 1985.

Sabben-Clare, E. E., D. J. Bradley, and K. Kirkwood, eds. *Health in Tropical Africa during the Colonial Period*. Oxford: Clarendon Press, 1980.

Sandford, Stephen. *Management of Pastoral Development in the Third World*. Chichester, England: John Wiley & Sons, 1983.

Schweitzer, Georg, ed. *Emin Pasha, His Life and Work Compiled from His Journals, Letters, Scientific Notes, and from Official Documents*. 2 vols. Westminster, England: Archibald Constable, 1898.

Sen, Amartya. *Poverty and Famines: An Essay on Entitlement and Deprivation*. Oxford: Clarendon Press, 1981.

Skaife, Sydney H. *African Insect Life*. Rev. ed., ed. John Ledger with photographs by Anthony Bannister. Cape Town: C. Struik, 1979.

Soyinka, Wole. *Aké: The Years of Childhood*. London: Rex Collings, 1981.

Stanley, Henry M. *In Darkest Africa, or the Quest, Rescue, and Retreat of Emin, Governor of Equatoria*. 2 vols. London: Sampson, Low, Marston, Searle, and Rivington, 1890.

Stanley, N. F., and R. A. Joske, eds. *Changing Disease Patterns and Human Behaviour*. London: Academic Press, 1980.

Stanley, N. F., and M. P. Alpers, eds. *Man-Made Lakes and Human Health*. London: Academic Press, 1975.

Stebbing, Edward P. "The Threat of the Sahara." *Journal of the Royal African Society* 36 (May 1937): 1–35.

Suret-Canale, Jean. *L'Afrique noire*. Paris: Messidor-Editions sociales, 1982.

Sutton, J. E. G. "The Aquatic Civilization of Middle Africa." *Journal of African History* 15 (1974): 527–546.

Swift, Jeremy. "The Future of African Hunter-Gatherer and Pastoral Peoples." *Development and Change* 13 (April 1982): 159–181.

Swift, Jeremy. *The Sahara*. Amsterdam: Time-Life Books, 1975.

Taieb, Maurice. *Sur la terre des premiers hommes*. Paris: Editions Robert Laffont, 1985.

Theiler, Max, and Wilbur G. Downs. *The Arthropod-Borne Viruses of Vertebrates: An Account of the Rockefeller Foundation Virus Program, 1951–1970*. New Haven: Yale University Press, 1973.

Thomas, Elizabeth Marshall. *Warrior Herdsmen*. New York: Knopf, 1965.

Turnbull, Colin. *The Mountain People*. New York: Simon and Schuster, 1972.

UNESCO. *General History of Africa*. 8 vols. London: Heinemann, 1981–.

Updike, John. *The Coup*. New York: Knopf, 1978.

Wood, Alan. *The Groundnut Affair*. London: The Bodley Head, 1950.

Worthington, Edgar B. *Science in Africa: A Review of Scientific Research Relating to Tropical and Southern Africa*. Oxford: Oxford University Press, 1938.

Yellen, John. *Archaeological Approaches to the Present: Models for Reconstructing the Past*. New York: Academic Press, 1977.

Acknowledgments

For teaching me about science in Africa and for allowing me to accompany them on their journeys, I am indebted to my African hosts. They are the true heroes of this story. Its virtues are their own. I am doubly indebted to those among them who read portions of the manuscript: Jeremy Swift, Richard Moorehead, Jamie Skinner, Stephen Cobb, Caroline Moorehead, Thomas Odhiambo, Robert Dransfield, Ken McKaye, Jay Stauffer, Laurence Stifel, Nilsa Bosque-Pérez, Alison Brooks, Noel Boaz, Jack Harris, Catherine Smith, Leith Smith, Tim White, Donald Johanson, Mary Leakey, Richard Leakey, Robert Shope, Thomas Aitken, Wilbur Downs, Luc Montagnier, and Oyewale Tomori.

Traveling in Africa is an expensive proposition, so I would like to thank those editors who sent me out to report the news: Les Line and Ruth Norris at *Audubon*, Robert Shnayerson and Signe Hammer at *Science Digest*, and Don Moser and Marlane Liddell at *Smithsonian*. Other assistance came from Patrice Adcroft, Dick Teresi, and Kathleen Stein at *Omni*.

My father, Nathan Bass, helped research the book by supplying me with a wealth of clippings. My mother, Audrey Bass, kept the mail and other aid coming in my direction. The library research assistance of Lynn Mayo, Linda Brown, Joan Wolek, Kristin Leimkuhler, and Corinne Jorgensen was invaluable. For logistical support, my thanks go to Donna Lewis, the Crèche Municipale of the rue de Fleurus, the Cambridge University Joint Colleges Nursery, and the Clinton Child Care Center.

I am enormously grateful to those friends who read the manuscript in its entirety, sometimes more than once: Dana Brand, Sheila Fisher, Bill Pietz, Jeff Seroy, and Roberta Krueger. Nan Talese was the patron saint who blessed this book at its inception. Joe Kanon and Harry Foster delivered the offspring. Peg Anderson copy edited the manuscript, Rafael Palacios Commelin drew the maps, Geraldine Krueger compiled the index, and Nat Sobel represented the author. My wife and daughter, to whom this work is dedicated, aided my African project with great patience and love.

Index